# סדור אור שלום
# לשבת ויום טוב

SIDDUR OR SHALOM

*for*

*Shabbat and Festivals*

# סדור אור שלום
# לשבת ויום טוב

# *SIDDUR OR SHALOM*
## *for*
## *Shabbat and Festivals*

Rabbi Daniel Pressman
Rabbi Ronald Isaacs

KTAV Publishing House, Inc.
Jersey City, New Jersey

U.S. Postal Service:
Library of Congress
Cataloging in Publication Division
101 Independence Avenue, S.E.
Washington, DC 20540-4320

Commercial courier (e.g., FedEx, UPS):
Library of Congress
CIP 20540-4320
9140 East Hampton Drive
Capitol Heights, MD 20743

Library of Congress Cataloging-in-Publication Data

Siddur. Sabbath. English & Hebrew
Siddur Or shalom for Shabbat and festivals / Daniel Pressman, Ronald Isaacs.
p. cm.
Text in Hebrew and Hebrew transliteration, with English translation
ISBN 978-1-60280-151-6
1. Sabbath – Liturgy – Texts. 2. Siddurim – Texts. 3. Mahzorim – Texts. 4. Judaism – Liturgy – Texts. 5. Siddur. Sabbath. 6. Mahzor. I. Pressman, Daniel. II. Isaacs, Ronald H. III. Mahzor. English & Hebrew. IV. Title.
EM675.S3Z5567 2010
296,4'5 – dc22

2010036583

Published by
KTAV Publishing House, Inc.
930 Newark Avenue
Jersey City, NJ 07306
orders@ktav.com
www.ktav.com
Tel: (201) 963-9524
Fax: (201) 963-0102

# CONTENTS


Key to Transliteration . . . . . . . . . . . . . . . . . . . . . . . . . . . 1
Introduction . . . . . . . . . . . . . . . . . . . . . . . . . . . . . . . . . 3
Acknowledgements . . . . . . . . . . . . . . . . . . . . . . . . . . . . 5
P'sukei D'Zimrah . . . . . . . . . . . . . . . . . . . . . . . . . . . . . 20
Shaḥarit . . . . . . . . . . . . . . . . . . . . . . . . . . . . . . . . . . . 28
Blessings of the Shema . . . . . . . . . . . . . . . . . . . . . . . . . . 34
Amidah . . . . . . . . . . . . . . . . . . . . . . . . . . . . . . . . . . . 58
Hallel . . . . . . . . . . . . . . . . . . . . . . . . . . . . . . . . . . . . 82
Torah Service . . . . . . . . . . . . . . . . . . . . . . . . . . . . . . . 98
Torah Blessings . . . . . . . . . . . . . . . . . . . . . . . . . . . . . . 104
Birkat Ha-Gomeil . . . . . . . . . . . . . . . . . . . . . . . . . . . . 106
Prayers for the Recovery of Those in Need of Healing . . . . . . . 108
Blessings Before and After the Haftarah . . . . . . . . . . . . . . . . 114
Prayer for our Country . . . . . . . . . . . . . . . . . . . . . . . . . . 120
Prayer for the State of Israel . . . . . . . . . . . . . . . . . . . . . . 122
Announcing the New Month . . . . . . . . . . . . . . . . . . . . . . . 124
Service for Returning the Torah . . . . . . . . . . . . . . . . . . . . . 126
Musaf . . . . . . . . . . . . . . . . . . . . . . . . . . . . . . . . . . . . 136
Shabbat Minḥah . . . . . . . . . . . . . . . . . . . . . . . . . . . . . . 172
Havdalah . . . . . . . . . . . . . . . . . . . . . . . . . . . . . . . . . . 216

### *Readings for Special Occasions*

Yizkor . . . . . . . . . . 220
Prayers for Sukkot . . . . . . . . . . 226
Geshem: Prayer for Rain . . . . . . . . . . 230
Simḥat Torah Prayers. . . . . . . . . . . 234
Prayers for Shabbat Ḥanukah . . . . . . . . . . 240
Tal: Prayer for Dew. . . . . . . . . . . 242
The Song of Songs. . . . . . . . . . . 246
Yom Ha-Atzma'ut: Israel Independence Day . . . . . . . . . . 247
Hatikvah . . . . . . . . . . 248
Shavuot: The Ten Commandments . . . . . . . . . . 250
Ma'ariv Evening Service. . . . . . . . . . . 251

## KEY TO TRANSLITERATION

The transliteration scheme follows that of the *Ḥumash Etz Ḥayim*. It is largely self-explanatory, though you will find a few hints below. Of course, we hope that this aid to participation will inspire you to take the plunge into learning to read Hebrew. It's not much harder than reading transliteration, and it will open the door to a wider world of participation in Jewish worship. In the meantime, we hope this will enhance your worship experience.

| Representation | Hebrew Letter | Pronunciation |
|---|---|---|
| . [dot | א or ע | [break] |
| a | | **ar**m |
| h | ה | **h**oly (or, at end of word, silent) |
| ḥ | ח | as in **ḥ**allah or **ḥ**azzan |
| I | | gr**i**n or pol**i**ce |
| kh | כ ך | like Scottish "lo**ch**" |
| o | וֹ | h**o**me |
| tz | צ ץ | bli**tz** |
| u | וּ | pl**u**me |
| ‘ | | like Australian "g'day" |
| ai | Th**ai**land | |
| ei | **ei**ght | |
| oi | וֹי | c**oi**n |
| ui | וּי | ch**ew**y |

*SPECIAL SYMBOL*

♪ A musical note precedes the Hebrew words to be chanted by Ḥazzan or other prayer leader. Local custom should be followed when it differs from this siddur.

# Introduction

Praying is easy and praying is hard. Praying is easy for some of us because words of praise are natural for us, or because we were raised with the formal prayers and they flow easily from our lips. Prayer is hard for some of us because we don't yet read Hebrew, or because we're not certain what to do, or because we're not sure what we believe.

We are both congregational Rabbis. We have led thousands of services, and we know full well the challenges of worship. This siddur comes from our experience in helping people to gain more ease, fluency, understanding and involvement in prayer.

It helps us to know that our Rabbis recognized the difficulties and challenges of prayer long ago. The Talmud teaches, "When one worships, his mind must concentrate on [the blessings of the Amidah]. If he cannot concentrate on them all, he should at least concentrate on one. Which one? Rav Safra said in the name of a scholar of the school of Rabbi, 'On *Avot* '[the first blessing of the Amidah]." (Babylonian Talmud Berakhot 34a)

Pretty amazing! Our holiest of Rabbis noticed that it is hard to concentrate on prayer, and that even when we do, it's difficult to sustain that focus. So they gave us guidance for those days when we are distracted: at least focus on the first blessing of the Amidah. Elsewhere they taught that the first six words of the Shema are also crucial for kavvanah.

Kavvanah is an important word for worship. Dr. David Blumenthal defines it as "spiritual consciousness-raising…, a technique for broadening one's awareness of what one is doing. " Kavvanah can be as simple and basic as knowing how to say the words and understand their meaning, and as deep as engaging so closely with the words that we feel that they are flowing from the deepest wells of our hearts and souls.

This *siddur* is designed to clear away some of the obstacles to prayer. It offers a clear, gender-neutral translation. It transliterates every passage likely to be sung or recited out loud. That transliteration follows the Hebrew phrase-by-phrase, to help reassure beginning readers. We also hope this will help people to learn to read Hebrew. People often are unsure where to stand up, sit down, bow, or perform other "choreography" of the service. Customs differ, but we have included directions for the most common practices, with explanations of why these are done.

We have abridged the beginning parts of the service on the basis of a teaching of Rabbi Yehudah he-Ḥasid in *Sefer Ḥasidim*, an 11$^{th}$ century pietistic work, "It is better to pray with a little with concentration than to pray much without feeling.…It is better to praise God with few words and without hurry, than to rush and say many phrases."

Finally, we have added comments and kavvanot to enhance people's understanding and spiritual consciousness-raising.

It is our devout hope that these enhancements will lead worshipers into a deeper engagement with prayer. Rabbi Milton Steinberg wrote, "Prayer is the bridge between man and God." May all of us grow in knowledge and spirit so that we can cross that bridge with devotion and kavvanah.

# Acknowledgements

I want to thank many teachers who, through both their writings and through personal instruction, have enhanced my *kavvanah*, including Elliot Dorff, Gail Dorph, Jules Harlow, Abraham Joshua Heschel, Lawrence Hoffman, Barry Holtz, Reuven Hammer, Issachar Jacobson, Shimon Potok, and Bernard Septimus.

Thanks also to my first teachers of Judaism and prayer, my parents, Rabbi Jacob and Marjorie Pressman, and to the wonderful synagogue where I grew up and first led a congregation in worship, Temple Beth Am, in Los Angeles, California.

My first pulpit, Congregation Ner Tamid of South Bay, in Palos Verdes, California, and especially my home synagogue for the last 30 years, Congregation Beth David, Saratoga, California, gave me the opportunity to explore the challenges of worship together with other seekers.

Rabbi Ronald Isaacs has invited me to partner with him on three siddur projects. I thank him for his friendship and insight, and I admire him for his scholarship and discipline.

I thank my children, Aliza, Benjamin, and Rebecca, and my son-in-law, Craig Chosiad, for their encouragement and love.

My late wife, Beverly, taught me so much about goodness, kindness, and authentic observance of mitzvot. She was devoted to the role of music in worship, and her beautiful voice enhanced many people's prayer experience. I dedicate this book to her memory.

Rabbi Daniel Pressman

I too want to thank my many teachers and students who have helped me to learn to pray with more fervor and understanding. A special thank you to Rabbi Shamai Kanter, an inspiring teacher and colleague who opened my eyes to the beauty of *tefillah.* I also want to thank my many camp counselors at Camp Ramah in Canada, Glen Spey and the Poconos for the opportunity to experiment with prayer techniques through the use of music, psycho-drama and film.

My writing partner Daniel Pressman is a special friend and colleague. He is a skilled writer, a master educator and more importantly, a mensch par excellence. Working with him has been most pleasurable!

Lastly, I want to thank my wife Leora for her loving companionship and creativity in all the worship services that she has led in my synagogue, Temple Sholom. I dedicate this *siddur* to her, and to my children Zachary and Keren, my son-in-law Aryeh and my two grandkids Mimi and Caleb.

Rabbi Ronald Isaacs

We want to thank Rabbi Judith Bachrach Kempler, who read and corrected the text with tremendous care. We both want to thank Adam Bengal, editor extraordinaire, and in particular, Bernie Scharfstein, one of the great treasures of American Jewish life, for his personal dedication to this project.

# סדור אור שלום
# לשבת ויום טוב

# SIDDUR OR SHALOM

*for*

*Shabbat and Festivals*

# Mah Tovu

*How wonderful it is to be here!*

Mah tovu,
ohalekha Ya·akov
mishk'notekha Yisra·el.
Va-ani b'rov ḥasdekha
avo veitekha,
eshtaḥaveh
el heikhal kodsh'kha b'yir·atekha.
Adonai, ahavti m'on beitekha,
u-m'kom mishkan k'vodekha.
Va-ani eshtaḥaveh v'ekhra·ah,
evr'khah lifnei Adonai osi.
Va-ani t'filati l'kha, Adonai,
eit ratzon.
Elohim b'rov ḥasdekha,
aneini be-emet yisḥekha.

מַה טֹּבוּ
אֹהָלֶיךָ יַעֲקֹב,
מִשְׁכְּנֹתֶיךָ יִשְׂרָאֵל.
וַאֲנִי בְּרֹב חַסְדְּךָ
אָבוֹא בֵיתֶךָ,
אֶשְׁתַּחֲוֶה
אֶל הֵיכַל קָדְשְׁךָ בְּיִרְאָתֶךָ.
יְיָ אָהַבְתִּי מְעוֹן בֵּיתֶךָ,
וּמְקוֹם מִשְׁכַּן כְּבוֹדֶךָ.
וַאֲנִי אֶשְׁתַּחֲוֶה וְאֶכְרָעָה,
אֶבְרְכָה לִפְנֵי יְיָ עֹשִׂי.
וַאֲנִי תְפִלָּתִי לְךָ יְיָ,
עֵת רָצוֹן,
אֱלֹהִים בְּרָב חַסְדֶּךָ,
עֲנֵנִי בֶּאֱמֶת יִשְׁעֶךָ.

# Mah Tovu

***How wonderful it is to be here!***

How wonderful are your tents, O Jacob, your dwelling places, O Israel! I, because of your great lovingkindess, will enter Your house. I will bow down to Your holy sanctuary, with reverence for you. Adonai, I love Your house, the place where Your glory dwells. I will bow, bend my knee, and offer blessings before Adonai, my Maker. As for me, Adonai, may my prayer come before You at the right moment. God, out of Your great mercy, answer me with Your true salvation.

The pagan prophet Balaam was hired to curse the Israelites during their wilderness wanderings. When he saw their beautifully arranged camp set on a hilltop, Balaam was so moved that he blessed the Israelites with the words Mah Tovu. Our Rabbis understood the word "tents" to refer to synagogues, and so we recite these words when we first enter the synagogue sanctuary. This is an opportunity to shift our mental gears from the ordinary to the holy. Ask yourself, "What does it mean to me to enter this sacred space?"

# Birkhot Ha-Shaḥar

| | |
|---|---|
| Barukh atah Adonai | בָּרוּךְ אַתָּה יְיָ |
| Eloheinu Melekh ha-olam, | אֱלֹהֵינוּ מֶלֶךְ הָעוֹלָם, |
| asher natan la-sekhvi vinah | אֲשֶׁר נָתַן לַשֶּׂכְוִי בִינָה |
| l'havḥin bein yom u-vein lailah. | לְהַבְחִין בֵּין יוֹם וּבֵין לָיְלָה. |
| Barukh atah Adonai | בָּרוּךְ אַתָּה יְיָ |
| Eloheinu Melekh ha-olam, | אֱלֹהֵינוּ מֶלֶךְ הָעוֹלָם, |
| she-asani b'tzalmo. | שֶׁעָשַׂנִי בְּצַלְמוֹ. |
| Barukh atah Adonai | בָּרוּךְ אַתָּה יְיָ |
| Eloheinu Melekh ha-olam, | אֱלֹהֵינוּ מֶלֶךְ הָעוֹלָם, |
| she-asani Yisra·el. | שֶׁעָשַׂנִי יִשְׂרָאֵל. |
| Barukh atah Adonai | בָּרוּךְ אַתָּה יְיָ |
| Eloheinu Melekh ha-olam, | אֱלֹהֵינוּ מֶלֶךְ הָעוֹלָם, |
| she-asani ben- (bat-) ḥorin. | שֶׁעָשַׂנִי בֶּן־ (בַּת־) חוֹרִין. |
| Barukh atah Adonai | בָּרוּךְ אַתָּה יְיָ |
| Eloheinu Melekh ha-olam, | אֱלֹהֵינוּ מֶלֶךְ הָעוֹלָם, |
| pokei·aḥ ivrim. | פּוֹקֵחַ עִוְרִים. |

# Birkhot Ha-Shaḥar

Praised are You, Adonai our God, Ruler of the Universe…
…who gave us the knowledge to tell day from night,
…who made me in God's image,
…who made me a Jew,
…who made me free,
…who opens the eyes of the blind,
…who clothes the unclothed,
…who frees the the bound,
…who helps those who are bent over by trouble stand straight,
…who spreads out the earth over the waters,
…who made for me everything I need,
…who prepares the way for our footsteps,
…who gives the people of Israel strength,
…who crowns the people of Israel with glory,
…who gives strength to the weary.
…who removes sleep from my eyes and slumber from my eyelids.

When we first wake up and begin our day, it's a good time to thank God for ordinary things that we might take for granted, such as our minds, our eyesight, and the ability to walk.

| | |
|---|---|
| Barukh atah Adonai | בָּרוּךְ אַתָּה יְיָ |
| Eloheinu Melekh ha-olam, | אֱלֹהֵינוּ מֶלֶךְ הָעוֹלָם, |
| malbish arumim. | מַלְבִּישׁ עֲרֻמִּים. |
| Barukh atah Adonai | בָּרוּךְ אַתָּה יְיָ |
| Eloheinu Melekh ha-olam, | אֱלֹהֵינוּ מֶלֶךְ הָעוֹלָם, |
| matir asurim. | מַתִּיר אֲסוּרִים. |
| Barukh atah Adonai | בָּרוּךְ אַתָּה יְיָ |
| Eloheinu Melekh ha-olam, | אֱלֹהֵינוּ מֶלֶךְ הָעוֹלָם, |
| zokeif k'fufim. | זוֹקֵף כְּפוּפִים. |
| Barukh atah Adonai | בָּרוּךְ אַתָּה יְיָ |
| Eloheinu Melekh ha-olam, | אֱלֹהֵינוּ מֶלֶךְ הָעוֹלָם, |
| roka ha-aretz al ha-mayim. | רוֹקַע הָאָרֶץ עַל הַמָּיִם. |
| Barukh atah Adonai | בָּרוּךְ אַתָּה יְיָ |
| Eloheinu Melekh ha-olam, | אֱלֹהֵינוּ מֶלֶךְ הָעוֹלָם, |
| she-asah li kol-tzorki. | שֶׁעָשָׂה לִי כָּל צָרְכִּי. |
| Barukh atah Adonai | בָּרוּךְ אַתָּה יְיָ |
| Eloheinu Melekh ha-olam, | אֱלֹהֵינוּ מֶלֶךְ הָעוֹלָם, |
| ha-meikhin mitz·adei-gaver. | הַמֵּכִין מִצְעֲדֵי גָבֶר. |
| Barukh atah Adonai | בָּרוּךְ אַתָּה יְיָ |
| Eloheinu Melekh ha-olam, | אֱלֹהֵינוּ מֶלֶךְ הָעוֹלָם, |
| ozeir Yisra·el big'vurah. | אוֹזֵר יִשְׂרָאֵל בִּגְבוּרָה. |
| Barukh atah Adonai | בָּרוּךְ אַתָּה יְיָ |
| Eloheinu Melekh ha-olam, | אֱלֹהֵינוּ מֶלֶךְ הָעוֹלָם, |
| oteir Yisra·el b'tif·arah. | עוֹטֵר יִשְׂרָאֵל בְּתִפְאָרָה. |
| Barukh atah Adonai | בָּרוּךְ אַתָּה יְיָ |
| Eloheinu Melekh ha-olam, | אֱלֹהֵינוּ מֶלֶךְ הָעוֹלָם, |
| ha-notein la-ya·eif ko·aḥ. | הַנּוֹתֵן לַיָּעֵף כֹּחַ. |
| Barukh atah Adonai | בָּרוּךְ אַתָּה יְיָ |
| Eloheinu Melekh ha-olam, | אֱלֹהֵינוּ מֶלֶךְ הָעוֹלָם, |
| ha-ma·avir sheinah mei-einai | הַמַּעֲבִיר שֵׁנָה מֵעֵינָי |
| u-t'numah mei-af·apai. | וּתְנוּמָה מֵעַפְעַפָּי. |

## MORNING BLESSINGS KAVVANAH

Thank you, God, for giving me understanding,
And for creating me in Your image.

Thank you, God, because I am Jewish,
And because I am free.

Thank you, God, for giving me sight
And clothes to wear.

Thank you, God that I can move freely
And stand up straight.

Thank you, God, for making this wonderful world
That has everything I need.

Thank you, God that I woke up today with energy.
May I be grateful all this day for Your many gifts.

**Commentary:** These fifteen blessings are based on the Babylonian Talmud Berakhot 60b, where the rabbis teach that as one experiences the phenomena of the new day, one ought to praise God for providing them. Originally these blessings were recited at home when performing one's regular daily morning routine of arising from bed, washing, dressing. In later years, because many people lacked the knowledge to say these prayers by themselves, they were included in the prayerbook as part of the preliminary morning service. As you recite these blessings, use this time to be aware of how these simple things, which we often take for granted, make our daily life possible. This awareness can also sensitize us to the struggles of those with disabilities.

**Prayer Motions:** The Code of Jewish Law (Oraḥ Ḥayim 46) suggests a variety of actions to accompany the various blessings of the morning. For example,

While dressing one should recite "clothes the unclothed."
When resting one's hands on one's eyes one recites "who opens the eyes of the blind."
When sitting one recites "who frees the bound"
When standing one recites "who helps those who are bent over by trouble stand straight."
When putting on one's shoes one recites "who made for me everything I need."
When putting on a belt one recites "who gives the people of Israel strength."
When putting on a hat one recites "who crowns the people of Israel with glory."
When washing one's face one recites "who removes sleep from my eyes."

## THE PSALM FOR SHABBAT

| | |
|---|---|
| Mizmor shir l'yom ha-Shabbat. | מִזְמוֹר שִׁיר לְיוֹם הַשַּׁבָּת. |
| Tov l'hodot la'Adonai, | טוֹב לְהֹדוֹת לַייָ, |
| u-l'zamer l'shimkha elyon. | וּלְזַמֵּר לְשִׁמְךָ עֶלְיוֹן. |
| L'hagid ba-boker ḥasdekha, | לְהַגִּיד בַּבֹּקֶר חַסְדֶּךָ, |
| ve-emunat'kha ba-leilot. | וֶאֱמוּנָתְךָ בַּלֵּילוֹת. |
| Alei asor va·alei navel, | עֲלֵי עָשׂוֹר וַעֲלֵי נָבֶל, |
| alei higayon b'khinor. | עֲלֵי הִגָּיוֹן בְּכִנּוֹר. |
| Ki simaḥtani Adonai | כִּי שִׂמַּחְתַּנִי יְיָ |
| b'fo·alekha, | בְּפָעֳלֶךָ, |
| b'ma·asei yadekha aranein. | בְּמַעֲשֵׂי יָדֶיךָ אֲרַנֵּן. |
| Ma gad'lu ma·asekha Adonai, | מַה גָּדְלוּ מַעֲשֶׂיךָ יְיָ, |
| m'od am'ku maḥ'sh'votekha. | מְאֹד עָמְקוּ מַחְשְׁבֹתֶיךָ. |
| Ish ba·ar lo yeida, | אִישׁ בַּעַר לֹא יֵדָע, |
| u-kh'sil lo yavin et zot. | וּכְסִיל לֹא יָבִין אֶת זֹאת. |
| Bif'ro·aḥ r'sha·im k'mo eisev, | בִּפְרֹחַ רְשָׁעִים כְּמוֹ עֵשֶׂב, |
| va-yatzitzu kol po·alei aven, | וַיָּצִיצוּ כָּל פֹּעֲלֵי אָוֶן, |
| l'hisham'dam adei ad. | לְהִשָּׁמְדָם עֲדֵי עַד. |
| V'atah marom l'olam Adonai. | וְאַתָּה מָרוֹם לְעֹלָם יְיָ. |

## THE PSALM FOR SHABBAT

It is good to gives thanks to Adonai,
To sing praises to Your Name, God on high.

To tell of Your lovingkindness in the morning,
Of Your faithfulness at night,
To the music of harp and stringed instruments.

Adonai, Your works make me happy,
I sing with joy about Your handiwork.

How great are Your works, Adonai.
Your thoughts are very deep.

Unthinking people don't know this,
The foolish can't understand it:

Wicked people may grow as quickly as grass,
But they will be destroyed forever.
For You are always on high.

**Psalm 92** was originally recited by the Levites in the Temple as the Psalm for Shabbat. The Psalm's contents seem to have little connection to Shabbat. Thus various legends have arisen to explain this association. In one midrash (Avot de-Rabbi Natan A1), evening arrives on Friday night, the day of Adam and Eve's creation. Adam is afraid of the dark and attributes the lack of light to his transgression in the Garden of Eden, not realizing that darkness will come each and every evening. The next morning, when Adam sees the light of the rising sun he rejoices and offers an ox as an offering to God. Three groups of angels then descend with their musical instruments and together with Adam, they sing a Psalm of praise to God, as it is said: "A Song for Shabbat. It is good to give thanks to Adonai, to sing praises to Your name, God on high."

The Psalm concludes by comparing righteous people to the date palm and cedar tree. The date palm gives sweet fruit and the cedar has very strong wood. The righteous person will have the best qualities of both – productive and generous, strong and resolute.

| | |
|---|---|
| Ki hineih oy'vekha, Adonai, | כִּי הִנֵּה אֹיְבֶיךָ, יְיָ, |
| ki hineih oy'vekha yoveidu, | כִּי הִנֵּה אֹיְבֶיךָ יֹאבֵדוּ, |
| yitpar'du kol po·alei aven. | יִתְפָּרְדוּ כָּל פֹּעֲלֵי אָוֶן. |
| Va-tarem kir'eim karni, | וַתָּרֶם כִּרְאֵים קַרְנִי, |
| baloti b'shemen ra·anan. | בַּלֹּתִי בְּשֶׁמֶן רַעֲנָן. |
| Va-tabeit eini b'shurai, | וַתַּבֵּט עֵינִי בְּשׁוּרָי, |
| b'kamim alai m'rei·im | בַּקָּמִים עָלַי מְרֵעִים |
| tishma·nah oznai. | תִּשְׁמַעְנָה אָזְנָי. |
| Tzaddik ka-tamar yifraḥ, | צַדִּיק כַּתָּמָר יִפְרָח, |
| k'erez bal'vanon yisgeh. | כְּאֶרֶז בַּלְּבָנוֹן יִשְׂגֶּה. |
| Sh'tulim b'veit Adonai, | שְׁתוּלִים בְּבֵית יְיָ, |
| b'ḥatzrot Eloheinu yafriḥu. | בְּחַצְרוֹת אֱלֹהֵינוּ יַפְרִיחוּ. |
| Od y'nuvun b'seivah, | עוֹד יְנוּבוּן בְּשֵׂיבָה, |
| d'sheinim v'ra·ananim yih'yu. | דְּשֵׁנִים וְרַעֲנַנִּים יִהְיוּ. |
| L'hagid ki yashar Adonai, | לְהַגִּיד כִּי יָשָׁר יְיָ, |
| tzuri v'lo avlatah bo. | צוּרִי וְלֹא עַוְלָתָה בּוֹ. |

## PSALM 27

*(From the first day of the month of Elul until the end of Sukkot we read this Psalm)*

| | |
|---|---|
| L'David. | לְדָוִד, |
| Adonai ori v'yishi, | יְיָ אוֹרִי וְיִשְׁעִי |
| mi-mi ira. | מִמִּי אִירָא, |
| Adnoi ma·oz ḥayyai, | יְיָ מָעוֹז חַיַּי |
| mi-mi efḥad. | מִמִּי אֶפְחָד. |
| Bi-k'rov alai m'rei·im | בִּקְרֹב עָלַי מְרֵעִים |
| le-ekhol et b'sari, | לֶאֱכֹל אֶת בְּשָׂרִי, |
| Tzarai v'oy'vai li | צָרַי וְאֹיְבַי לִי, |
| heimah kashlu v'nafa'lu. | הֵמָּה כָשְׁלוּ וְנָפָלוּ. |
| Im taḥaneh alai maḥaneh | אִם תַּחֲנֶה עָלַי מַחֲנֶה |
| lo yira libi, | לֹא יִירָא לִבִּי, |
| Im takum alai milḥamah | אִם תָּקוּם עָלַי מִלְחָמָה |
| b'zot ani votei·aḥ. | בְּזֹאת אֲנִי בוֹטֵחַ. |
| Aḥat sha·alti mei-eit Adonai, | אַחַת שָׁאַלְתִּי מֵאֵת יְיָ, |
| otah avakeish: | אוֹתָהּ אֲבַקֵּשׁ, |

Your enemies, Adonai, Your enemies will be destroyed,
All evil-doers will be scattered.

But You have lifted me up, refreshed me with sweet oil.

My eyes have seen the defeat of my enemies;
I have heard the downfall of those who attacked me.

The righteous shall blossom like the date-palm,
They shall grow like a cedar of Lebanon.

Planted in Adonai's house,
they blossom in our God's courts.
They still give fruit even in old age,
sleek and fresh.

So that they may tell that God is upright.
God is my Rock, in whom there is no wrong.

## PSALM 27

*(From the first day of the month of Elul until the end of Sukkot we read this Psalm)*

A Psalm of David:
Adonai is my light and my help, whom shall I fear?
Adonai is the strength of my life, of whom shall I be afraid?

*When my enemies try to hurt me, they will stumble and fall.*
*Even if an army stands against me, my heart will feel no fear;*

One thing I asked of Adonai, and continue to seek:
To live in Adonai's House all the days of my life;
In order to see God's beauty and to visit in God's Temple.

*God will shelter me in a safe sukkah on an evil day,*
*Hide me in God's tent, lift me high upon a rock,*
*Out of danger's reach.*

| | |
|---|---|
| Shivti b'veit Adonai | שִׁבְתִּי בְּבֵית יְיָ |
| kol y'mei ḥayai, | כׇּל יְמֵי חַיַּי, |
| La-ḥazot b'no·am Adonai | לַחֲזוֹת בְּנֹעַם יְיָ |
| u-l'vakeir b'heikhalo. | וּלְבַקֵּר בְּהֵיכָלוֹ. |
| Ki yitzp'neini b'sukkoh | כִּי יִצְפְּנֵנִי בְּסֻכֹּה |
| b'yom ra·ah, | בְּיוֹם רָעָה, |
| Yastireini b'seiter ohalo, | יַסְתִּרֵנִי בְּסֵתֶר אׇהֳלוֹ, |
| b'tzur y'rom'meini. | בְּצוּר יְרוֹמְמֵנִי. |
| V'atah yarum roshi | וְעַתָּה יָרוּם רֹאשִׁי |
| al oy'vai s'vivotai, | עַל אֹיְבַי סְבִיבוֹתַי, |
| v-ezb'ḥah v'ohalo | וְאֶזְבְּחָה בְאׇהֳלוֹ |
| zivḥei t'ru·ah, | זִבְחֵי תְרוּעָה, |
| Ashirah va-azam'rah la-Adonai. | אָשִׁירָה וַאֲזַמְּרָה לַייָ. |
| Sh'ma Adonai, koli ekra, | שְׁמַע יְיָ קוֹלִי אֶקְרָא, |
| v'ḥoneini va-aneini. | וְחׇנֵּנִי וַעֲנֵנִי. |
| L'kha amar libi | לְךָ אָמַר לִבִּי, |
| bak'shu fanai, | בַּקְּשׁוּ פָנָי, |
| Et panekha Adonai avakeish. | אֶת פָּנֶיךָ יְיָ אֲבַקֵּשׁ. |
| Al tasteir panekha mi-meni, | אַל תַּסְתֵּר פָּנֶיךָ מִמֶּנִּי, |
| At tat b'af avdekha, | אַל תַּט בְּאַף עַבְדֶּךָ, |
| ezrati hayita, | עֶזְרָתִי הָיִיתָ, |
| Al tit'sheini v'al ta·azveini | אַל תִּטְּשֵׁנִי וְאַל תַּעַזְבֵנִי |
| Elohei yish·i. | אֱלֹהֵי יִשְׁעִי. |
| Ki avi v'imi azavuni | כִּי אָבִי וְאִמִּי עֲזָבוּנִי, |
| Va-Adonai ya·asfeini. | וַייָ יַאַסְפֵנִי. |
| Horeini Adonai darkekha | הוֹרֵנִי יְיָ דַּרְכֶּךָ, |
| u-n'ḥeini b'oraḥ mishor | וּנְחֵנִי בְּאֹרַח מִישׁוֹר, |
| l'ma·an shor'rai. | לְמַעַן שׁוֹרְרָי. |
| Al tit'neini b'nefesh tzarai, | אַל תִּתְּנֵנִי בְּנֶפֶשׁ צָרָי, |
| Ki kamu vi eidei sheker | כִּי קָמוּ בִי עֵדֵי שֶׁקֶר |
| vifei·aḥ ḥamas. | וִיפֵחַ חָמָס. |
| Lulei he-emanti lir·ot | לוּלֵא הֶאֱמַנְתִּי, לִרְאוֹת |
| b'tuv Adonai b'eretz ḥayyim. | בְּטוּב יְיָ, בְּאֶרֶץ חַיִּים. |
| Kaveih el Adonai, | קַוֵּה אֶל יְיָ, |
| ḥazak v'ya·ameitz libekha | חֲזַק וְיַאֲמֵץ לִבֶּךָ, |
| v'kaveih el Adonai. | וְקַוֵּה אֶל יְיָ. |

I can raise my head high above my enemies all around me. I can worship in God's Tent with happy shofar sounds

*In times of danger and fear, God is my trusted shield.*
*Even if my father and mother left me, God would take me in.*

I never stopped believing that I would see
Adonai's goodness in the land of the living.

*Hope in Adonai. Be strong and let your heart be brave.*
*Hope in Adonai.*

**Psalm 27** is a very personal and intimate psalm, reminding us that although God is our Judge, the Almighty is also our light and our help. It is recited from the beginning of the Hebrew month of Elul until the end of Sukkot. One interpretation is: "Adonai is my light" reminds us of Rosh Hashanah as our process of self-evaluation shines a light of awareness on our misdeeds..

# P'sukei D'zimrah

## BARUKH SHE-AMAR

| | |
|---|---|
| Barukh she-amar | בָּרוּךְ שֶׁאָמַר |
| v'haya ha-olam, | וְהָיָה הָעוֹלָם, |
| barukh Hu. | בָּרוּךְ הוּא, |
| Barukh oseh v'reishit, | בָּרוּךְ עֹשֶׂה בְרֵאשִׁית, |
| barukh omeir v'oseh, | בָּרוּךְ אוֹמֵר וְעוֹשֶׂה, |
| Barukh gozeir u-m'kayeim, | בָּרוּךְ גּוֹזֵר וּמְקַיֵּם, |
| barukh m'raḥeim al ha-aretz, | בָּרוּךְ מְרַחֵם עַל הָאָרֶץ, |
| Barukh m'raḥeim al ha-b'riyot, | בָּרוּךְ מְרַחֵם עַל הַבְּרִיּוֹת, |
| barukh m'shaleim sakhar tov | בָּרוּךְ מְשַׁלֵּם שָׂכָר טוֹב |
| li-rei·av, | לִירֵאָיו, |
| Barukh ḥai la-ad | בָּרוּךְ חַי לָעַד |
| v'kayam la-netzaḥ, | וְקַיָּם לָנֶצַח, |
| barukh podeh u-matzil, | בָּרוּךְ פּוֹדֶה וּמַצִּיל, |
| barukh sh'mo. | בָּרוּךְ שְׁמוֹ. |
| | |
| Barukh Atah Adonai, | בָּרוּךְ אַתָּה יְיָ |
| Eloheinu Melekh ha-olam, | אֱלֹהֵינוּ מֶלֶךְ הָעוֹלָם, |
| ha-Eil, | הָאֵל |
| ha-av ha-raḥaman, | הָאָב הָרַחֲמָן, |
| ham'hulal b'fi amo, | הַמְהֻלָּל בְּפִי עַמּוֹ, |
| m'shubaḥ u-m'fo·ar | מְשֻׁבָּח וּמְפֹאָר |
| bil'shon ḥasidav | בִּלְשׁוֹן חֲסִידָיו |
| va-avodav. | וַעֲבָדָיו, |
| U-v'shirei David avdekha | וּבְשִׁירֵי דָוִד עַבְדֶּךָ. |
| n'halelkha Adonai Eloheinu, | נְהַלֶּלְךָ יְיָ אֱלֹהֵינוּ |
| bish'vaḥot u-viz'mirot, | בִּשְׁבָחוֹת וּבִזְמִירוֹת, |
| n'gadelkha u-n'shabeiḥakha | וּנְגַדֶּלְךָ וּנְשַׁבֵּחֲךָ |
| u-n'fa·erkha | וּנְפָאֶרְךָ |
| v'nazkir shimkha | וְנַזְכִּיר שִׁמְךָ, |
| v'namlikh'kha | וְנַמְלִיכְךָ, |
| Malkeinu Eloheinu, | מַלְכֵּנוּ אֱלֹהֵינוּ, |

# P'sukei D'zimrah

## BARUKH SHE-AMAR

*It is the custom to stand for this prayer. The traditional reason for this is that this prayer dates back to the Men of the Great Assembly (perhaps 410–310 BCE), who were very holy and whose teachings had prophetic authority.*

**Naming and praising God**

Praised is the One who spoke – and the world was!
Praised is God.
Praised is the One who made Creation.
Praised is the One who speaks and it is done.
Praised is the One who decides and it happens.
Praised is the One who has mercy on the world.
Praised is the One who has mercy on all creatures.
Praised is the One who rewards those who respect God.
Praised is the One who lives forever and exists eternally.
Praised is the One who redeems and rescues.
Praised be God's name.

Praised are You, Adonai our God, Ruler of the universe, God, merciful Parent, You are praised in song by Your people, praised and glorified by Your loyal servants. We will sing to You, Adonai our God, with the songs written by Your servant David. We will tell how great You are with praises and Psalms.

***Barukh She-amar***: We begin the *P'sukei D'zimra* by thanking God for creating the world. You can read the phrases in the blessing's first paragraph as different names of God. In fact, *mi she-amar v'haya ha-olam* [The One who spoke and the word was] is one of the names of God found in the Talmud. When we think of this prayer in this way, we deepen our understanding of God's multifaceted nature. When we conclude by saying barukh sh'mo, "praised be God's name," we understand that no one name, no one description, can contain God's greatness. As you recite this prayer, consider different ways that you have experienced God's presence.

| | |
|---|---|
| יָחִיד, חֵי הָעוֹלָמִים, | yaḥid ḥei ha-olamim. |
| מֶלֶךְ מְשֻׁבָּח וּמְפֹאָר עֲדֵי עַד | Melekh m'shubaḥ u-m'fo·ar adei |
| שְׁמוֹ הַגָּדוֹל. | ad sh'mo ha-gadol. |
| בָּרוּךְ אַתָּה יְיָ, | Barukh Atah Adonai, Melekh |
| מֶלֶךְ מְהֻלָּל בַּתִּשְׁבָּחוֹת. | m'hulal ba-tishbaḥot. |

## ASHREI

### *The joy of praising God*

*The verses are often read responsively, with the congregation reading the starred lines.*

| | |
|---|---|
| אַשְׁרֵי יוֹשְׁבֵי | Ashrei yos'hvei |
| בֵיתֶךָ, | veitekha, |
| עוֹד יְהַלְלוּךָ סֶּלָה. | od y'hal'lukha selah. |
| *אַשְׁרֵי הָעָם שֶׁכָּכָה לּוֹ, | *Ashrei ha-am she-kakha lo, |
| אַשְׁרֵי הָעָם | ashrei ha-am |
| שֶׁיְיָ אֱלֹהָיו. | she-Adonai Elohav. |
| תְּהִלָּה לְדָוִד, | T'hilah l'David |
| אֲרוֹמִמְךָ אֱלוֹהַי הַמֶּלֶךְ, | Aromimkha Elohai ha-Melekh, |
| וַאֲבָרְכָה שִׁמְךָ לְעוֹלָם וָעֶד. | va-avar'kha shimkha l'olam va·ed. |
| *בְּכָל יוֹם אֲבָרְכֶךָּ, | *B'khol yom avar'kheka, |
| וַאֲהַלְלָה שִׁמְךָ לְעוֹלָם וָעֶד. | va·ahal'lah shimkha l'olam va·ed. |
| גָּדוֹל יְיָ וּמְהֻלָּל מְאֹד, | Gadol Adonai u-m'hulal m'od, |
| וְלִגְדֻלָּתוֹ אֵין חֵקֶר. | v'lig'dulato ein ḥeiker. |
| *דּוֹר לְדוֹר | *Dor l'dor |
| יְשַׁבַּח מַעֲשֶׂיךָ, | y'shabaḥ ma·asekha, |
| וּגְבוּרֹתֶיךָ יַגִּידוּ. | u-g'vurotekha yagidu. |
| הֲדַר כְּבוֹד הוֹדֶךָ, | Hadar k'vod hodekha, |
| וְדִבְרֵי נִפְלְאֹתֶיךָ אָשִׂיחָה. | v'divrei nifl'otekha asiḥah. |
| *וֶעֱזוּז נוֹרְאוֹתֶיךָ יֹאמֵרוּ, | *Ve-ezuz nor'otekha yomeiru, |
| וּגְדֻלָּתְךָ אֲסַפְּרֶנָּה. | u-g'dulat'kha asap'renah. |
| זֵכֶר רַב טוּבְךָ יַבִּיעוּ, | Zeikher rav tuv'kha yabi·u, |
| וְצִדְקָתְךָ יְרַנֵּנוּ. | v'tzidkat'kha y'raneinu. |
| *חַנּוּן וְרַחוּם יְיָ, | *Ḥanun v'raḥum Adonai, |
| אֶרֶךְ אַפַּיִם וּגְדָל חָסֶד. | erekh apayim ug'dol ḥased. |

Unique One, Who lives forever, You are the Ruler that we praise, whose great name is wonderful forever. Praised are You, Adonai, Ruler whom we praise with songs.

## ASHREI

### *The joy of praising God*

Happy are they who live in Your house;
They shall continue to praise You. (Psalm 84:5)

Happy are the people for whom this is so;
Happy are the people whose God is Adonai. (Psalm 144:15)

A Psalm of David.
א I will honor you, my God and Ruler,
I will praise Your name forever and ever.
ב Every day I will praise You,
And sing praises to Your name forever and ever.
ג Great is Adonai and greatly praised;
There is no limit to God's greatness.
ד One generation shall praise Your deeds to another,
And tell about Your mighty deeds.
ה I will speak about Your splendor and glory,
And Your wonderful deeds.

**Ashrei** calls upon all people to glorify God's majesty, emphasizing the Almighty's providential care for all of God's creation. The Babylonian Talmud (Berakhot 4a) teaches that the Rabbis guarantee a place in the World-to-Come to any person who recites Ashrei three times a day. This is because it contains the verse, "You open Your hand and feed everything that lives to its heart's content." God is recognized as the ultimate source in the maintenance of all of life. Ashrei's prominence among the psalms is also reflected in the Jewish legal ruling that if a person arrives late at services and has time to recite only a single psalm before continuing to pray with the rest of the congregation, that it ought to be Ashrei.

Ashrei is written as an alphabetical acrostic, following the order of the Hebrew alphabet. This makes it easier for the prayer to be memorized.

| | |
|---|---|
| Tov Adonai lakol, | טוֹב יְיָ לַכֹּל, |
| v'raḥamav al kol ma·asav. | וְרַחֲמָיו עַל כָּל מַעֲשָׂיו. |
| *Yodukha Adonai kol ma·asekha, | *יוֹדְוּךָ יְיָ כָּל מַעֲשֶׂיךָ, |
| va-ḥasidekha y'var'khukha. | וַחֲסִידֶיךָ יְבָרְכוּכָה. |
| K'vod malkhut'kha yomeiru, | כְּבוֹד מַלְכוּתְךָ יֹאמֵרוּ, |
| u-g'vurat'kha y'dabeiru | וּגְבוּרָתְךָ יְדַבֵּרוּ. |
| *L'hodi·a liv'nei ha-adam g'vurotav, | *לְהוֹדִיעַ לִבְנֵי הָאָדָם גְּבוּרֹתָיו, |
| u-kh'vod hadar malkhuto | וּכְבוֹד הֲדַר מַלְכוּתוֹ. |
| Malkhut'kha malkhut kol olamim, | מַלְכוּתְךָ מַלְכוּת כָּל עֹלָמִים, |
| u-memshalt'kha b'khol dor va-dor | וּמֶמְשַׁלְתְּךָ בְּכָל דֹּר וָדֹר. |
| *Someikh Adonai l'khol ha-nof'lim, | *סוֹמֵךְ יְיָ לְכָל הַנֹּפְלִים, |
| v'zokeif l'khol hak'fufim. | וְזוֹקֵף לְכָל הַכְּפוּפִים. |
| Einei khol eilekha y'sabeiru, | עֵינֵי כֹל אֵלֶיךָ יְשַׂבֵּרוּ, |
| v'Atah notein lahem | וְאַתָּה נוֹתֵן לָהֶם |
| et okhlam b'ito. | אֶת אָכְלָם בְּעִתּוֹ. |
| *Pote'aḥ et yadekha, | *פּוֹתֵחַ אֶת יָדֶךָ, |
| u-masbi·a l'khol ḥai ratzon. | וּמַשְׂבִּיעַ לְכָל חַי רָצוֹן. |
| Tzadik Adonai b'khol d'rakhav, | צַדִּיק יְיָ בְּכָל דְּרָכָיו, |
| v'ḥasid b'khol ma·asav. | וְחָסִיד בְּכָל מַעֲשָׂיו. |
| *Karov Adonai l'khol kor'av, | *קָרוֹב יְיָ לְכָל קֹרְאָיו, |
| l'khol asher yikra·uhu ve-emet. | לְכֹל אֲשֶׁר יִקְרָאֻהוּ בֶאֱמֶת. |
| R'tzon y'rei·av ya·aseh, | רְצוֹן יְרֵאָיו יַעֲשֶׂה, |
| v'et shav·atam yishmah v'yoshi·eim. | וְאֶת שַׁוְעָתָם יִשְׁמַע וְיוֹשִׁיעֵם. |
| *Shomeir Adonai et kol ohavav | *שׁוֹמֵר יְיָ אֶת כָּל אֹהֲבָיו, |
| v'et kol har'sha·im yashmid | וְאֵת כָּל הָרְשָׁעִים יַשְׁמִיד. |
| T'hilat Adonai y'daber pi, | תְּהִלַּת יְיָ יְדַבֶּר פִּי, |
| Vi-varekh kol basar | וִיבָרֵךְ כָּל בָּשָׂר |
| sheim kodsho l'olam va·ed. | שֵׁם קָדְשׁוֹ לְעוֹלָם וָעֶד. |
| *Va-anaḥnu n'vareikh Yah, | *וַאֲנַחְנוּ נְבָרֵךְ יָהּ, |
| mei-atah v'ad olam. | מֵעַתָּה וְעַד עוֹלָם, |
| Hal'luyah. | הַלְלוּיָהּ. |

ו They will talk about the power of Your mighty acts;
And I will tell of Your greatness.

ז They recall Your great goodness,
And sing of Your righteousness.

ח Adonai is gracious and caring, patient and very kind.

ט Adonai is good to all,
And merciful to everything God made.

י All Your works shall praise You, Adonai,
And Your faithful ones shall bless You.

כ They shall speak of the glory of Your rule,
And talk of Your might,

ל To announce to humanity God's greatness,
The splendor and glory of God's rule.

מ God, You rule forever,
Your kingdom is for all generations.

ס God holds up all who fall,
And helps all who are bent over stand straight.

ע The eyes of all look to You with hope,
And You give them their food at the right time.

פ You open Your hand,
And feed everything that lives to its heart's content.

צ Adonai is good in every way,
And kind in every deed.

ק Adonai is near to all who call,
To all who call to God sincerely.

ר God does the wishes of those who respect God,
God hears their cry and saves them.

ש Adonai protects all who love God,
But God will destroy the wicked.

ת My mouth shall speak praises of God,
And all beings shall bless God's holy name
Forever and ever. (Psalm 145)

We shall praise God,
Now and forever. Halleluyah. (Psalm 115:18)

## PSALM 150

| | |
|---|---|
| הַלְלוּיָהּ, | Hal'luyah, |
| הַלְלוּ אֵל בְּקָדְשׁוֹ, | Hal'lu Eil b'kodsho, |
| הַלְלוּהוּ | hal'luhu |
| בִּרְקִיעַ עֻזּוֹ. | bir'ki·a uzo. |
| הַלְלוּהוּ בִגְבוּרֹתָיו, | Hal'luhu vig'vurotav, |
| הַלְלוּהוּ כְּרֹב גֻּדְלוֹ. | hal'luhu k'rov gud-lo. |
| הַלְלוּהוּ בְּתֵקַע שׁוֹפָר, | Hal'luhu b'teika shofar, |
| הַלְלוּהוּ בְּנֵבֶל וְכִנּוֹר. | Hal'luhu b'neivel v'khinor. |
| הַלְלוּהוּ בְּתֹף וּמָחוֹל, | Hal'luhu b'tof u-maḥol, |
| הַלְלוּהוּ בְּמִנִּים וְעֻגָב. | Hal'luhu b'minim v'ugav. |
| הַלְלוּהוּ בְצִלְצְלֵי שָׁמַע, | Hal'luhu v'tzil-tz'lei shama, |
| הַלְלוּהוּ בְּצִלְצְלֵי תְרוּעָה. | Hal'luhu b'tzil-tz'lei t'ru·ah. |
| ♪ כֹּל הַנְּשָׁמָה תְּהַלֵּל יָהּ | Kol ha-n'shamah t'haleil Ya. |
| הַלְלוּיָהּ. | Hal'luyah! |
| כֹּל הַנְּשָׁמָה תְּהַלֵּל יָהּ | Kol ha-n'shamah t'haleil Ya |
| הַלְלוּיָהּ. | Hal'luyah! |

## PSALM 150

Halleluyah! Praise God in God's holy place.
Praise God in the heavens.

Praise God for mighty deeds,
Praise God for endless greatness.

Praise God with the sound of the Shofar,
Praise God with harp and lyre.

Praise God with drum and dance,
Praise God with lute and pipe.

Praise God with loud cymbals,
Praise God with clashing cymbals.
Let everything that breathes praise God.

**Psalm 150:** This is the last Psalm in the Book of Psalms. It tells us that we can praise God not just with words, but also with music and dance, with our bodies and with our voices. In fact, sometimes our joy is too great to be expressed in words. So we end the Book of Psalms, and this part of the service, on a note of exaltation and joy.

## SHOKHEIN AD

***Though words are inadequate, nevertheless we still praise God.***

| | |
|---|---|
| Shokhein ad, | שׁוֹכֵן עַד, |
| marom v'kadosh sh'mo. | מָרוֹם וְקָדוֹשׁ שְׁמוֹ. |
| v'khatuv: | וְכָתוּב, |
| ran'nu tzadikim bAdonai, | רַנְּנוּ צַדִּיקִים בַּייָ, |
| la-y'sharim navah t'hilah. | לַיְשָׁרִים נָאוָה תְהִלָּה. |
| B'fi y'sharim | בְּפִי יְשָׁרִים |
| tit-halal, | תִּתְהַלָּל, |
| u-v'divrei tzadikim | וּבְדִבְרֵי צַדִּיקִים |
| titbarakh | תִּתְבָּרַךְ, |
| uvil'shon ḥasidim | וּבִלְשׁוֹן חֲסִידִים |
| titromam, | תִּתְרוֹמָם, |
| u-v'kerev k'doshim | וּבְקֶרֶב קְדוֹשִׁים |
| titkadash. | תִּתְקַדָּשׁ. |

| | |
|---|---|
| U-v'mak-halot | וּבְמַקְהֲלוֹת |
| riv'vot am'kha beit Yisra·el | רִבְבוֹת עַמְּךָ בֵּית יִשְׂרָאֵל, |
| b'rina | בְּרִנָּה |
| yitpa·ar shimkha Malkenu | יִתְפָּאַר שִׁמְךָ מַלְכֵּנוּ, |
| b'khol dor va-dor. | בְּכָל דּוֹר וָדוֹר, |
| She-ken ḥovat | שֶׁכֵּן חוֹבַת |
| kol ha-y'tzurim l'fanekha | כָּל הַיְצוּרִים לְפָנֶיךָ |
| Adonai Eloheinu vei-lohei avoteinu, | יְיָ אֱלֹהֵינוּ וֵאלֹהֵי אֲבוֹתֵינוּ, |
| l'hodot l'halleil l'shabei·aḥ, | לְהוֹדוֹת, לְהַלֵּל, לְשַׁבֵּחַ, |
| l'fa·er l'romeim l'hadeir, | לְפָאֵר, לְרוֹמֵם, לְהַדֵּר, |
| l'vareikh l'aleh ul'kaleis | לְבָרֵךְ, לְעַלֵּה וּלְקַלֵּס, |
| al kol divrei | עַל כָּל דִּבְרֵי |
| shirot v'tishb'ḥot | שִׁירוֹת וְתִשְׁבְּחוֹת |
| David ben Yishai | דָּוִד בֶּן יִשַׁי |
| avd'kha m'shiḥekha. | עַבְדְּךָ מְשִׁיחֶךָ. |

## SHOKHEIN AD

***Though words are inadequate,***
***nevertheless we still praise God.***

God dwells forever – high and holy is God's name. (Isaiah 57:15) As the Psalmist wrote: "Good people, rejoice in Adonai; how lovely it is when the upright praise God."

You are praised by the mouth of the upright.
You are blessed by the words of the righteous.
You are exalted by the tongue of the faithful.
You are sanctified in the midst of the holy ones.

Tens of thousands of Your people gather in every generation joyously to praise Your name, our Ruler. Indeed, it is the duty of all creatures before you, Adonai our God and God of our ancestors, to thank, to extol, to praise, to glorify, to exalt, to honor, to bless, to raise high, and to acclaim You, and to add our own praises to the songs of David, Your royal servant.

**You are praised:** These words all speak of the value of praising God. Why is praise such a major part of our worship? Does God need it? Surely not. So we must conclude that *we* need it. Our prayers prompt us to express praise and gratitude, "to add our own praises to the songs of David." It's like raising children, reminding them consistently to say "please" and "thank you," prodding them to put some coins in the tzedakah box. Rabbi Abraham Joshua Heschel wrote, "Wonder or radical amazement is the chief characteristic of the religious person's attitude toward history and nature. One attitude is alien to his spirit: taking things for granted, regarding events as a natural course of things." When we praise, bless and exalt God, we open our eyes and our hearts to take in God's wonders and God's presence.

Just as the *P'sukei D'zimrah* begins with a blessing – *Barukh She-amar* – so it ends with a blessing praising God who, because God gives life to the world, is emphatically deserving of our praise.

Yishtabaḥ shimkha la-ad, Malkeinu,
ha-Eil ha-Melekh hagadol
v'hakadosh bashamayim uva-aretz.
Ki l'kha na·eh,
Adonai, Eloheinu
vei-lohei avoteinu,
shir u-sh'vaḥah, haleil v'zimrah,
oz umemshalah,
netzaḥ, g'dulah ug'vurah,
t'hilah v'tiferet,
k'dusha umal'khut,
b'rakhot v'hoda·ot
mei-Atah v'ad olam.
Barukh Atah Adonai
Eil Melekh gadol batishbaḥot,
Eil
ha-hoda·ot,
Adon ha-nifla·ot,
ha-boḥeir b'shirei zimrah,
Melekh
Eil
ḥei ha-olamim.

יִשְׁתַּבַּח שִׁמְךָ לָעַד מַלְכֵּנוּ,
הָאֵל הַמֶּלֶךְ הַגָּדוֹל וְהַקָּדוֹשׁ
בַּשָּׁמַיִם וּבָאָרֶץ.
כִּי לְךָ נָאֶה,
יְיָ אֱלֹהֵינוּ
וֵאלֹהֵי אֲבוֹתֵינוּ,
שִׁיר וּשְׁבָחָה, הַלֵּל וְזִמְרָה,
עֹז וּמֶמְשָׁלָה,
נֶצַח, גְּדֻלָּה וּגְבוּרָה,
תְּהִלָּה וְתִפְאֶרֶת,
קְדֻשָּׁה וּמַלְכוּת.
בְּרָכוֹת וְהוֹדָאוֹת
מֵעַתָּה וְעַד עוֹלָם.
בָּרוּךְ אַתָּה יְיָ,
אֵל מֶלֶךְ גָּדוֹל בַּתִּשְׁבָּחוֹת,
אֵל
הַהוֹדָאוֹת,
אֲדוֹן הַנִּפְלָאוֹת,
הַבּוֹחֵר בְּשִׁירֵי זִמְרָה,
מֶלֶךְ,
אֵל,
חֵי הָעוֹלָמִים.

May Your name be praised forever, our Ruler, great and holy God, in heaven and on earth. Adonai our God and God of our ancestors, it is proper to sing songs of glory to You, songs of praise, singing of your strength and sovereignty, victory and greatness, power, praise and splendor, holiness and mastery; singing praises and thanks now and forever. Praised are You, Adonai, God and Ruler, great in praises, God of thanksgivings, Sovereign of wonders, who chooses songs of praise, Ruler, God, Life-giver of the universe.

This prayer emphasizes that we sing our praises and prayers. Non-Jews visiting Jewish services for the first time often comment that they noticed how much of the service is sung. One aspect of Jewish prayer is the *nusaḥ*, the different modes for chanting prayers on weekdays, Shabbat, festivals and High Holy days. In addition, there are many melodies, and new ones all the time. We notice it when we go to a different synagogue if they have different melodies for prayers than from our own synagogue. In short, music and song are a central part of Jewish worship. What are some of your favorite melodies? How has song played a part in your own prayer life?

## ḤATZI KADDISH

*Leader:*

| | |
|---|---|
| Yit-gadal v'yit-kadash sh'mei rabba, | יִתְגַּדַּל וְיִתְקַדַּשׁ שְׁמֵהּ רַבָּא. |
| b'al'ma di v'ra | בְּעָלְמָא דִּי בְרָא |
| khir'utei | כִרְעוּתֵהּ, |
| v'yam-likh malkhutei | וְיַמְלִיךְ מַלְכוּתֵהּ |
| b'ḥayeikhon u-v'yomeikhon | בְּחַיֵּיכוֹן וּבְיוֹמֵיכוֹן |
| u-v'ḥayei d'khol beit Yisra·el, | וּבְחַיֵּי דְכָל בֵּית יִשְׂרָאֵל, |
| ba'agala u-viz'man kariv, | בַּעֲגָלָא וּבִזְמַן קָרִיב, |
| v'imru, Amen. | וְאִמְרוּ אָמֵן. |

*Congregation and Leader:*

| | |
|---|---|
| Y'hei sh'mei rabba m'va-rakh, | יְהֵא שְׁמֵהּ רַבָּא מְבָרַךְ |
| l'alam ul-al'mei al-maya. | לְעָלַם וּלְעָלְמֵי עָלְמַיָּא. |

*Leader:*

| | |
|---|---|
| Yitbarakh v'yishtabaḥ | יִתְבָּרַךְ וְיִשְׁתַּבַּח |
| v'yitpa·ar v'yitromam v'yitnasei | וְיִתְפָּאַר וְיִתְרוֹמַם וְיִתְנַשֵּׂא |
| v'yit-hadar v'yit·aleh v'yit-halal | וְיִתְהַדָּר וְיִתְעַלֶּה וְיִתְהַלָּל |
| sh'mei d'kud'sha, b'rikh Hu, | שְׁמֵהּ דְּקֻדְשָׁא בְּרִיךְ הוּא, |
| L'eila [u-l'eila mi-kol] | לְעֵלָּא (וּלְעֵלָּא מִכָּל) |
| min kol birkhata v'shirata | מִן כָּל בִּרְכָתָא וְשִׁירָתָא |
| tushb'ḥata v'neḥemata | תֻּשְׁבְּחָתָא וְנֶחֱמָתָא, |
| da·amiran b'al'ma, | דַּאֲמִירָן בְּעָלְמָא, |
| v'imru Amen. | וְאִמְרוּ אָמֵן. |

## ḤATZI KADDISH

May God's great name be made great and holy in the world that God created according to God's will. May God establish the Divine kingdom soon, in our days, quickly and in the near future, and let us say, Amen.

*Congregation and Leader together:*

May God's great name be praised forever and ever.

Blessed, praised, glorified and raised high, honored and elevated be the name of the Holy Blessed One, far beyond all blessings and songs, praises and comforts which people can say, and let us say: Amen.

# Blessings of the Shema

## BARKHU

***Let us praise God.***

*We rise. The leader begins, bowing at the word "Barukh," and straightening up at the word "Adonai."*

| | |
|---|---|
| Bar'khu et Adonai ha-m'vorakh. | בָּרְכוּ אֶת יְיָ הַמְבֹרָךְ |

*The congregation responds, bowing at the word "Barukh," and straightening up at the word "Adonai."*

| | |
|---|---|
| Barukh Adonai ha-m'vorakh<br>l'olam va·ed. | בָּרוּךְ יְיָ הַמְבֹרָךְ<br>לְעוֹלָם וָעֶד |

*The leader repeats:*

| | |
|---|---|
| Barukh Adonai ha-m'vorakh<br>l'olam va·ed | בָּרוּךְ יְיָ הַמְבֹרָךְ<br>לְעוֹלָם וָעֶד |

# Blessings of the Shema

## BARKHU

***Let us praise God.***

*We rise. The leader begins, bowing at the word "Barukh," and straightening up at the word "Adonai."*

Praise Adonai, who is to be praised.

*The congregation responds, bowing at the word "Barukh," and straightening up at the word "Adonai." The leader then repeats.*

Praised be Adonai who is to be praised forever and ever.

*We sit down.*

Praised are You, Adonai our God, Ruler of the universe, who forms light and creates darkness, who makes peace and creates everything.

*Why do we bow here? It says in the First Book of Chronicles (29:20): "David said to the whole assemblage, 'Now bless Adonai God.' All the assemblage blessed Adonai, God of their ancestors, and bowed their heads low to Adonai."*

## YOTZEIR OR

***Shema blessing #1: Creation. Example: morning light.***

| | |
|---|---|
| Barukh Atah Adonai, | בָּרוּךְ אַתָּה יְיָ, |
| Eloheinu Melekh ha-olam, | אֱלֹהֵינוּ מֶלֶךְ הָעוֹלָם, |
| yotzeir or u-vorei ḥoshekh | יוֹצֵר אוֹר וּבוֹרֵא חֹשֶׁךְ, |
| oseh shalom | עֹשֶׂה שָׁלוֹם |
| u-vorei et ha-kol. | וּבוֹרֵא אֶת הַכֹּל. |

## HA-KOL YODUKHA

*On Shabbat, a Yom Tov and Ḥol Ha-mo·ed:*

הַכֹּל יוֹדוּךָ, וְהַכֹּל יְשַׁבְּחוּךָ, וְהַכֹּל יֹאמְרוּ, אֵין קָדוֹשׁ כַּיְיָ.
הַכֹּל יְרוֹמְמוּךָ סֶּלָה, יוֹצֵר הַכֹּל.
הָאֵל הַפּוֹתֵחַ בְּכָל יוֹם דַּלְתוֹת שַׁעֲרֵי מִזְרָח,
וּבוֹקֵעַ חַלּוֹנֵי רָקִיעַ, מוֹצִיא חַמָּה מִמְּקוֹמָהּ,
וּלְבָנָה מִמְּכוֹן שִׁבְתָּהּ, וּמֵאִיר לָעוֹלָם כֻּלּוֹ וּלְיוֹשְׁבָיו,
שֶׁבָּרָא בְּמִדַּת הָרַחֲמִים.
הַמֵּאִיר לָאָרֶץ וְלַדָּרִים עָלֶיהָ בְּרַחֲמִים.
וּבְטוּבוֹ מְחַדֵּשׁ בְּכָל יוֹם תָּמִיד מַעֲשֵׂה בְרֵאשִׁית.
הַמֶּלֶךְ הַמְרוֹמָם לְבַדּוֹ מֵאָז,
הַמְשֻׁבָּח וְהַמְפֹאָר וְהַמִּתְנַשֵּׂא מִימוֹת עוֹלָם.
אֱלֹהֵי עוֹלָם, בְּרַחֲמֶיךָ הָרַבִּים רַחֵם עָלֵינוּ.
אֲדוֹן עֻזֵּנוּ צוּר מִשְׂגַּבֵּנוּ,

## YOTZEIR OR

***Shema blessing #1: Creation. Example: morning light.***

Praised are You, Adonai our God, Ruler of the universe, who forms light and creates darkness, who makes peace and creates everything.

## HA-KOL YODUKHA

*On Shabbat, a Yom Tov and Ḥol Ha-mo·ed:*

All beings praise You, saying: there is none holy like Adonai. All applaud You, Creator of everything, God who opens the gates of the east every day, throws open the windows of the heavens, brings the sun from its place and the moon from its home, shines light to the whole world and to all who live in it – for You created it with Your attribute of mercy. You mercifully give light to the world and to all who live in it, and out of Your goodness You renew Creation every day. The Ruler who has been on high alone from of old, the One who was praised, glorified, and exalted from days of old, God of the universe, with Your great mercy have mercy on us, Adonai who gives us strength.

Rock who shelters us, Shield who saves us, our Shelter. None can compare to You and there is none other than You; there is

**Yotzeir Or:** Light follows us through the Jewish year and the Jewish lifetime. We light candles to begin and end Shabbat and Holy Days. We kindle Hanukah candles in the darkest days of winter. There are customs to light candles at a Brit Milah, a wedding, and, during the week of Shivah following a death. Torah is compared to light. Light symbolizes holiness and God's presence. God created light on Day One of Creation. With this prayer, we remind ourselves of the glory of God's creation, and the miracle of light. We are asked to open our eyes and appreciate that daily light that we can so easily take for granted. Notice that the verbs are in the present tense: Creation is ongoing. Right now, somewhere in the universe, new stars are being born. How can we not praise God?

| | |
|---|---|
| Magein yish-einu | מָגֵן יִשְׁעֵנוּ, |
| Misgav ba-adeinu. | מִשְׂגָּב בַּעֲדֵנוּ. |
| Ein k'erk'keha v'ein zulatekha, | אֵין כְּעֶרְכֶּךָ וְאֵין זוּלָתֶךָ, |
| efes bilt'ekha u-mi domeh lakh. | אֶפֶס בִּלְתֶּךָ, וּמִי דּוֹמֶה לָּךְ. |
| Ein k'erk'kha Adonai Eloheinu | אֵין כְּעֶרְכְּךָ, יְיָ אֱלֹהֵינוּ, |
| ba-olam ha-zeh, | בָּעוֹלָם הַזֶּה, |
| v'ein zulat'kha Malkeinu | וְאֵין זוּלָתְךָ מַלְכֵּנוּ |
| l'ḥayei ha-olam ha-ba. | לְחַיֵּי הָעוֹלָם הַבָּא. |
| Efes bilt'kha go·aleinu | אֶפֶס בִּלְתְּךָ גּוֹאֲלֵנוּ |
| limot ha-mashi·aḥ, | לִימוֹת הַמָּשִׁיחַ, |
| v'ein domeh l'kha | וְאֵין דּוֹמֶה לְּךָ |
| moshi·einu lit'ḥiyat ha-meitim. | מוֹשִׁיעֵנוּ לִתְחִיַּת הַמֵּתִים. |

## EL ADON

| | |
|---|---|
| Eil | אֵל |
| Adon al kol ha-ma·asim, | אָדוֹן עַל כָּל הַמַּעֲשִׂים, |
| barukh | בָּרוּךְ |
| um'vorakh b'fi kol n'shama | וּמְבֹרָךְ בְּפִי כָּל נְשָׁמָה, |
| Godlo v'tuvo malei olam, | גָּדְלוֹ וְטוּבוֹ מָלֵא עוֹלָם, |
| da'at ut'vunah sov'vim oto. | דַּעַת וּתְבוּנָה סֹבְבִים אוֹתוֹ. |
| Hamitga-eh al ḥayot ha-kodesh, | הַמִּתְגָּאֶה עַל חַיּוֹת הַקֹּדֶשׁ, |
| v'nehdar b'khavod al ha-merkavah | וְנֶהְדָּר בְּכָבוֹד עַל הַמֶּרְכָּבָה, |
| Z'khut u-mishor lifnei khi·so, | זְכוּת וּמִישׁוֹר לִפְנֵי כִסְאוֹ, |
| ḥesed v'raḥamim lifnei kh'vodo | חֶסֶד וְרַחֲמִים לִפְנֵי כְבוֹדוֹ. |
| Tovim m'orot | טוֹבִים מְאוֹרוֹת |
| she-bara Eloheinu, | שֶׁבָּרָא אֱלֹהֵינוּ, |
| y'tzaram b'da·at | יְצָרָם בְּדַעַת |
| b'vinah uv'haskel | בְּבִינָה וּבְהַשְׂכֵּל, |
| Ko·ah u'g'vurah natan bahem, | כֹּחַ וּגְבוּרָה נָתַן בָּהֶם, |
| lih'yot moshlim | לִהְיוֹת מוֹשְׁלִים |
| b'kerev tevel | בְּקֶרֶב תֵּבֵל. |
| M'le-im ziv um'fikim nogah, | מְלֵאִים זִיו וּמְפִיקִים נֹגַהּ, |
| na·eh zivam b'khol ha-olam | נָאֶה זִיוָם בְּכָל הָעוֹלָם, |
| S'meiḥim b'tzeitam | שְׂמֵחִים בְּצֵאתָם |
| v'sasim b'vo·am, | וְשָׂשִׂים בְּבוֹאָם, |

nothing without You and who is like You? None can compare to You in this world, and there is none other than You, our Ruler, in the life of the world to come. There is none other than You, our Redeemer, in the days of the Messiah, and none like You, our Redeemer, in the revival of the dead.

## EL ADON

God, Sovereign over all creation, is blessed, and praised by all that breathes.
God's greatness and goodness fill the world.
Knowledge and understanding surround God.
God is above the heavenly beings, and wonderful in glory.
Goodness and uprightness stand before God's throne;
kindness and mercy before God's glory.
The heavenly lights that our God created are good.
God made them wisely, putting strength and power into them to oversee the earth.
They shine brightly, their glow is beautiful throughout the world.
They rise with joy and set with happiness,

**El Adon** is an alphabetical acrostic, whose words have been attributed to the mystics of the eighth century. The hymn is a praise of God who created the sun, moon and the stars. Just as these heavenly bodies obey and proclaim God's sovereignty, so we too prepare to do the same.

| | |
|---|---|
| osim b'eimah | עֹשִׂים בְּאֵימָה |
| r'tzon konam | רְצוֹן קוֹנָם. |
| P'er v'khavod not'nim lish'mo, | פְּאֵר וְכָבוֹד נוֹתְנִים לִשְׁמוֹ, |
| tzoholah v'rinah | צׇהֳלָה וְרִנָּה |
| l'zeikher malkhuto | לְזֵכֶר מַלְכוּתוֹ, |
| Kara la-shemesh | קָרָא לַשֶּׁמֶשׁ |
| va-yizraḥ or, | וַיִּזְרַח אוֹר, |
| ra·ah v'hitkin | רָאָה וְהִתְקִין |
| tzurat hal'vanah | צוּרַת הַלְּבָנָה. |
| Shevaḥ not'nim lo | שֶׁבַח נוֹתְנִים לוֹ |
| kol tz'va marom | כׇּל צְבָא מָרוֹם, |
| Tiferet ug'dulah, | תִּפְאֶרֶת וּגְדֻלָּה, |
| s'rafim v'ofanim | שְׂרָפִים וְאוֹפַנִּים |
| v'hayot hakodesh | וְחַיּוֹת הַקֹּדֶשׁ. |

לָאֵל אֲשֶׁר שָׁבַת מִכׇּל הַמַּעֲשִׂים, בַּיּוֹם הַשְּׁבִיעִי הִתְעַלָּה וְיָשַׁב עַל כִּסֵּא כְבוֹדוֹ, תִּפְאֶרֶת עָטָה לְיוֹם הַמְּנוּחָה, עֹנֶג קָרָא לְיוֹם הַשַּׁבָּת. זֶה שֶׁבַח שֶׁל יוֹם הַשְּׁבִיעִי, שֶׁבּוֹ שָׁבַת אֵל מִכׇּל מְלַאכְתּוֹ, וְיוֹם הַשְּׁבִיעִי מְשַׁבֵּחַ וְאוֹמֵר, מִזְמוֹר שִׁיר לְיוֹם הַשַּׁבָּת, טוֹב לְהוֹדוֹת לַייָ. לְפִיכָךְ יְפָאֲרוּ וִיבָרְכוּ לָאֵל כׇּל יְצוּרָיו, שֶׁבַח יְקָר וּגְדֻלָּה יִתְּנוּ לָאֵל מֶלֶךְ יוֹצֵר כֹּל, הַמַּנְחִיל מְנוּחָה לְעַמּוֹ יִשְׂרָאֵל בִּקְדֻשָּׁתוֹ, בְּיוֹם שַׁבַּת קֹדֶשׁ. שִׁמְךָ יְיָ אֱלֹהֵינוּ יִתְקַדַּשׁ, וְזִכְרְךָ מַלְכֵּנוּ יִתְפָּאַר, בַּשָּׁמַיִם מִמַּעַל וְעַל הָאָרֶץ מִתָּחַת. תִּתְבָּרַךְ מוֹשִׁיעֵנוּ עַל שֶׁבַח מַעֲשֵׂה יָדֶיךָ, וְעַל מְאוֹרֵי אוֹר שֶׁעָשִׂיתָ יְפָאֲרוּךָ סֶּלָה.

*If Yom Tov falls on a weekday, begin here:*

### *Ha-me·ir La-aretz* / You Give Light to the World

הַמֵּאִיר לָאָרֶץ וְלַדָּרִים עָלֶיהָ בְּרַחֲמִים. וּבְטוּבוֹ מְחַדֵּשׁ בְּכׇל יוֹם תָּמִיד מַעֲשֵׂה בְרֵאשִׁית. מָה רַבּוּ מַעֲשֶׂיךָ יְיָ. כֻּלָּם בְּחׇכְמָה עָשִׂיתָ, מָלְאָה הָאָרֶץ קִנְיָנֶךָ. הַמֶּלֶךְ הַמְרוֹמָם לְבַדּוֹ מֵאָז. הַמְשֻׁבָּח וְהַמְפֹאָר וְהַמִּתְנַשֵּׂא מִימוֹת עוֹלָם. אֱלֹהֵי עוֹלָם, בְּרַחֲמֶיךָ הָרַבִּים רַחֵם עָלֵינוּ, אֲדוֹן עֻזֵּנוּ צוּר מִשְׂגַּבֵּנוּ, מָגֵן יִשְׁעֵנוּ מִשְׂגָּב בַּעֲדֵנוּ. אֵל בָּרוּךְ גְּדוֹל דֵּעָה. הֵכִין וְפָעַל זׇהֳרֵי חַמָּה. טוֹב יָצַר כָּבוֹד לִשְׁמוֹ. מְאוֹרוֹת נָתַן סְבִיבוֹת עֻזּוֹ, פִּנּוֹת צְבָאָיו קְדוֹשִׁים, רוֹמְמֵי שַׁדַּי. תָּמִיד מְסַפְּרִים, כְּבוֹד אֵל וּקְדֻשָּׁתוֹ. תִּתְבָּרַךְ יְיָ אֱלֹהֵינוּ עַל שֶׁבַח מַעֲשֵׂה יָדֶיךָ. וְעַל מְאוֹרֵי אוֹר שֶׁעָשִׂיתָ יְפָאֲרוּךָ סֶּלָה.

faithfully doing God's will.
They bring glory and honor to God's name,
causing rejoicing and joyous song at the mention of God's rule.
God called to the sun and it shone with light;
God set the phases of the moon.
All the heavenly beings praise God's glory and greatness.

To God who ceased from all activity on the seventh day, rising up to sit on the Throne of Glory. God wrapped the day of rest in splendor, calling the Shabbat a day of delight. This is the praise of the seventh day, that on it God from all creative work. The seventh day itself speaks praise: "A Psalm sung by the Shabbat day: It is good to thank God." Therefore all that God made should glorify and bless God, offering praise, honor, and greatness to God who is the Ruler and Creator of all; who granted rest to the people of Israel on the holy Shabbat day. Your Name, Adonai our God, will be made holy and Your memory, our Ruler, will be exalted in the heavens above and on the earth below. May you, our Savior, be praised by the works of Your power and glorified by the sources of light that You made.

*If Yom Tov falls on a weekday, begin here:*

## *Ha-me·ir La-aretz* / You Give Light to the World

With mercy You give light to the world and to those who live in it, and because You are good, You renew Creation every day. "How great are Your works, Adonai, You made them all with wisdom, the earth is filled with Your possessions."

The blessed God, with great knowledge, prepared and made the rays of the sun. The Good One created for the glory of God's name. God placed lights around God's stronghold. The leaders of God's holy hosts exalt Shaddai, always telling of God's glory and holiness. Be praised, Adonai our God, for the praiseworthy works of Your power, and for the lights which You made – they will glorify You forever. The Ruler who alone was exalted from the beginning, who was praised, glorified, and elevated for eternity. God of the Universe, have mercy on us in your great mercy. Ruler of our strength, our rocklike refuge, shield of our salvation, be our shelter.

*On all days continue here:*

## TITBARAKH TZUREINU

תִּתְבָּרַךְ צוּרֵנוּ מַלְכֵּנוּ וְגֹאֲלֵנוּ בּוֹרֵא קְדוֹשִׁים יִשְׁתַּבַּח שִׁמְךָ לָעַד מַלְכֵּנוּ, יוֹצֵר מְשָׁרְתִים, וַאֲשֶׁר מְשָׁרְתָיו כֻּלָּם, עוֹמְדִים בְּרוּם עוֹלָם, וּמַשְׁמִיעִים בְּיִרְאָה יַחַד בְּקוֹל, דִּבְרֵי אֱלֹהִים חַיִּים וּמֶלֶךְ עוֹלָם. כֻּלָּם אֲהוּבִים, כֻּלָּם גִּבּוֹרִים, וְכֻלָּם עֹשִׂים בְּאֵימָה וּבְיִרְאָה רְצוֹן קוֹנָם. וְכֻלָּם פּוֹתְחִים אֶת פִּיהֶם בִּקְדֻשָּׁה וּבְטָהֳרָה, בְּשִׁירָה וּבְזִמְרָה, וּמְבָרְכִים וּמְשַׁבְּחִים, וּמְפָאֲרִים וּמַעֲרִיצִים, וּמַקְדִּישִׁים וּמַמְלִיכִים.

אֶת שֵׁם הָאֵל, הַמֶּלֶךְ הַגָּדוֹל, הַגִּבּוֹר וְהַנּוֹרָא, קָדוֹשׁ הוּא וְכֻלָּם מְקַבְּלִים עֹל מַלְכוּת שָׁמַיִם זֶה מִזֶּה. וְנוֹתְנִים רְשׁוּת זֶה לָזֶה, לְהַקְדִּישׁ לְיוֹצְרָם בְּנַחַת רוּחַ, בְּשָׂפָה בְרוּרָה וּבִנְעִימָה, קְדֻשָּׁה כֻּלָּם כְּאֶחָד עוֹנִים וְאוֹמְרִים בְּיִרְאָה:

קָדוֹשׁ, קָדוֹשׁ, קָדוֹשׁ, יְיָ צְבָאוֹת, מְלֹא כָל הָאָרֶץ כְּבוֹדוֹ.

וְהָאוֹפַנִּים וְחַיּוֹת הַקֹּדֶשׁ בְּרַעַשׁ גָּדוֹל מִתְנַשְּׂאִים לְעֻמַּת שְׂרָפִים, לְעֻמָּתָם מְשַׁבְּחִים וְאוֹמְרִים:

| | |
|---|---|
| Barukh k'vod Adonai mim'komo. | בָּרוּךְ כְּבוֹד יְיָ מִמְּקוֹמוֹ. |
| L'eil barukh n'imot yiteinu. | לְאֵל בָּרוּךְ נְעִימוֹת יִתֵּנוּ, |
| L'Melekh Eil ḥai v'kayam, | לְמֶלֶךְ אֵל חַי וְקַיָּם |
| z'mirot yomeiru | זְמִירוֹת יֹאמֵרוּ |
| v'tishbaḥot yashmi·u, | וְתִשְׁבָּחוֹת יַשְׁמִיעוּ, |
| ki hu l'vado po·el g'vurot, | כִּי הוּא לְבַדּוֹ פּוֹעֵל גְּבוּרוֹת, |
| oseh ḥadashot, | עֹשֶׂה חֲדָשׁוֹת, |
| ba·al milḥamot,zorei·a tz'dakot, | בַּעַל מִלְחָמוֹת, זוֹרֵעַ צְדָקוֹת, |
| matzmi·aḥ y'shu·ot, borei r'fu·ot, | מַצְמִיחַ יְשׁוּעוֹת, בּוֹרֵא רְפוּאוֹת, |
| nora t'hilot, Adon ha-nifla·ot, | נוֹרָא תְהִלּוֹת, אֲדוֹן הַנִּפְלָאוֹת, |
| ham'ḥadeish b'tuvob'khol yom tamid | הַמְחַדֵּשׁ בְּטוּבוֹ בְּכָל יוֹם תָּמִיד |
| ma·aseih v'reishit, | מַעֲשֵׂה בְרֵאשִׁית. |
| ka-amur: | כָּאָמוּר, |
| l'oseh orim g'dolim, | לְעֹשֵׂה אוֹרִים גְּדֹלִים, |
| ki l'olam ḥasdo. | כִּי לְעוֹלָם חַסְדּוֹ. |
| Or ḥadash al Tziyon ta·ir, | אוֹר חָדָשׁ עַל צִיּוֹן תָּאִיר, |
| v'nizkeh khulanu m'heirah l'oro. | וְנִזְכֶּה כֻלָּנוּ מְהֵרָה לְאוֹרוֹ. |
| Barukh Atah Adonai | בָּרוּךְ אַתָּה יְיָ, |
| yotzeir ha-m'orot. | יוֹצֵר הַמְּאוֹרוֹת. |

*On all days continue here:*

## TITBARAKH TZUREINU

You shall be praised forever, our Rock and Ruler. You created holy beings that serve You on high. They all praise You in one voice, with the words of the living God, the Ruler of the universe. These beloved, pure and mighty beings all open their mouths in holy songs of praise and blessing, to glorify and make holy…

The Name of the great, powerful and awe-inspiring God and Ruler, the Holy One. They each accept God's authority, and allow each other to tell their Creator's holiness. Gently, clearly and sweetly, they all sing in harmony, declaring:

"Holy, holy, holy is the Adonai Tz'va-ot.
The whole world is filled with God's glory."

*Then other heavenly beings rise up and praise God:*

"Praised be Adonai's glory from God's place."

They offer lovely melodies to the Blessed God. To the Ruler, the living and eternal God, they chant songs and proclaim praises, for God alone does great things, creates anew, masters war, sows righteousness, causes salvation to bloom, creates healing, is awesome in praise and God of wonders – God out of goodness renews creation every day, perpetually, as it says: "[Praise] the One who made the great lights, for God's kindness is everlasting."

Cause a new light to shine upon Zion, and may we all soon be able to enjoy its light. Praised are You, Adonai, Creator of the heavenly lights.

**Kavvanah:** What does it mean to say that God is holy? It means that God is unique and exalted, but it also means that God made the world in such a way that it can be sanctified. When we do mitzvot, we fulfill that God-given potential for holiness.

## AHAVAH RABBAH

***Shema blessing #2: Revelation. Thank You God, for the loving gift of Torah***

| | |
|---|---|
| Ahavah rabbah ahavtanu, | אַהֲבָה רַבָּה אֲהַבְתָּנוּ, |
| Adonai Eloheinu, | יְיָ אֱלֹהֵינוּ, |
| ḥemlah g'dolah viteirah | חֶמְלָה גְדוֹלָה וִיתֵרָה |
| ḥamalta aleinu. | חָמַלְתָּ עָלֵינוּ. |
| Avinu Malkeinu, | אָבִינוּ מַלְכֵּנוּ, |
| ba·avur avoteinu | בַּעֲבוּר אֲבוֹתֵינוּ |
| she-bat'ḥu v'kha | שֶׁבָּטְחוּ בְךָ, |
| vat'lam'deim ḥukei ḥayyim, | וַתְּלַמְּדֵם חֻקֵּי חַיִּים, |
| kein t'ḥoneinu ut'lam'deinu. | כֵּן תְּחָנֵּנוּ וּתְלַמְּדֵנוּ. |
| Avinu ha-av ha-raḥaman, | אָבִינוּ, הָאָב הָרַחֲמָן, |
| ham'raḥeim, | הַמְרַחֵם, |
| raḥeim aleinu v'tein b'libeinu | רַחֵם עָלֵינוּ, וְתֵן בְּלִבֵּנוּ |
| l' havin ul'haskil | לְהָבִין וּלְהַשְׂכִּיל, |
| lish'mo·a, lil'mod ul'lameid, | לִשְׁמֹעַ, לִלְמֹד וּלְלַמֵּד, |
| lishmor v'la·asot ul'kayeim | לִשְׁמֹר וְלַעֲשׂוֹת וּלְקַיֵּם |
| et kol divrei talmud Toratekha | אֶת כָּל דִּבְרֵי תַלְמוּד תּוֹרָתֶךָ |
| b'ahavah. | בְּאַהֲבָה. |
| v'ha·eir eineinu b'Toratekha, | וְהָאֵר עֵינֵינוּ בְּתוֹרָתֶךָ, |
| v'dabeik libeinu | וְדַבֵּק לִבֵּנוּ |
| b'mitzvotekha, | בְּמִצְוֹתֶיךָ, |
| v'yaḥeid l'vaveinu | וְיַחֵד לְבָבֵנוּ |
| l'ahavah ul'yir·ah et sh'mekha, | לְאַהֲבָה וּלְיִרְאָה אֶת שְׁמֶךָ, |
| v'lo neivosh l'olam va·ed. | וְלֹא נֵבוֹשׁ לְעוֹלָם וָעֶד. |
| Ki v'sheim kodsh'kha ha-gadol | כִּי בְשֵׁם קָדְשְׁךָ הַגָּדוֹל |
| v'ha-nora bataḥnu, | וְהַנּוֹרָא בָּטָחְנוּ, |
| nagilah v'nism'ḥah bishu·atekha. | נָגִילָה וְנִשְׂמְחָה בִּישׁוּעָתֶךָ. |

## AHAVAH RABBAH

### *Shema blessing #2: Revelation. Thank You God, for the loving gift of Torah*

With great love have You loved us, Adonai our God; with great and extra tenderness You have pitied us. Our Parent, our Ruler, for the sake of our ancestors who trusted in You, and whom You taught life-giving laws, be kind to us, too, and teach us. Our merciful Parent, treat us with mercy, and help our minds to understand Your Torah, teaching us to listen, to learn and to teach, to observe, to do, and to fulfill all its words with love. Light up our eyes with Your Torah and cause our hearts to hold tight to Your commandments. Unify our hearts to love and respect Your name so that we will never be ashamed. For we trust in Your holy, great, and awe-inspiring Name – may we rejoice in Your saving power.

**Ahavah Rabbah:** Rabbi Bachya ibn Pekuda in his great work, *Ḥovot Ha-Levavot* states: "One should be aware of the Divine's overwhelming goodness to him, and that due to God's great kindness and beneficence, the Divine bestowed good upon him from the very beginning, not because the person deserved it, and not because the Divine had any need to do so, but rather out of generosity, goodness and kindness."

This prayer gives us a lens for viewing the world. When we take our very existence as a loving gift, just waking in the morning is a wonder. The astonishing richness and variety of nature, the beauty revealed in every leaf and flower, the grandeur of the earth's structure, the very fact that we can feel awe and gratitude – these are God's gifts of love to us. In particular, the Torah offers us God's love through guidance on the path to righteousness, compassion and holiness.

Close your eyes and try to remember a time when you felt so embraced by human love that it seemed that its very source might be from God. Now try to recall an experience of Torah–studying a biblical story, reading from the scroll, or touching the Torah in procession was so powerful that you felt yourself in God's presence. Now try to picture the Torah as a gift from God, a gift of love and joy. Torah is also a light that shines through the darkness. Picture it illuminating your eyes, mind and heart. The Torah is also a beautiful gown, clothing God's Presence. Picture the Torah as life–giving medicine, that can heal the hurts of the world and offer vitamins to our souls.

Help us God, to learn Torah, to love and live Torah, so that we will truly treasure Your loving gift.

וַהֲבִיאֵנוּ לְשָׁלוֹם
מֵאַרְבַּע כַּנְפוֹת הָאָרֶץ,
וְתוֹלִיכֵנוּ קוֹמְמִיּוּת לְאַרְצֵנוּ,
כִּי אֵל
פּוֹעֵל יְשׁוּעוֹת אָתָּה,
וּבָנוּ בָחַרְתָּ
מִכָּל עַם וְלָשׁוֹן.
וְקֵרַבְתָּנוּ
לְשִׁמְךָ הַגָּדוֹל סֶלָה בֶּאֱמֶת,
לְהוֹדוֹת לְךָ וּלְיַחֶדְךָ בְּאַהֲבָה.
בָּרוּךְ אַתָּה יְיָ,
הַבּוֹחֵר בְּעַמּוֹ יִשְׂרָאֵל
בְּאַהֲבָה.

Va-havi·einu l'shalom
mei-arba kanfot ha-aretz,
v'tolikheinu kom'miyut l'artzeinu,
ki Eil
po·eil y'shu·ot Atah,
u-vanu vaḥarta
mi-kol am v'lashon,
v'keiravtanu
l'shimkha ha-gadol selah be-emet,
l'hodot l'kha ul'yaḥedkha b'ahavah.
Barukh Atah Adonai
ha-boḥeir b'amo Yisra·el
b'ahavah.

Gather us in peace from the four corners of the earth,* and lead us to our land with our heads held high, for You are a God who is able to rescue. You have chosen us from among all peoples and brought us near to You, to thank You sincerely, and to announce with love that You are One. Praised are You, Adonai, who lovingly chooses the people of Israel.

* It is the custom to gather the four corners of the tallit, holding the tzitzit in your hand, when you say the words *Arba kanot ha-aretz*, "the four corners of the earth."

## SH'MA

### *Proclaiming God's oneness*

*Many people have the custom of closing their eyes when they recite the first line of the Shema in order to block out all distractions so that they can concentrate on this great truth: there is a God, one and unique.*

| | |
|---|---|
| Sh'ma Yisra·el Adonai Eloheinu | שְׁמַע יִשְׂרָאֵל, יְיָ אֱלֹהֵינוּ, |
| Adonai eḥad. | יְיָ אֶחָד. |

*(The next line is said silently, except on Yom Kippur)*

| | |
|---|---|
| Barukh shem k'vod malkhuto | בָּרוּךְ שֵׁם כְּבוֹד מַלְכוּתוֹ |
| l'olam va·ed. | לְעוֹלָם וָעֶד. |

| | |
|---|---|
| V'ahavta et Adonai Elohekha | וְאָהַבְתָּ אֵת יְיָ אֱלֹהֶיךָ, |
| b'khol l'vav'kha, | בְּכָל לְבָבְךָ, |
| u-v'khol nafsh'kha, | וּבְכָל נַפְשְׁךָ, |
| u-v'khol m'odekha. | וּבְכָל מְאֹדֶךָ. |
| v'hayu had'varim ha-eileh, | וְהָיוּ הַדְּבָרִים הָאֵלֶּה, |
| asher anokhi m'tzav'kha ha-yom | אֲשֶׁר אָנֹכִי מְצַוְּךָ הַיּוֹם, |
| al l'vavekha. | עַל לְבָבֶךָ. |
| v'shinantam l'vanekha, | וְשִׁנַּנְתָּם לְבָנֶיךָ, |
| v'dibarta bam, | וְדִבַּרְתָּ בָּם, |
| b'shivt'kha b'veitekha, | בְּשִׁבְתְּךָ בְּבֵיתֶךָ, |
| u-v'lekht'kha va-derekh, | וּבְלֶכְתְּךָ בַדֶּרֶךְ, |
| u-v'shokhb'kha u-v'kumekha. | וּבְשָׁכְבְּךָ, וּבְקוּמֶךָ. |
| Uk'shartam l'ot | וּקְשַׁרְתָּם לְאוֹת |
| al yadekha, | עַל יָדֶךָ, |
| v'hayu l'totafot bein einekha. | וְהָיוּ לְטֹטָפֹת בֵּין עֵינֶיךָ. |
| Ukh'tavtam | וּכְתַבְתָּם |
| al m'zuzot beitekha | עַל מְזֻזוֹת בֵּיתֶךָ |
| u-visharekha. | וּבִשְׁעָרֶיךָ. |

## SH'MA

### *Proclaiming God's oneness*

*Many people have the custom of closing their eyes when they recite the first line of the Shema in order to block out all distractions so that they can concentrate on this great truth: there is a God, one and unique*

**Listen, Israel, Adonai is our God, Adonai is One.**

*(The next line is said silently, except on Yom Kippur)*

Praised be God's glorious name forever.

You will love Adonai your God with all your mind, soul, and might. Take to heart these words which I command you today. Teach them carefully to your children. Repeat them at home and away, morning and night. Bind them as a sign on your hand, and let them be a symbol above your eyes. Write them on the doorposts of your homes and on your gates.

**Shema:** With these words we proclaim to the world and to ourselves that God is, that God is one, and that God is unique. The large Hebrew letter "ayin" at the end of Shema and the larger letter "dalet" at the end of "eḥad" spell "ayd", meaning "witness." Imagine that you are a witness before a court of all the countless people who believe that nothing in life is connected to anything else, that there are no causes or effects, no unifying principles–and you bravely, anxiously, not sure of your own evidence but wanting desperately to believe that harmony is possible–you are going to say Shema Yisrael: "I want to believe there is one unifying God." (Richard Levy, On Wings of Light)

**V'ahavata:** We are here commanded to show our love for God through thought, word and deed.

## V'HAYA IM SHAMO·A

### *If You Will Really Listen*

וְהָיָה אִם שָׁמֹעַ תִּשְׁמְעוּ אֶל מִצְוֹתַי, אֲשֶׁר אָנֹכִי מְצַוֶּה אֶתְכֶם הַיּוֹם, לְאַהֲבָה אֶת יְיָ אֱלֹהֵיכֶם וּלְעָבְדוֹ, בְּכָל לְבַבְכֶם וּבְכָל נַפְשְׁכֶם.

וְנָתַתִּי מְטַר אַרְצְכֶם בְּעִתּוֹ, יוֹרֶה וּמַלְקוֹשׁ, וְאָסַפְתָּ דְגָנֶךָ וְתִירשְׁךָ וְיִצְהָרֶךָ. וְנָתַתִּי עֵשֶׂב בְּשָׂדְךָ לִבְהֶמְתֶּךָ, וְאָכַלְתָּ וְשָׂבָעְתָּ.

הִשָּׁמְרוּ לָכֶם פֶּן יִפְתֶּה לְבַבְכֶם, וְסַרְתֶּם וַעֲבַדְתֶּם אֱלֹהִים אֲחֵרִים וְהִשְׁתַּחֲוִיתֶם לָהֶם.

וְחָרָה אַף יְיָ בָּכֶם, וְעָצַר אֶת הַשָּׁמַיִם וְלֹא יִהְיֶה מָטָר, וְהָאֲדָמָה לֹא תִתֵּן אֶת יְבוּלָהּ, וַאֲבַדְתֶּם מְהֵרָה מֵעַל הָאָרֶץ הַטֹּבָה אֲשֶׁר יְיָ נֹתֵן לָכֶם.

וְשַׂמְתֶּם אֶת דְּבָרַי אֵלֶּה עַל לְבַבְכֶם וְעַל נַפְשְׁכֶם, וּקְשַׁרְתֶּם אֹתָם לְאוֹת עַל יֶדְכֶם, וְהָיוּ לְטוֹטָפֹת בֵּין עֵינֵיכֶם.

וְלִמַּדְתֶּם אֹתָם אֶת בְּנֵיכֶם לְדַבֵּר בָּם, בְּשִׁבְתְּךָ בְּבֵיתֶךָ,וּבְלֶכְתְּךָ בַדֶּרֶךְ, וּבְשָׁכְבְּךָ, וּבְקוּמֶךָ.

וּכְתַבְתָּם עַל מְזוּזוֹת בֵּיתֶךָ וּבִשְׁעָרֶיךָ. לְמַעַן יִרְבּוּ יְמֵיכֶם וִימֵי בְנֵיכֶם עַל הָאֲדָמָה אֲשֶׁר נִשְׁבַּע יְיָ לַאֲבֹתֵיכֶם לָתֵת לָהֶם, כִּימֵי הַשָּׁמַיִם עַל הָאָרֶץ.

## V'HAYA IM SHAMO·A

### *If You Will Really Listen*

If you will really listen to my commandments which I command you today, to love Adonai your God and to serve God with all your heart and soul, then I will give your land rain at the proper season – rain in autumn and rain in spring – and you will gather in your grain and wine and oil. I will give grass in the fields for your cattle, and you will eat your fill. Beware that you are not tempted to turn aside and worship other gods. For then God will be angry at you and will shut up the skies and there will be no rain, and the earth will not give you its produce, and you will quickly disappear from the good land which the God is giving to you. So keep these words in mind and take them to heart, and bind them as a sign upon your hand, and let them be a symbol between your eyes. Teach them to your children, speaking of them at home and away, when you lie down and when you get up. Write them upon the doorposts of your house and upon your gates, so that your days and the days of your children will last long on the land which Adonai promised to your ancestors, to give to them for as long as the heavens and earth last. (Deuteronomy 11:13–21)

**Vehaya Im Shamo·a:** The second paragraph of the Shema asks us to pay attention to the consequences of our actions and the acceptance of the authority of mitzvot. Now close your eyes and try to focus on one single mitzvah that you very much enjoy performing. Reflect on that mitzvah and think about the specific actions that it inspires you to perform. In what ways has doing this particular mitzvah changed your life or way of living life. Always, remember, too, that everything you do bears a consequence. So be careful with your actions!

## VAYOMER

### *The Passage about the* **Tzitzit**

| | |
|---|---|
| Vayomer Adonai el Moshe leimor. | וַיֹּאמֶר יְיָ אֶל מֹשֶׁה לֵּאמֹר. |
| Dabeir el b'nei Yisra·el | דַּבֵּר אֶל בְּנֵי יִשְׂרָאֵל |
| v'amarta aleihem | וְאָמַרְתָּ אֲלֵהֶם, |
| v'asu lahem **tzitzit** | וְעָשׂוּ לָהֶם צִיצִת |
| al kanfei vigdeihem | עַל כַּנְפֵי בִגְדֵיהֶם |
| l'dorotam | לְדֹרֹתָם, |
| v'natnu al **tzitzit** | וְנָתְנוּ עַל צִיצִת |
| ha-kanaf | הַכָּנָף |
| p'til t'kheilet. | פְּתִיל תְּכֵלֶת. |
| v'haya lakhem l'**tzitzit** | וְהָיָה לָכֶם לְצִיצִת, |
| ur'item oto | וּרְאִיתֶם אֹתוֹ |
| uz'khartem | וּזְכַרְתֶּם |
| et kol mitzvot Adonai | אֶת כָּל מִצְוֹת יְיָ, |
| va-asitem otam, | וַעֲשִׂיתֶם אֹתָם, |
| v'lo taturu aḥarei l'vavkhem | וְלֹא תָתוּרוּ אַחֲרֵי לְבַבְכֶם |
| v'aḥarei eineikhem | וְאַחֲרֵי עֵינֵיכֶם, |
| asher atem zonim | אֲשֶׁר אַתֶּם זֹנִים |
| aḥareihem. | אַחֲרֵיהֶם. |
| L'ma-an tizk'ru | לְמַעַן תִּזְכְּרוּ |
| va-asitem et kol mitzvotai | וַעֲשִׂיתֶם אֶת כָּל מִצְוֹתָי, |
| vih'yitem k'doshim lEiloheikhem. | וִהְיִיתֶם קְדֹשִׁים לֵאלֹהֵיכֶם. |
| Ani Adonai Eloheikhem | אֲנִי יְיָ אֱלֹהֵיכֶם, |
| asher hotzeiti etkhem | אֲשֶׁר הוֹצֵאתִי אֶתְכֶם |
| mei-eretz Mitzrayim | מֵאֶרֶץ מִצְרַיִם, |
| lih'yot lakhem lEilohim, | לִהְיוֹת לָכֶם לֵאלֹהִים, |
| ani Adonai Eloheikhem. | אֲנִי יְיָ אֱלֹהֵיכֶם. |

*Leader:*

| | |
|---|---|
| Adonai Eloheikhem emet. | יְיָ אֱלֹהֵיכֶם אֱמֶת. ♪ |

## VAYOMER

### *The Passage about the* Tzitzit

*It is the custom to kiss the gathered* ***tzitzit*** *at each mention of the word* ***tzitzit****, and again at the conclusion, "Adonai Eloheikhem emet." The Mishnah B'rurah explains this, "Because the verse says with regard to* ***tzitzit*** *that 'When they look at them they will remember.' Seeing the* ***tzitzit*** *will bring us to remembering the mitzvot, and remembering the mitzvot will bring us to keeping the mizvot."*

Adonai said to Moses: Speak to the people of Israel and tell them to make fringes for the corners of their clothes in all future generations. They shall put a blue thread in the fringe of each corner. When they look at them they will remember all of Adonai's *mitzvot,* and do them, and their hearts or their eyes won't lead them astray. This is in order that you will remember and do all My *mitzvot,* and you will be holy for your God. I am Adonai your God, who took you out of the land of Egypt to be your God. I, Adonai, am your God. (Numbers 15:37–41)

*One common practice is to kiss the* ***tzitzit*** *and let them go at the words "la'ad kayamet."*

**Vayomer Adonai:** Close your eyes and try to picture Moses the Prophet being commanded by God to tell the children of Israel to put blue fringes on the corners of their garments. Why do you think God chose the color blue? Do you see any connection between the knotted **tzitzit** cords of the tallit and tying a string around your finger in order to remember something? Picture the blue of heaven reflected in the blue sea, that it might become a tzitzit of remembrance for you.

## GE·ULAH

**אֱמֶת וְיַצִּיב**, וְנָכוֹן וְקַיָּם, וְיָשָׁר וְנֶאֱמָן, וְאָהוּב וְחָבִיב, וְנֶחְמָד וְנָעִים, וְנוֹרָא וְאַדִּיר, וּמְתֻקָּן וּמְקֻבָּל, וְטוֹב וְיָפֶה הַדָּבָר הַזֶּה עָלֵינוּ לְעוֹלָם וָעֶד. אֱמֶת אֱלֹהֵי עוֹלָם מַלְכֵּנוּ, צוּר יַעֲקֹב, מָגֵן יִשְׁעֵנוּ,

| | |
|---|---|
| L'dor va-dor | לְדֹר וָדֹר |
| hu kayyam u-sh'mo kayyam | הוּא קַיָּם, וּשְׁמוֹ קַיָּם, |
| v'khiso nakhon | וְכִסְאוֹ נָכוֹן, |
| u-malkhuto ve-emunato | וּמַלְכוּתוֹ וֶאֱמוּנָתוֹ |
| la-ad kayamet. | לָעַד קַיָּמֶת. |

וּדְבָרָיו חָיִים וְקַיָּמִים, נֶאֱמָנִים וְנֶחֱמָדִים לָעַד וּלְעוֹלְמֵי עוֹלָמִים. עַל אֲבוֹתֵינוּ וְעָלֵינוּ, עַל בָּנֵינוּ וְעַל דּוֹרוֹתֵינוּ, וְעַל כָּל דּוֹרוֹת זֶרַע יִשְׂרָאֵל עֲבָדֶיךָ.

**עַל הָרִאשׁוֹנִים** וְעַל הָאַחֲרוֹנִים, דָּבָר טוֹב וְקַיָּם לְעוֹלָם וָעֶד, אֱמֶת וֶאֱמוּנָה חֹק וְלֹא יַעֲבֹר. אֱמֶת שָׁאַתָּה הוּא יְיָ אֱלֹהֵינוּ וֵאלֹהֵי אֲבוֹתֵינוּ, מַלְכֵּנוּ מֶלֶךְ אֲבוֹתֵינוּ, גֹּאֲלֵנוּ גֹּאֵל אֲבוֹתֵינוּ, יוֹצְרֵנוּ צוּר יְשׁוּעָתֵנוּ, פּוֹדֵנוּ וּמַצִּילֵנוּ מֵעוֹלָם שְׁמֶךָ, אֵין אֱלֹהִים זוּלָתֶךָ.

| | |
|---|---|
| Ezrat avoteinu | עֶזְרַת אֲבוֹתֵינוּ |
| Atah Hu mei-olam… | אַתָּה הוּא מֵעוֹלָם |

מָגֵן וּמוֹשִׁיעַ לִבְנֵיהֶם אַחֲרֵיהֶם בְּכָל דּוֹר וָדוֹר. בְּרוּם עוֹלָם מוֹשָׁבֶךָ, וּמִשְׁפָּטֶיךָ וְצִדְקָתְךָ עַד אַפְסֵי אָרֶץ. אַשְׁרֵי אִישׁ שֶׁיִּשְׁמַע לְמִצְוֹתֶיךָ, וְתוֹרָתְךָ וּדְבָרְךָ יָשִׂים עַל לִבּוֹ. אֱמֶת, אַתָּה הוּא אָדוֹן לְעַמֶּךָ, וּמֶלֶךְ גִּבּוֹר לָרִיב רִיבָם. אֱמֶת, אַתָּה הוּא רִאשׁוֹן וְאַתָּה הוּא אַחֲרוֹן, וּמִבַּלְעָדֶיךָ אֵין לָנוּ מֶלֶךְ גּוֹאֵל וּמוֹשִׁיעַ. מִמִּצְרַיִם גְּאַלְתָּנוּ, יְיָ אֱלֹהֵינוּ, וּמִבֵּית עֲבָדִים פְּדִיתָנוּ. כָּל בְּכוֹרֵיהֶם הָרַגְתָּ, וּבְכוֹרְךָ גָּאָלְתָּ, וְיַם סוּף בָּקַעְתָּ, וְזֵדִים טִבַּעְתָּ, וִידִידִים הֶעֱבַרְתָּ, וַיְכַסּוּ מַיִם צָרֵיהֶם, אֶחָד מֵהֶם לֹא נוֹתָר. עַל זֹאת שִׁבְּחוּ אֲהוּבִים וְרוֹמְמוּ אֵל, וְנָתְנוּ יְדִידִים זְמִרוֹת שִׁירוֹת וְתִשְׁבָּחוֹת, בְּרָכוֹת וְהוֹדָאוֹת, לְמֶלֶךְ אֵל חַי וְקַיָּם, רָם וְנִשָּׂא, גָּדוֹל וְנוֹרָא, מַשְׁפִּיל גֵּאִים, וּמַגְבִּיהַּ שְׁפָלִים,

## GE·ULAH

### *Redemption*

***Shema blessing #3: Redemption. God has rescued us from danger, and will redeem us some day.***

You always helped our ancestors, You were a shield
And a rescuer to their children in every generation.

Though You live in the heights of the universe,
Your justice and Your goodness reach
To the ends of the earth.

Happy is the person who obeys Your commandments,
And takes Your words and Your Torah to heart.

Truly You are the Leader of Your people,
And a mighty Ruler to take their side.

Truly You are first and You are last,
And we have no Ruler or Rescuer besides You.

You saved us from Egypt, Adonai our God,
And You freed us from the slave-house.

You split the Red Sea and drowned the evil-doers;
You brought the loved ones through,
And covered their enemies with water.

Give praises to God on high,
Who brings down those who are arrogant
Who raises up those who are brought low,
Who answers those who call for help.

Moses and the Israelites sang a song to You with great joy, as they all said:

| | |
|---|---|
| מוֹצִיא אֲסִירִים, וּפוֹדֶה עֲנָוִים, | Motzi asirim u-fodeh anavim |
| וְעוֹזֵר דַּלִּים, | v'ozeir dalim |
| וְעוֹנֶה לְעַמּוֹ | v'oneh l'amo |
| בְּעֵת שַׁוְּעָם אֵלָיו. | b'eit shav·am eilav. |
| תְּהִלּוֹת לְאֵל עֶלְיוֹן, | T'hilot l'Eil Elyon |
| בָּרוּךְ הוּא וּמְבֹרָךְ. | barukh Hu u-m'vorakh. |
| מֹשֶׁה וּבְנֵי יִשְׂרָאֵל | Moshe uv'nei Yisra·el |
| לְךָ עָנוּ שִׁירָה בְּשִׂמְחָה רַבָּה, | l'kha anu shirah b'simḥah rabbah, |
| וְאָמְרוּ כֻלָּם: | v'am'ru khulam: |
| | |
| מִי כָמֹכָה בָּאֵלִם יְיָ, | Mi khamokha ba-eilim Adonai, |
| מִי כָּמֹכָה | mi kamokha |
| נֶאְדָּר בַּקֹּדֶשׁ, | ne·dar ba-kodesh, |
| נוֹרָא תְהִלֹּת, עֹשֵׂה פֶלֶא. | nora t'hilot, oseih feleh. |
| | |
| שִׁירָה חֲדָשָׁה שִׁבְּחוּ גְאוּלִים | Shirah ḥadashah shib'ḥu g'ulim |
| לְשִׁמְךָ עַל שְׂפַת הַיָּם, | l'shimkha al s'fat ha-yam. |
| יַחַד כֻּלָּם | Yaḥad kulam |
| הוֹדוּ וְהִמְלִיכוּ | hodu v'himlikhu |
| וְאָמְרוּ: | v'am'ru. |
| | |
| יְיָ יִמְלֹךְ לְעוֹלָם וָעֶד. | Adonai yimlokh l'olam va·ed. |
| | |
| צוּר יִשְׂרָאֵל, | Tzur Yisra·el, |
| קוּמָה בְּעֶזְרַת יִשְׂרָאֵל, | *kumah b'ezrat Yisra·el, |
| וּפְדֵה | uf'dei |
| כִנְאֻמֶךָ יְהוּדָה וְיִשְׂרָאֵל. | khin'umekha Y'hudah v'Yisra·el. |
| גֹּאֲלֵנוּ | Go·aleinu |
| יְיָ צְבָאוֹת שְׁמוֹ, | Adonai Tz'va·ot sh'mo |
| קְדוֹשׁ יִשְׂרָאֵל. | k'dosh Yisra·el. |
| בָּרוּךְ אַתָּה יְיָ | Barukh Atah Adonai, |
| גָּאַל יִשְׂרָאֵל. | ga·al Yisra·el. |

* We rise here before the Amidah.

"Who is like You, Adonai, among the mighty?
Who is like You, glorious in holiness,
Awesome in praises, doing wonders." (Exodus 15:11)

With a new song those who were rescued
Sang at the shore of the sea,
Together they thanked You and announced Your power:

"Adonai will rule forever and ever." (Exodus 15:18)

Rock of Israel, rise up to help Israel,*
And rescue Judah and Israel as You promised.

You are our Savior, *Adonai Tz'va·ot* is Your name.
Praised are You, Adonai, who rescued Israel.

---

* We rise here before the Amidah.

**Mi Khamokha:** Close your eyes and picture yourself as one of the Israelites leaving Egypt after 400 years of slavery. Now imagine yourself seeing the spectacular view of the sea splitting open, and your ability to literally walk through the water. How do you feel now? What do you feel like singing when you reach the other side of the Red Sea?

Moses now begins to sing and you feel yourself drawn into his melody. Miriam, his sister, plays the timbrel and dances with the women in joyous rapture. Now your own body begins to sway to and fro, back and forth. You are in a state of ecstasy and the song permeates your entire being. For once in your life you truly feel free and at peace. How can you ever forget this moment?

# Amidah

## AVOT

### *God of our Ancestors*

| | |
|---|---|
| Adonai, s'fatai tiftaḥ, | אֲדֹנָי שְׂפָתַי תִּפְתָּח |
| u-fi yaggid t'hilatekha. | וּפִי יַגִּיד תְּהִלָּתֶךָ. |

*Before starting, we take three steps backward, leaving our earthly realm, and three steps forward, entering the Presence of God. As we recite the words Adonai, s'fatai tiftaḥ "Adonai, open my lips," we walk three steps forward to enter God's presence. Then at the beginning and end of the first blessing, bend your knees at "Barukh," bend over from your waist at "atah," and straighten up at "Adonai."*

| | |
|---|---|
| Barukh Atah Adonai | בָּרוּךְ אַתָּה יְיָ |
| Eloheinu vEilohei avoteinu, | אֱלֹהֵינוּ וֵאלֹהֵי אֲבוֹתֵינוּ, |
| Elohei Avraham, | אֱלֹהֵי אַבְרָהָם, |
| Elohei Yitzhak vEilohei | אֱלֹהֵי יִצְחָק, וֵאלֹהֵי |
| Ya'akov, | יַעֲקֹב, |
| [Elohei Sarah, Elohei Rivkah, | (אֱלֹהֵי שָׂרָה, אֱלֹהֵי רִבְקָה, |
| Elohei Raḥel vEilohei Le·ah] | אֱלֹהֵי רָחֵל, וֵאלֹהֵי לֵאָה,) |
| ha-Eil ha-gadol ha-gibor v'ha-nora | הָאֵל הַגָּדוֹל הַגִּבּוֹר וְהַנּוֹרָא, |
| Eil elyon, | אֵל עֶלְיוֹן, |
| gomeil ḥasadim tovim | גּוֹמֵל חֲסָדִים טוֹבִים, |
| v'koneih hakol | וְקֹנֵה הַכֹּל, |
| v'zokheir ḥasdei avot, | וְזוֹכֵר חַסְדֵי אָבוֹת, |
| u-meivi go·eil | וּמֵבִיא גוֹאֵל |
| liv'nei v'neihem | לִבְנֵי בְנֵיהֶם, |
| l'ma·an sh'mo b'ahavah. | לְמַעַן שְׁמוֹ בְּאַהֲבָה. |

*On Shabbat Shuvah, the Shabbat between Rosh Hashanah and Yom Kippur:*

| | |
|---|---|
| *Zokhrei-nu l'ḥayim,* | זָכְרֵנוּ לְחַיִּים, |
| *Melekh ha-feitz b'chayim,* | מֶלֶךְ חָפֵץ בַּחַיִּים, |
| *v'khat-vei nu b'sefer ha-kayyim* | וְכָתְבֵנוּ בְּסֵפֶר הַחַיִּים, |
| *l'ma·an-kha Elohim ḥayim.* | לְמַעַנְךָ אֱלֹהִים חַיִּים. |

# Amidah

## AVOT

### *God of our Ancestors*

God, open my lips so that my mouth may speak your praise.

*Before starting, we take three steps backward, leaving our earthly realm, and three steps forward, entering the Presence of God. As we recite the words Adonai, s'fatai tiftaḥ "Adonai, open my lips," we walk three steps forward to enter God's presence. Then at the beginning and end of the first blessing, bend your knees at "Barukh," bend over from your waist at "atah," and straighten up at "Adonai."*

Praised are You, Adonai our God and God of our ancestors, God of Abraham, God of Isaac, and God of Jacob, [God of Sarah, God of Rebecca. God of Rachel and God of Leah]*, the great, strong and awe-inspiring God, God on high. You act with lovingkindness and create everything. God remembers the loving deeds of our ancestors, and will bring a redeemer to their children's children because that is God's loving nature.

Remember us for life, Ruler who wants life, and write us in the Book of Life, for Your sake, living God.

* In recent years many Jews have begun to include the matriarchs in the Avot blessing, in order to acknowledge their great contributions to the formation of Judaism. Some congregations leave the choice of whether or not to include this phrase up to the prayer leader, which is why it is in parentheses.

Once the Baal Shem Tov stopped on the threshold of a House of Prayer and refused to go in. "I cannot go in," he said. "It is crowded with teaching and prayers from wall to wall and from floor to ceiling. How could there be room for me? And when he saw that those around him were staring at him and did not know what he meant, he added: "The words from the lips of those whose teaching and praying does not come from hearts lifted to heaven cannot rise, but fill the house from wall to wall and from floor to ceiling." (Martin Buber)

May a person who recites the Amidah privately do so out loud? We have learned the answer from Hannah, Samuel the Prophet's mother: "Now Hannah was praying in her heart. Only her lips moved, but her voice could not be heard" [I Samuel 1:13] (Midrash, Deuteronomy Rabbah 2:1)

| | |
|---|---|
| Melekh ozeir u-moshi·a u-magein. | מֶלֶךְ עוֹזֵר וּמוֹשִׁיעַ וּמָגֵן. |
| Barukh Atah Adonai | בָּרוּךְ אַתָּה יְיָ, |
| magein Avraham [u-fokeid Sarah]. | מָגֵן אַבְרָהָם (וּפֹקֵד שָׂרָה). |

## G'VUROT

### *God's benevolent power*

| | |
|---|---|
| Atah gibor l'olam Adonai, | אַתָּה גִּבּוֹר לְעוֹלָם אֲדֹנָי, |
| m'ḥayeih meitim Atah, | מְחַיֵּה מֵתִים אַתָּה, |
| rav l'hoshi·a. | רַב לְהוֹשִׁיעַ. |

*From Sh'mini Atzeret until Pesaḥ, we pray for rain:*

| | |
|---|---|
| mashiv haru·aḥ u-morid ha-gashem | מַשִּׁיב הָרוּחַ וּמוֹרִיד הַגֶּשֶׁם. |

| | |
|---|---|
| M'khalkeil ḥayim b'ḥesed, | מְכַלְכֵּל חַיִּים בְּחֶסֶד, |
| m'ḥayei meitim b'raḥamim rabim, | מְחַיֵּה מֵתִים בְּרַחֲמִים רַבִּים, |
| someikh nofl'im | סוֹמֵךְ נוֹפְלִים, |
| v'rofei ḥolim | וְרוֹפֵא חוֹלִים, |
| u-matir asurim, | וּמַתִּיר אֲסוּרִים, |
| um'kayeim emunato | וּמְקַיֵּם אֱמוּנָתוֹ |
| lisheinei afar. | לִישֵׁנֵי עָפָר, |
| Mi khamokha, ba·al g'vurot | מִי כָמְוֹךָ בַּעַל גְּבוּרוֹת |
| u-mi domeh lakh, | וּמִי דּוֹמֶה לָּךְ, |
| Melekh meimit um'ḥayeih | מֶלֶךְ מֵמִית וּמְחַיֶּה |
| u-matzmi·aḥ y'shu·a. | וּמַצְמִיחַ יְשׁוּעָה. |

You are a helping, saving and shielding Ruler. Praised are You, Adonai, Shield of Abraham (and Guardian of Sarah).

## G'VUROT

### *God's benevolent power*

You are mighty forever, Adonai, giving life to the dead with Your great saving power.

*From Sh'mini Atzeret until Pesaḥ, we pray for rain:*

You cause the wind to blow and the rain to fall.

You support the living with kindness, you give life to the dead with great mercy. You support the fallen, heal the sick and set free those in prison. You keep faith with those who sleep in the dust. Who is like You, Sovereign of mighty deeds, and who can compare to You, Ruler of life and death who causes salvation to bloom.

God is the God of our ancestors and was their protector and continues to protect us now. God appeared differently to each of them and is different to each of us. God is the God of history, awesome and all-powerful. We appeal to the "merit" of our ancestors as a way of urging God to care for us as well as feeling ourselves a part of the continuity of Jewish history. The rabbis teach us that we mention each of the patriarchs and matriarchs separately because every human being has his or her own unique relationship with God and each person has his or her own way of thinking about our One God. What was Abraham's God like? What about Isaac's and Jacob's? What was Sarah, Rebecca, Rachel and Leah's God like? What other people's ideas of God are models for you today?

We declare God's power to perform wondrous deeds and God's deep concern for providing for all our needs. God's power is so great that God can even revive the dead. But notice that God's great power is used for compassionate ends of support, healing, and liberation.

Focus on the memory of someone who has died whom you yearn to be restored to life. Imagine how it would feel with that person alive again in your midst? You might then thank God for the power that will someday make that imaging come true. (*On Wings of Light*, Richard Levy)

*On Shabbat Shuvah, the Shabbat between Rosh Hashanah and Yom Kippur:*

| | |
|---|---|
| Mi khamocha av ha-rachamim, | מִי כָמוֹךָ אַב הָרַחֲמִים, |
| zokheir y'tzurav l'hayyim b'rahamim. | זוֹכֵר יְצוּרָיו לְחַיִּים בְּרַחֲמִים |

| | |
|---|---|
| v'ne·eman Atah | וְנֶאֱמָן אַתָּה |
| l'haḥayot meitim. | לְהַחֲיוֹת מֵתִים. |
| Barukh Atah Adonai, | בָּרוּךְ אַתָּה יְיָ, |
| m'ḥayeih ha-meitim. | מְחַיֵּה הַמֵּתִים. |

## K'DUSHAH

### *We praise God's holiness.*

*We rise up on our toes for each "kadosh" to show our desire to come closer to God. Some also stand on tiptoe for "Barukh" and "Yimlokh."*

| | |
|---|---|
| N'kadeish et shimkha ba-olam | נְקַדֵּשׁ אֶת שִׁמְךָ בָּעוֹלָם, |
| k'sheim she-makdishim oto | כְּשֵׁם שֶׁמַּקְדִּישִׁים אוֹתוֹ |
| bish'mei marom, | בִּשְׁמֵי מָרוֹם, |
| kakatuv al yad n'vi·ekha | כַּכָּתוּב עַל יַד נְבִיאֶךָ, |
| v'kara zeh el zeh v'amar. | וְקָרָא זֶה אֶל זֶה וְאָמַר: |

| | |
|---|---|
| Kadosh kadosh kadosh | קָדוֹשׁ, קָדוֹשׁ, קָדוֹשׁ, |
| Adonai Tz'va·ot, | יְיָ צְבָאוֹת, |
| m'lo khol ha-aretz k'vodo. | מְלֹא כָל הָאָרֶץ כְּבוֹדוֹ. |

| | |
|---|---|
| Az b'kol ra·ash gadol | אָז בְּקוֹל רַעַשׁ גָּדוֹל |
| adir v'ḥazak | אַדִּיר וְחָזָק, |
| mashmi·im kol, | מַשְׁמִיעִים קוֹל, |
| mitnas'im l'umat s'rafim, | מִתְנַשְּׂאִים לְעֻמַּת שְׂרָפִים, |
| l'u·matam barukh yomeiru. | לְעֻמָּתָם בָּרוּךְ יֹאמֵרוּ: |

| | |
|---|---|
| Barukh k'vod Adonai mim'komo. | בָּרוּךְ כְּבוֹד יְיָ מִמְּקוֹמוֹ |

| | |
|---|---|
| Mim'kom'kha Malkeinu tofi·a | מִמְּקוֹמְךָ מַלְכֵּנוּ תוֹפִיעַ, |
| v'timlokh aleinu | וְתִמְלֹךְ עָלֵינוּ, |
| ki m'ḥakim anaḥnu lakh. | כִּי מְחַכִּים אֲנַחְנוּ לָךְ. |
| Matai timlokh b'Tziyon, | מָתַי תִּמְלֹךְ בְּצִיּוֹן, |

*On Shabbat Shuvah, the Shabbat between Rosh Hashanah and Yom Kippur:*

Who is like you, Merciful Parent? You remember those You created with the merciful gift of life.

You are trustworthy in giving life to the dead.

Praised are You, who gives life to the dead.

## K'DUSHAH

**_We praise God's holiness._**

*We rise up on our toes for each "kadosh" to show our desire to come closer to God. Some also stand on tiptoe for "Barukh" and "Yimlokh."*

We shall tell of Your holiness on earth just as it is told in the heavens above. As Your prophet wrote, the angels called to one another, saying:

"Holy, holy, holy is *Adonai Tz'eva·ot*, the whole world is filled with God's glory." (Isaiah 6:3)

Then the Serafim responded in a mighty chorus:

"Praised is God's glory from God's place." (Ezekiel 3:12)

Our Ruler, show Yourself to us from Your place, and rule over us for we are waiting for You. When will You rule in Zion? Soon, in our days, may You establish Yourself there forever. May You be made great and holy in Jerusalem Your city for all generations and forever. May our eyes see Your kingdom as described in righteous David's psalms of Your might:

| | |
|---|---|
| b'karov b'yameinu | בְּקָרוֹב בְּיָמֵינוּ, |
| l'olam va·ed tishkon. | לְעוֹלָם וָעֶד תִּשְׁכּוֹן. |
| Titgadal v'titkadash | תִּתְגַּדַּל וְתִתְקַדַּשׁ |
| b'tokh Y'rushalayim ir'kha | בְּתוֹךְ יְרוּשָׁלַיִם עִירְךָ, |
| l'dor va-dor ul'neitzaḥ n'tzaḥim. | לְדוֹר וָדוֹר וּלְנֵצַח נְצָחִים. |
| V'eineinu tir·enah malkhutekha, | וְעֵינֵינוּ תִרְאֶינָה מַלְכוּתֶךָ, |
| ka-davar ha-amur b'shirei u-zekha, | כַּדָּבָר הָאָמוּר בְּשִׁירֵי עֻזֶּךָ, |
| al y'dei David m'shi·aḥ tzidkekha. | עַל יְדֵי דָוִד מְשִׁיחַ צִדְקֶךָ: |
| | |
| Yimlokh Adonai l'olam, | יִמְלֹךְ יְיָ לְעוֹלָם, |
| Elohayikh Tziyon l'dor va-dor. | אֱלֹהַיִךְ צִיּוֹן, לְדֹר וָדֹר, |
| Hal'luyah. | הַלְלוּיָהּ. |
| | |
| L'dor va-dor | לְדוֹר וָדוֹר |
| nagid godlekha | נַגִּיד גָּדְלֶךָ, |
| u-l'netzaḥ n'tzaḥim | וּלְנֵצַח נְצָחִים |
| k'dushat'kha nakdish. | קְדֻשָּׁתְךָ נַקְדִּישׁ, |
| v'shivḥakha Eloheinu | וְשִׁבְחֲךָ, אֱלֹהֵינוּ, |
| mipinu lo yamush | מִפִּינוּ לֹא יָמוּשׁ |
| l'olam va·ed, | לְעוֹלָם וָעֶד, |
| ki Eil Melekh | כִּי אֵל מֶלֶךְ |
| gadol v'kadosh Atah. | גָּדוֹל וְקָדוֹשׁ אָתָּה. |
| Barukh Atah Adonai, | בָּרוּךְ אַתָּה יְיָ, |
| ha-Eil ha-kadosh | הָאֵל הַקָּדוֹשׁ |

*On Shabbat Shuvah, the Shabbat between Rosh Hashanah and Yom Kippur:*

| | |
|---|---|
| [ha-Melekh ha-kadosh]. | הַמֶּלֶךְ הַקָּדוֹשׁ. |

Adonai will rule forever, your God, O Zion, for all generations. Halleluyah. (Psalm 146:10)

For all generations we will tell Your greatness, and we will add our holiness to Yours forever and ever. We will never stop praising You, for You are a great and holy God.

*When reading the Amidah silently, substitute this blessing for the K'dushah:*

You are holy and Your name is holy and holy beings praise You every day.

Praised are You Adonai, holy God.

*On Shabbat Shuvah, the Shabbat between Rosh Hashanah and Yom Kippur:*

Praised are You Adonai, the Holy Ruler.

**K'dushah:** God is *kadosh* – holy – and we aspire to holiness. We symbolize our desire for holiness by rising up on our toes each time we say "*kadosh*," and at the first words of the other two verses quoted here. But how do we actually achieve holiness in our lives? Not by separating from the world, but by bringing God's holiness into the world through the mitzvot, through compassion, through kindness, and through righteousness. So, as you pray the K'dushah, ask yourself, how have I brought holiness into my life and into the world this past week, and promise yourself that you will try to ask, "How can I make this moment *kadosh*?" during the coming week.

The K'dushah prayer is recited standing, feet straight and together. The custom is to rise on our tiptoes while reciting the words "holy, holy holy", thus mimicking the angels themselves. During the time of its recitation no one should enter or leave the prayer service. The K'dushah reminds us that God is separate, unique and beyond earthly pressures in God's rule. Praising God's holiness, the K'dushah gives us a picture of heavenly beings praising God above, and human beings praising God on earth. You could almost say that we sing in harmony with the heavenly realm.

**K'dushah:** Focus on one experience you have had of God's greatness, awesomeness or goodness. How did that experience affect you? Did it change your actions, your belief? How could you let it change you now. (*On Wings of Light*, Richard Levy)

## K'DUSHAT HA-YOM

*The holiness of the (Shabbat) day*

### Yismaḥ Moshe

| | |
|---|---|
| Yismaḥ Moshe | יִשְׂמַח מֹשֶׁה |
| b'mat'nat ḥelko, | בְּמַתְּנַת חֶלְקוֹ, |
| ki eved ne·eman karata lo. | כִּי עֶבֶד נֶאֱמָן קָרָאתָ לוֹ. |
| K'lil tiferet | כְּלִיל תִּפְאֶרֶת |
| b'rosho natata, | בְּרֹאשׁוֹ נָתַתָּ, |
| b'omdo l'fanekha al har Sinai. | בְּעָמְדוֹ לְפָנֶיךָ עַל הַר סִינָי. |
| Ush'nei luḥot avanim | וּשְׁנֵי לוּחוֹת אֲבָנִים |
| horid b'yado, | הוֹרִיד בְּיָדוֹ, |
| v'khatuv bahem | וְכָתוּב בָּהֶם |
| sh'mirat Shabbat, | שְׁמִירַת שַׁבָּת, |
| v'khein katuv b'Toratekha. | וְכֵן כָּתוּב בְּתוֹרָתֶךָ: |

### V'sham'ru

| | |
|---|---|
| V'sham'ru v'nei Yisra·el | וְשָׁמְרוּ בְנֵי יִשְׂרָאֵל |
| et ha-Shabbat | אֶת הַשַּׁבָּת, |
| la·asot et ha-Shabbat l'dorotam | לַעֲשׂוֹת אֶת הַשַּׁבָּת לְדֹרֹתָם |
| b'rit olam. | בְּרִית עוֹלָם. |
| Beini u-vein B'nei Yisra·el | בֵּינִי וּבֵין בְּנֵי יִשְׂרָאֵל |
| ot hi l'olam | אוֹת הִיא לְעֹלָם, |
| ki sheishet yamim asah Adonai | כִּי שֵׁשֶׁת יָמִים עָשָׂה יְיָ |
| et ha-shamayim v'et ha-aretz | אֶת הַשָּׁמַיִם וְאֶת הָאָרֶץ, |
| u-vayom ha-sh'vi-i | וּבַיּוֹם הַשְּׁבִיעִי |
| shavat va-yinafash. | שָׁבַת וַיִּנָּפַשׁ. |

| | |
|---|---|
| v'lo natato, Adonai Eloheinu, | וְלֹא נְתַתּוֹ יְיָ אֱלֹהֵינוּ |
| l'goyyai ha-aratzot, | לְגוֹיֵי הָאֲרָצוֹת, |
| v'lo hinḥalto, | וְלֹא הִנְחַלְתּוֹ |
| malkeinu, | מַלְכֵּנוּ |
| l'ov'dei f'silim, | לְעוֹבְדֵי פְסִילִים, |
| v'gam bim'nuḥato | וְגַם בִּמְנוּחָתוֹ |
| lo yishk'nu areilim, | לֹא יִשְׁכְּנוּ עֲרֵלִים. |

## K'DUSHAT HA-YOM

*The holiness of the (Shabbat) day*

### Yismaḥ Moshe

Moses was happy because You, God, gave him a gift: You called him a faithful servant, crowning him with glory as he stood before You on Mount Sinai. He brought down two stone tablets, with the command to observe the Shabbat written on them. So it is written in Your Torah.

### V'sham'ru

The people of Israel shall keep the Shabbat, to make Shabbat in every generation as a forever covenant. It is a sign between Me and the people of Israel forever, that in six days Adonai made the heavens and the earth, and on the seventh day God stopped working and rested.

Adonai our God, you did not give the Shabbat to other peoples and nations.

During the week, there are thirteen blessings in the middle of the Amidah. On Shabat and Ḥagim, there is just one: *K'dushat Ha-yom* – the sanctification of the day. In the Friday night Kabbalat service, it contains the *Va-y'khulu* passage from the Creation story, tying the Amidah to the theme of Creation. In the Shabbat Shaḥarit Amidah, we refer to Moses bringing down the two Tablets of the Commandments with the mitzvah of Shabbat written on them, as well as another key passage for Shabbat observance, known as the *V'sham'ru*. This ties in with the theme of Revelation. At the Shabbat Minḥah service, we find the theme of Redemption, a time when Shabbat will be fulfilled with perfection. The language of this version of the *K'dushat Ha-yom* is one of joy and delight. Moses rejoices at God's giving him the privilege of bringing the Torah to us, in particular the Holy Shabbat. Later on, we find that God called the Shabbat *ḥemdat Yamim*, the most treasured of days. Just as Moses rejoiced to be the messenger bringing this gift, we rejoice every Shabbat when we use this gift.

| | |
|---|---|
| ki l'Yisra·el am'kha | כִּי לְיִשְׂרָאֵל עַמְּךָ |
| n'tato b'ahava, | נְתַתּוֹ בְּאַהֲבָה, |
| l'zera Ya·akov | לְזֶרַע יַעֲקֹב |
| asher bam baḥarta. | אֲשֶׁר בָּם בָּחָרְתָּ. |
| Am m'kad'shei sh'vi·i, | עַם מְקַדְּשֵׁי שְׁבִיעִי, |
| kulam yisb'u | כֻּלָּם יִשְׂבְּעוּ |
| v'yit·an'gu mi-tuvekha. | וְיִתְעַנְּגוּ מִטּוּבֶךָ, |
| v'hashvi·i ratzita bo | וּבַשְּׁבִיעִי רָצִיתָ בּוֹ |
| v'kidashto, | וְקִדַּשְׁתּוֹ, |
| ḥemdat yamim oto karata, | חֶמְדַּת יָמִים אוֹתוֹ קָרָאתָ, |
| zeikher | זֵכֶר |
| l'ma·asei v'reishit. | לְמַעֲשֵׂה בְרֵאשִׁית. |

## Eloheinu vEilohei Avoteinu

| | |
|---|---|
| Eloheinu vEilohei avoteinu, | אֱלֹהֵינוּ וֵאלֹהֵי אֲבוֹתֵינוּ, |
| r'tzei vim'nuḥateinu. | רְצֵה בִמְנוּחָתֵנוּ, |
| Kad'sheinu b'mitz-votekha | קַדְּשֵׁנוּ בְּמִצְוֹתֶיךָ, |
| v'tein ḥelkeinu b'Toratekha, | וְתֵן חֶלְקֵנוּ בְּתוֹרָתֶךָ, |
| sab'einu mi-tuvekha | שַׂבְּעֵנוּ מִטּוּבֶךָ, |
| v'samḥeinu bishu·atekha, | וְשַׂמְּחֵנוּ בִּישׁוּעָתֶךָ, |
| v'taheir libeinu l'ov-d'kha be·emet. | וְטַהֵר לִבֵּנוּ לְעָבְדְּךָ בֶּאֱמֶת, |
| v'hanḥileinu | וְהַנְחִילֵנוּ |
| Adonai Eloheinu | יְיָ אֱלֹהֵינוּ |
| b'ahavah uv'ratzon | בְּאַהֲבָה וּבְרָצוֹן |
| Shabbat kod-shekha. | שַׁבַּת קָדְשֶׁךָ, |
| v'yanuḥu vo Yisra·el | וְיָנוּחוּ בוֹ יִשְׂרָאֵל |
| m'kad'shei sh'mekha. | מְקַדְּשֵׁי שְׁמֶךָ. |
| Barukh Atah Adonai, | בָּרוּךְ אַתָּה יְיָ, |
| m'kadeish ha-Shabbat. | מְקַדֵּשׁ הַשַּׁבָּת. |

You lovingly gave it to Your people Israel, Jacob's children, whom You chose. The people who make the seventh day holy – may they all be satisfied and delighted in Your goodness. You favored the seventh day and made it holy, calling it the most treasured of days, a day to remember the Creation of the world.

**Eloheinu vEilohei Avoteinu**

Our God and God of our ancestors, be pleased with our Shabbat rest, make us holy with Your mitzvot and let us share in Your Torah. Satisfy us with Your goodness and make us happy with Your help. Purify our hearts so that we can serve you truly. Adonai our God, let us receive Your holy Shabbat with love and favor, so that Your people Israel who make Your name holy will rest on it. Praised are You Adonai, who makes the Shabbat holy.

## *K'DUSHAT HAYOM FOR FESTIVALS*

אַתָּה בְחַרְתָּנוּ מִכָּל הָעַמִּים, אָהַבְתָּ אוֹתָנוּ וְרָצִיתָ בָּנוּ, וְרוֹמַמְתָּנוּ מִכָּל הַלְּשׁוֹנוֹת, וְקִדַּשְׁתָּנוּ בְּמִצְוֹתֶיךָ, וְקֵרַבְתָּנוּ מַלְכֵּנוּ לַעֲבוֹדָתֶךָ, וְשִׁמְךָ הַגָּדוֹל וְהַקָּדוֹשׁ עָלֵינוּ קָרָאתָ.

וַתִּתֶּן לָנוּ יְיָ אֱלֹהֵינוּ בְּאַהֲבָה (שַׁבָּתוֹת לִמְנוּחָה וּ) מוֹעֲדִים לְשִׂמְחָה, חַגִּים וּזְמַנִּים לְשָׂשׂוֹן, אֶת יוֹם (הַשַּׁבָּת הַזֶּה וְאֶת יוֹם)

*On Pesaḥ:*

חַג הַמַּצּוֹת הַזֶּה, זְמַן חֵרוּתֵנוּ

*On Shavuot:*

חַג הַשָּׁבֻעוֹת הַזֶּה,זְמַן מַתַּן תּוֹרָתֵנוּ

*On Sukkot:*

חַג הַסֻּכּוֹת הַזֶּה, זְמַן שִׂמְחָתֵנוּ

*On Sh'mini Atzeret and Simchat Torah:*

הַשְּׁמִינִי חַג הָעֲצֶרֶת הַזֶּה, זְמַן זְמַן שִׂמְחָתֵנוּ

(בְּאַהֲבָה) מִקְרָא קֹדֶשׁ, זֵכֶר לִיצִיאַת מִצְרָיִם.

אֱלֹהֵינוּ וֵאלֹהֵי אֲבוֹתֵינוּ, יַעֲלֶה וְיָבֹא, וְיַגִּיעַ, וְיֵרָאֶה, וְיֵרָצֶה, וְיִשָּׁמַע, וְיִפָּקֵד, וְיִזָּכֵר זִכְרוֹנֵנוּ וּפִקְדוֹנֵנוּ, וְזִכְרוֹן אֲבוֹתֵינוּ, וְזִכְרוֹן מָשִׁיחַ בֶּן דָּוִד עַבְדֶּךָ, וְזִכְרוֹן יְרוּשָׁלַיִם עִיר קָדְשֶׁךָ, וְזִכְרוֹן כָּל עַמְּךָ בֵּית יִשְׂרָאֵל לְפָנֶיךָ, לִפְלֵיטָה, לְטוֹבָה, לְחֵן וּלְחֶסֶד וּלְרַחֲמִים, לְחַיִּים וּלְשָׁלוֹם, בְּיוֹם

לְפֶסַח: חַג הַמַּצּוֹת הַזֶּה.
לְסֻכּוֹת: חַג הַסֻּכּוֹת הַזֶּה.
לְשָׁבֻעוֹת: חַג הַשָּׁבוּעוֹת הַזֶּה.

זָכְרֵנוּ, יְיָ אֱלֹהֵינוּ, בּוֹ לְטוֹבָה, וּפָקְדֵנוּ בוֹ לִבְרָכָה, וְהוֹשִׁיעֵנוּ בוֹ לְחַיִּים. וּבִדְבַר יְשׁוּעָה וְרַחֲמִים, חוּס וְחָנֵּנוּ, וְרַחֵם עָלֵינוּ וְהוֹשִׁיעֵנוּ, כִּי אֵלֶיךָ עֵינֵינוּ, כִּי אֵל מֶלֶךְ חַנּוּן וְרַחוּם אָתָּה.

וְהַשִּׂיאֵנוּ, יְיָ אֱלֹהֵינוּ, אֶת בִּרְכַּת מוֹעֲדֶיךָ, לְחַיִּים וּלְשָׁלוֹם, לְשִׂמְחָה וּלְשָׂשׂוֹן, כַּאֲשֶׁר רָצִיתָ וְאָמַרְתָּ לְבָרְכֵנוּ. (לשבת אֱלֹהֵינוּ וֵאלֹהֵי אֲבוֹתֵינוּ, רְצֵה בִמְנוּחָתֵנוּ,) קַדְּשֵׁנוּ בְּמִצְוֹתֶיךָ, וְתֵן חֶלְקֵנוּ בְּתוֹרָתֶךָ, שַׂבְּעֵנוּ מִטּוּבֶךָ, וְשַׂמְּחֵנוּ בִּישׁוּעָתֶךָ, וְטַהֵר לִבֵּנוּ לְעָבְדְּךָ בֶּאֱמֶת, וְהַנְחִילֵנוּ יְיָ אֱלֹהֵינוּ (לשבת בְּאַהֲבָה וּבְרָצוֹן) בְּשִׂמְחָה וּבְשָׂשׂוֹן (לשבת שַׁבָּת וּ)מוֹעֲדֵי קָדְשֶׁךָ, וְיִשְׂמְחוּ בְךָ יִשְׂרָאֵל מְקַדְּשֵׁי שְׁמֶךָ. בָּרוּךְ אַתָּה יְיָ, מְקַדֵּשׁ (לשבת הַשַּׁבָּת וְ)יִשְׂרָאֵל וְהַזְּמַנִּים.

## *K'DUSHAT HAYOM FOR FESTIVALS*

You chose us from among all the peoples, you loved us. and were pleased with us. You raised us up by making us holy by Your *mitzvot*, and You brought us near, our Ruler, to worship You. We have been called by Your great and holy Name.

Adonai our God, You lovingly gave us holidays for joy, festivals and special times for happiness, including this day (of Shabbat and this)

*On Pesaḥ:*
Festival of Matzot, the time of our freedom,

*On Shavuot:*
Festival of Shavuot, the time of the giving of our Torah,

*On Sukkot:*
Festival of Sukkot, the time of our rejoicing,

*On Sh'mini Atzeret and Simḥat Torah:*
Festival of Sh'mini Atzeret, the time of our rejoicing, (with love) a holy day for gathering together, to remember the Exodus from Egypt.

Our God and God of our ancestors, please remember us, our ancestors, the Messiah, Your holy city Jerusalem, and your people Israel. Remember them for good, with mercy and lovingkindness, for life and for peace on this day of:

| | |
|---|---|
| *On Rosh Ḥodesh* | New Month |
| *On Pesaḥ*: | Festival of Matzot |
| *On Sukkot*: | Festival of Sukkot. |

Remember us, Adonai our God, for good; keep us in mind for blessing, and bring us to life. As You promised to protect and save us, have mercy on us and save us, for our eyes turn to You, for You are a kind and merciful Ruler.

Adonai our God, give us the blessing of Your Festivals for life and peace, for joy and happiness, as You have promised us You would bless us. Our God and God of our ancestors, [be pleased with our Shabbat rest,] make us holy with Your mitzvot and let Torah be Your gift to us, fill us up with Your goodness and make us happy by saving us. Make our hearts pure so that we can truly serve You. Adonai our God, [lovingly and willingly,] joyfully and happily give us Your gift of [Shabbat and] your holy days, so that Israel who treats Your Name as holy will always rejoice in You. Praised are You, Adonai, who makes [the Shabbat and] Israel and the special times holy.

## AVODAH

***We pray to God to accept our prayers.***

| | |
|---|---|
| R'tzeih Adonai Eloheinu | רְצֵה, יְיָ אֱלֹהֵינוּ, |
| b'am'kha Yisra·el u-vit'filatam, | בְּעַמְּךָ יִשְׂרָאֵל וּבִתְפִלָּתָם, |
| v'hasheiv et ha-avodah | וְהָשֵׁב אֶת הָעֲבוֹדָה |
| li-d'vir beitekha, | לִדְבִיר בֵּיתֶךָ, |
| u-t'filatam b'ahavah | וּתְפִלָּתָם בְּאַהֲבָה |
| t'kabeil b'ratzon. | תְקַבֵּל בְּרָצוֹן, |
| U-t'hi l'ratzon tamid | וּתְהִי לְרָצוֹן תָּמִיד |
| avodat Yisra·el amekha. | עֲבוֹדַת יִשְׂרָאֵל עַמֶּךָ. |

*On Rosh Ḥodesh and on Ḥol Ha-mo·ed, we add the prayer Ya·aleh v'yavo.*

| | | |
|---|---|---|
| Zokhreinu Adonai Eloheinu | | זָכְרֵנוּ, יְיָ אֱלֹהֵינוּ, |
| bo l'tovah | Amen! | בּוֹ לְטוֹבָה, |
| U'fokdeinu vo liv'rakha | Amen! | וּפָקְדֵנוּ בוֹ לִבְרָכָה, |
| v'hoshi·einu vo l'ḥayyim | Amen! | וְהוֹשִׁיעֵנוּ בוֹ לְחַיִּים. |

| | |
|---|---|
| v'teḥezenah eineinu | וְתֶחֱזֶינָה עֵינֵינוּ |
| b'shuv'kha l'Tziyon b'raḥamim. | בְּשׁוּבְךָ לְצִיּוֹן בְּרַחֲמִים. |
| Barukh Atah Adonai | בָּרוּךְ אַתָּה יְיָ, |
| ha-maḥazir sh'khinato l'Tziyon. | הַמַּחֲזִיר שְׁכִינָתוֹ לְצִיּוֹן. |

## AVODAH

### *We pray to God to accept our prayers.*

Adonai, be pleased with Your people Israel and with their prayer. Restore worship to Your Temple. May the prayer of Your people Israel always be accepted with love and favor.

*On Rosh Ḥodesh and on Ḥol Ha-mo•ed (the intermediate days of Pesaḥ and Sukkot), we add the prayer Yà•aleh v'yavo.*

Our God and God of our ancestors, may [what we pray for] ascend, come, and reach, appear, be accepted and heard, counted and remembered: our memory and our record, the memory of our ancestors, and the memory of the Messiah, the son of David Your servant; the memory of Jerusalem, Your holy city, and the memory of Your entire people, before You, for survival, for good, for grace, for lovingkindness, for mercy, for life and for peace on this…

The first day of the month
The festival of matzah
The Festival of Sukkot

Remember us on it, Adonai our God, for good; take note of us on it for blessing; and save us on it for life. In this matter of salvation and mercy, spare us and be gracious to us, and have mercy upon us and save us, for our eyes are turned toward You, for you are our God, sovereign, gracious and merciful.

May we see Your merciful return to Zion. Praised are You, Adonai, who restores Your presence to Zion.

**Avodah:** In the days of the Temple, this was a prayer asking God to accept our sacrifices. In fact, the word Avodah referred specifically to sacrificial worship. When prayer replaced sacrifices, it became a plea for God to be pleased with our prayers and to accept them. What makes our prayers acceptable to God? Right now, as I stand in silent prayer, what can I bring to my prayer to make it pleasing and proper? Is it understanding the words? Is it my desire to reach out before God and stand in God's presence? Or something else?

## MODIM

## *Thank You, God.*
## *We give thanks for God's daily miracles.*

*We bow, bending the knee at "modim," bowing from the waist at "anaḥnu", and standing straight again at "lakh".*

*When the Amidah is repeated, the congregation reads this paragraph silently.*

מוֹדִים אֲנַחְנוּ לָךְ, שָׁאַתָּה הוּא יְיָ אֱלֹהֵינוּ וֵאלֹהֵי אֲבוֹתֵינוּ, אֱלֹהֵי כָל בָּשָׂר, יוֹצְרֵנוּ, יוֹצֵר בְּרֵאשִׁית. בְּרָכוֹת וְהוֹדָאוֹת לְשִׁמְךָ הַגָּדוֹל וְהַקָּדוֹשׁ, עַל שֶׁהֶחֱיִיתָנוּ וְקִיַּמְתָּנוּ. כֵּן תְּחַיֵּנוּ וּתְקַיְּמֵנוּ, וְתֶאֱסוֹף גָּלֻיּוֹתֵינוּ לְחַצְרוֹת קָדְשֶׁךָ, לִשְׁמוֹר חֻקֶּיךָ וְלַעֲשׂוֹת רְצוֹנֶךָ, וּלְעָבְדְּךָ בְּלֵבָב שָׁלֵם, עַל שֶׁאֲנַחְנוּ מוֹדִים לָךְ. בָּרוּךְ אֵל הַהוֹדָאוֹת.

מוֹדִים אֲנַחְנוּ לָךְ, שָׁאַתָּה הוּא, יְיָ אֱלֹהֵינוּ וֵאלֹהֵי אֲבוֹתֵינוּ, לְעוֹלָם וָעֶד, צוּר חַיֵּינוּ, מָגֵן יִשְׁעֵנוּ, אַתָּה הוּא לְדוֹר וָדוֹר, נוֹדֶה לְּךָ וּנְסַפֵּר תְּהִלָּתֶךָ, עַל חַיֵּינוּ הַמְּסוּרִים בְּיָדֶךָ, וְעַל נִשְׁמוֹתֵינוּ הַפְּקוּדוֹת לָךְ, וְעַל נִסֶּיךָ שֶׁבְּכָל יוֹם עִמָּנוּ, וְעַל נִפְלְאוֹתֶיךָ וְטוֹבוֹתֶיךָ שֶׁבְּכָל עֵת, עֶרֶב וָבֹקֶר וְצָהֳרָיִם, הַטּוֹב, כִּי לֹא כָלוּ רַחֲמֶיךָ, וְהַמְרַחֵם, כִּי לֹא תַמּוּ חֲסָדֶיךָ, מֵעוֹלָם קִוִּינוּ לָךְ

*On Ḥanukah:*

| | |
|---|---|
| Al ha-nisim v'al ha-purkan, | עַל הַנִּסִּים, וְעַל הַפֻּרְקָן, |
| v'al ha-g'vurot, v'al ha-t'shu·ot, | וְעַל הַגְּבוּרוֹת, וְעַל הַתְּשׁוּעוֹת, |
| v'al ha-milḥamot | וְעַל הַמִּלְחָמוֹת, |
| she-asita la-avoteinu | שֶׁעָשִׂיתָ לַאֲבוֹתֵינוּ |
| ba-yamim ha-heim | בַּיָּמִים הָהֵם |
| ba-z'man ha-zeh. | בַּזְּמַן הַזֶּה. |

## MODIM

### *Thank You, God.*
### *We give thanks for God's daily miracles.*

*We bow, bending the knee at "modim," bowing from the waist at "anaḥnu", and standing straight again at "lakh".*

*When the Amidah is repeated, the congregation reads this paragraph silently.*

We thank You for being our God and God of our ancestors, God of all flesh, our Crafter who formed Creation. We offer praises and thanks to Your great and holy Name for keeping us alive and sustaining us. So may You keep your laws and do Your will, and serve you whole-heartedly. For this we thank You. Praised is the God to whom thanks is due.

We thank You for being our God and God of our ancestors for ever and ever. You are the Rock of our lives and our saving Shield. In every generation we will thank and praise You for our lives which are in Your power, for our souls which are in Your keeping, for Your miracles which are with us every day, and for your wonders and good things that are with us at all times, evening, morning, and noon. O Good One, Your mercies have never stopped. O Merciful One, your kindness has never stopped. We have always placed our hope in You.

*On Ḥanukah:*

We thank You, God, for the miracles, for the rescues, for the mighty deeds, for the saving acts, and for the wars that you fought for our ancestors long ago at this time of year.

The sixth blessing of the Amidah acknowledges, thanks and praises God for our lives and the daily miracles that are all around us. The custom is to bow at the beginning of the Modim prayer and at the end of the Modim blessing, indicating that we are bringing our prayer to an end

**Modim Kavanah/Reflections:**
Has something happened to you this week that seemed like a miracle? Has something occurred that makes you particularly grateful for being alive? What one thing would you especially like to thank God for now? Use this prayer, expressed with your own unique enthusiasm, to voice your gratitude, (*On Wings of Light*, Richard Levy)

בִּימֵי מַתִּתְיָהוּ בֶּן יוֹחָנָן כֹּהֵן גָּדוֹל, חַשְׁמוֹנַאי וּבָנָיו, כְּשֶׁעָמְדָה מַלְכוּת יָוָן הָרְשָׁעָה עַל עַמְּךָ יִשְׂרָאֵל לְהַשְׁכִּיחָם תּוֹרָתֶךָ, וּלְהַעֲבִירָם מֵחֻקֵּי רְצוֹנֶךָ, וְאַתָּה בְּרַחֲמֶיךָ הָרַבִּים עָמַדְתָּ לָהֶם בְּעֵת צָרָתָם, רַבְתָּ אֶת רִיבָם, דַּנְתָּ אֶת דִּינָם, נָקַמְתָּ אֶת נִקְמָתָם, מָסַרְתָּ גִּבּוֹרִים בְּיַד חַלָּשִׁים, וְרַבִּים בְּיַד מְעַטִּים, וּטְמֵאִים בְּיַד טְהוֹרִים, וּרְשָׁעִים בְּיַד צַדִּיקִים, וְזֵדִים בְּיַד עוֹסְקֵי תוֹרָתֶךָ. וּלְךָ עָשִׂיתָ שֵׁם גָּדוֹל וְקָדוֹשׁ בְּעוֹלָמֶךָ, וּלְעַמְּךָ יִשְׂרָאֵל עָשִׂיתָ תְּשׁוּעָה גְדוֹלָה וּפֻרְקָן כְּהַיּוֹם הַזֶּה. וְאַחַר כֵּן בָּאוּ בָנֶיךָ לִדְבִיר בֵּיתֶךָ, וּפִנּוּ אֶת הֵיכָלֶךָ, וְטִהֲרוּ אֶת מִקְדָּשֶׁךָ, וְהִדְלִיקוּ נֵרוֹת בְּחַצְרוֹת קָדְשֶׁךָ, וְקָבְעוּ שְׁמוֹנַת יְמֵי חֲנֻכָּה אֵלּוּ, לְהוֹדוֹת וּלְהַלֵּל לְשִׁמְךָ הַגָּדוֹל.

וְעַל כֻּלָּם יִתְבָּרַךְ וְיִתְרוֹמַם שִׁמְךָ מַלְכֵּנוּ תָּמִיד לְעוֹלָם וָעֶד.

*On Shabbat Shuvah, the Shabbat between Rosh Hashanah and Yom Kippur, add:*

וּכְתוֹב לְחַיִּים טוֹבִים כָּל בְּנֵי בְרִיתֶךָ.

וְכֹל הַחַיִּים יוֹדוּךָ סֶּלָה, וִיהַלְלוּ אֶת שִׁמְךָ בֶּאֱמֶת, הָאֵל יְשׁוּעָתֵנוּ וְעֶזְרָתֵנוּ סֶלָה. בָּרוּךְ אַתָּה יְיָ, הַטּוֹב שִׁמְךָ וּלְךָ נָאֶה לְהוֹדוֹת.

## BIRKAT KOHANIM (PRIESTLY BLESSING)

*When the Amidah is recited aloud.*

*Leader:*

יְבָרֶכְךָ יְיָ וְיִשְׁמְרֶךָ. (כֵּן יְהִי רָצוֹן)
Y'verekh'kha Adonai v'Yishm'rekha (Kein y'hi ratzon)

יָאֵר יְיָ פָּנָיו אֵלֶיךָ וִיחֻנֶּךָּ. (כֵּן יְהִי רָצוֹן)
Ya·eir Adonai panav eilekha vikhuneka. (Kein y'hi ratzon)

יִשָּׂא יְיָ פָּנָיו אֵלֶיךָ וְיָשֵׂם לְךָ שָׁלוֹם. (כֵּן יְהִי רָצוֹן)
Yisa Adonai panav eilekha v'yaseim l'kha shalom. (Kein y'hi ratzon)

In the days of Mattathias son of Yochanan, the High Priest, of the Hasmonean family, and his sons, when the evil Greek government rose up against Your people Israel, they tried to make them forget Your Torah and break Your laws. You, in Your great mercy, stood firm for them in their time of trouble. You defended them, you judged in their favor, you punished their enemies. You helped the weak to defeat the strong, the few to defeat the many, the pure to defeat the impure, the righteous to defeat the wicked, and the followers of Your Torah to defeat the sinners. Because you did this, Your Name was made great and holy before all the world. You won a great victory for Your people Israel that lasted until this day. Afterwards, Your children came into the holiest part of Your House, cleaned and purified Your Palace, and lit lights in the courtyards of Your Holy Place. They set these eight days of Hanukah as a time for thanking and Praising You.

For all these things, our Ruler, may Your name be blessed and honored forever.

*On Shabbat Shuvah, the Shabbat between Rosh Hashanah and Yom Kippur, add:*

Write us down for a good life.

May every living thing thank You and praise You sincerely, O God, our rescue and help. Praised are You, Your name is "the Good One," and it is good to thank You.

## BIRKAT KOHANIM (PRIESTLY BLESSING)

*When the Amidah is recited aloud.*

*Leader:*

Our God and God of our ancestors, bless us with the three-part blessing of the Torah, written by Your servant Moses, spoken by Aaron and his sons the Kohanim, Your holy people, as it is said:

| *Leader:* | *Congregation:* |
|---|---|
| May Adonai bless You and protect You. | So may it be God's will. |
| May Adonai show you favor and be gracious to you. | So may it be God's will. |
| May Adonai show you kindness and grant you peace | So may it be God's will. |

## BIRKAT SHALOM

***We pray for peace, the ultimate blessing.***

| | |
|---|---|
| Sim shalom | שִׂים שָׁלוֹם |
| ba-olam tovah uv'rakha, | בָּעוֹלָם טוֹבָה וּבְרָכָה, |
| ḥein va-ḥesed v'raḥamim | חֵן וָחֶסֶד וְרַחֲמִים, |
| aleinu v'al kol Yisra·el amekha. | עָלֵינוּ וְעַל כָּל יִשְׂרָאֵל עַמֶּךָ. |
| Bar'kheinu Avinu kulanu k'eḥad | בָּרְכֵנוּ, אָבִינוּ, כֻּלָּנוּ כְּאֶחָד |
| b'or panekha, | בְּאוֹר פָּנֶיךָ, |
| ki v'or panekha | כִּי בְאוֹר פָּנֶיךָ |
| natata lanu, Adonai Eloheinu, | נָתַתָּ לָּנוּ, יְיָ אֱלֹהֵינוּ, |
| Torat ḥayim v'ahavat ḥesed, | תּוֹרַת חַיִּים וְאַהֲבַת חֶסֶד, |
| u-tz'dakah uv'rakha v'raḥamim | וּצְדָקָה וּבְרָכָה וְרַחֲמִים |
| v'ḥayim v'shalom. | וְחַיִּים וְשָׁלוֹם, |
| v'tov b'einekha | וְטוֹב בְּעֵינֶיךָ |
| l'varekh et am'kha Yisra·el | לְבָרֵךְ אֶת עַמְּךָ יִשְׂרָאֵל |
| b'khol eit uv'khol sha·ah | בְּכָל עֵת וּבְכָל שָׁעָה |
| bish'lo-mekha. | בִּשְׁלוֹמֶךָ. |

*On Shabbat Shuvah, the Shabbat between Rosh Hashanah and Yom Kippur, say these words instead of the next paragraph:.*

| | |
|---|---|
| B'seifer ḥayyim, b'rakhah v'shalom, | בְּסֵפֶר חַיִּים, בְּרָכָה וְשָׁלוֹם, |
| u-farnasah tovah, n'zakheir | וּפַרְנָסָה טוֹבָה, נִזָּכֵר |
| v'nikateiv l'fanekha, | וְנִכָּתֵב לְפָנֶיךָ, |
| anaḥnu v'khol amkha beit Yisra·el. | אֲנַחְנוּ וְכָל עַמְּךָ בֵּית יִשְׂרָאֵל, |
| L'ḥayyim tovim u-l'shalom. | לְחַיִּים טוֹבִים וּלְשָׁלוֹם. |
| Barukh atah Adonai | בָּרוּךְ אַתָּה יְיָ, |
| oseh ha-shalom. | עוֹשֵׂה הַשָּׁלוֹם |

| | |
|---|---|
| Barukh Atah Adonai | בָּרוּךְ אַתָּה יְיָ, |
| ha-m'vareikh et amo Yisra·el | הַמְבָרֵךְ אֶת עַמּוֹ יִשְׂרָאֵל |
| ba-shalom. | בַּשָּׁלוֹם. |

## BIRKAT SHALOM

***We pray for peace, the ultimate blessing.***

Make peace in the world, with goodness, blessing, grace, lovingkindness and mercy for us and for all Your people Israel. Bless us, our Parent, all of us together, with Your light, by which You taught us Your Torah of life, love and kindness, justice and mercy, life and peace. May it be good in Your sight to bless Your people Israel at all times with peace.

*On Shabbat Shuvah, the Shabbat between Rosh Hashanah and Yom Kippur, say these words instead of the next paragraph:*

Remember us and write us down in the Book of life, blessing, peace, and support, along with the entire Jewish people, for a good life and for peace. Praised are You, Adonai, who makes peace.

Praised are You, Adonai, who blesses God's people Israel with peace.

A midrash says, "Blessings are of no use at all if peace is not with them." So we end the *Amidah*, the *Kaddish Shalem*, and the *Birkat Ha-mazon* with a prayer for peace. In the *Sim Shalom*, peace has an escort of other blessings: goodness, blessing, grace, lovingkindness and mercy. This reminds us that *shalom* means far more than just the absence of conflict. It is a positive state of tranquility, well-being, contentment and more. With *shalom*, people can live to their highest potential, free of danger, deprivation, and sorrow. As you pray this prayer, think: is there anything I can do to bring a little more *shalom* into my life, into my home, into my community, into the world?

## ELOHAI N'TZOR

***A prayer for self-mastery and purification.***

אֱלֹהַי, נְצוֹר לְשׁוֹנִי מֵרָע, וּשְׂפָתַי מִדַּבֵּר מִרְמָה, וְלִמְקַלְלַי נַפְשִׁי
תִדֹּם, וְנַפְשִׁי כֶּעָפָר לַכֹּל תִּהְיֶה. פְּתַח לִבִּי בְּתוֹרָתֶךָ, וּבְמִצְוֹתֶיךָ
תִּרְדּוֹף נַפְשִׁי. וְכָל הַחוֹשְׁבִים עָלַי רָעָה, מְהֵרָה הָפֵר עֲצָתָם
וְקַלְקֵל מַחֲשַׁבְתָּם. עֲשֵׂה לְמַעַן שְׁמֶךָ, עֲשֵׂה לְמַעַן יְמִינֶךָ, עֲשֵׂה
לְמַעַן קְדֻשָּׁתֶךָ, עֲשֵׂה לְמַעַן תּוֹרָתֶךָ. לְמַעַן יֵחָלְצוּן יְדִידֶיךָ,
הוֹשִׁיעָה יְמִינְךָ וַעֲנֵנִי. יִהְיוּ לְרָצוֹן אִמְרֵי פִי וְהֶגְיוֹן לִבִּי לְפָנֶיךָ, יְיָ
צוּרִי וְגוֹאֲלִי.

*Take three steps back and bow to the left at the word "oseh," to the right at "hu," and to the center at "aleinu."*

עֹשֶׂה שָׁלוֹם בִּמְרוֹמָיו, הוּא
יַעֲשֶׂה שָׁלוֹם עָלֵינוּ, וְעַל כָּל
יִשְׂרָאֵל, וְאִמְרוּ אָמֵן.

Oseh shalom bim'romav, hu ya·seh shalom aleinu, v'al kol Yisra·el, v'imru amen.

## ELOHAI N'TZOR

### *A prayer for self-mastery and purification.*

*This personal prayer by Mar ben Ravina is quoted in the Talmud. It appears here to encourage us to add our individual and personal prayers during this quiet time of reflection at the end of the silent prayer. Perhaps it was chosen because the first sentence goes well with the prelude to the Avot blessing, "God, open my lips so that my mouth may speak your praise."*

My God, prevent my tongue from saying bad things and my lips from telling lies. Help me to ignore people who say bad things about me. Open my heart to Your Torah, so that I can do Your mitzvot. If anyone wants to do me harm, quickly stop their ideas and spoil their plans. Do this because of Your love, Your holiness, and Your Torah: so that those You love will be free. May the words of my mouth and the thoughts of my heart find favor with You, my Rock and my Saver. May the One who makes peace up above give peace to us and to all the people of Israel. Amen.

**Elohai Netzor:** Watch your thoughts, they can become words.
Watch your words, they can become actions.
Watch your actions, they can become habits.
Watch your habits, they can become character.
Watch your character, it becomes your destiny.

The Hebrew word for "words" is "devarim". With a slight change in vowels, words can become "devorim" – bees that sting. How do people generally react to the words that you speak to them? Do they fall upon people like stinging bees, or like light and soft dew? This prayer, *Elohai N'tzor* – "Guard my tongue," – reminds us to be careful with our words!

# Hallel

*This section of the service, Hallel, mean's "praise." We add it on the three pilgrimage Festivals, Hanukah, and Rosh Ḥodesh (the new month). Hallel is recited while standing. This blessing is recited first by the leader and then repeated by the congregation:*

| | |
|---|---|
| Barukh Atah Adonai | בָּרוּךְ אַתָּה יְיָ |
| Eloheinu Melekh ha-olam, | אֱלֹהֵינוּ מֶלֶךְ הָעוֹלָם, |
| asher kid'shanu b'mitzvotav | אֲשֶׁר קִדְּשָׁנוּ בְּמִצְוֹתָיו, |
| v'tzivanu lik'ro et ha-hallel. | וְצִוָּנוּ לִקְרֹא אֶת הַהַלֵּל. |

## PSALM 113

| | |
|---|---|
| Hal'luyah. | הַלְלוּיָהּ, |
| Hal'lu, avdei Adonai, | הַלְלוּ עַבְדֵי יְיָ, |
| hal'lu et sheim Adonai. | הַלְלוּ אֶת שֵׁם יְיָ. |
| Y'hi sheim Adonai m'vorakh | יְהִי שֵׁם יְיָ מְבֹרָךְ, |
| mei-Atah v'ad olam. | מֵעַתָּה וְעַד עוֹלָם. |
| Mi-mizraḥ shemesh ad m'vo·o | מִמִּזְרַח שֶׁמֶשׁ עַד מְבוֹאוֹ, |
| m'hulal sheim Adonai. | מְהֻלָּל שֵׁם יְיָ. |
| Ram al kol goyim Adonai, | רָם עַל כָּל גּוֹיִם יְיָ, |
| al ha-shamayim k'vodo. | עַל הַשָּׁמַיִם כְּבוֹדוֹ. |
| Mi kAdonai Eloheinu, | מִי כַּייָ אֱלֹהֵינוּ, |
| ha-magbihi la-shavet, | הַמַּגְבִּיהִי לָשָׁבֶת. |
| Ha-mashpili lir'ot | הַמַּשְׁפִּילִי לִרְאוֹת, |
| ba-shamayim u-va·aretz. | בַּשָּׁמַיִם וּבָאָרֶץ. |
| M'kimi mei-afar dal, | ♪ מְקִימִי מֵעָפָר דָּל, |
| mei-ashpot yarim evyon, | מֵאַשְׁפֹּת יָרִים אֶבְיוֹן. |
| l'hoshivi im n'divim | לְהוֹשִׁיבִי עִם נְדִיבִים, |
| im n'divei amo. | עִם נְדִיבֵי עַמּוֹ. |
| Moshivi akeret ha-bayit, | מוֹשִׁיבִי עֲקֶרֶת הַבַּיִת, |
| eim ha-banim s'meiḥah. | אֵם הַבָּנִים שְׂמֵחָה, |
| Hal'luyah. | הַלְלוּיָהּ. |

# Hallel

*This blessing is recited first by the leader and then repeated by the congregation:*

Praised are You, Adonai our God, Ruler of the Universe, who made us holy through mitzvot and commanded us to read the Hallel.

## PSALM 113

Halleluyah! Praise Adonai, you who serve Adonai,
praise the name of Adonai.

May Adonai's Name be blessed now and forever.
From sunrise to sunset, Adonai's name is praised.

Adonai is above all the nations,
God's glory goes beyond the heavens.

Who is like Adonai our God, who is far above us,
yet "bends down" to look at the heavens and the earth.

God lifts up the poor from the dust,
the needy from the trash heap,
and seats them with the nobles of God's people.

He transforms the childless woman
into a mother joyful with her children. Hallelulah!

This section of the service is known as Hallel, since all of the psalms use either the word "hallel" (praise) or the concept of praise. The prayers are all recited while standing. During Temple times, all of these Psalms were accompanied by musical instruments and dancing which helped in the expression of joy as they were recited. Hallel is recited on each of our three pilgrimage festivals–Passover, Shavuot and Sukkot, as well as on Israel Independence Day, Jerusalem Day, and Rosh Hodesh (New Month).

**Psalm 113** speaks of God's greatness and concern for the downtrodden.

## PSALM 114

| | |
|---|---|
| B'tzeit Yisra·el mi-Mitzrayim, | בְּצֵאת יִשְׂרָאֵל מִמִּצְרָיִם, |
| beit Ya·akov | בֵּית יַעֲקֹב |
| mei·am lo·eiz. | מֵעַם לֹעֵז. |
| Hai-y'tah Y'hudah l'kodsho, | הָיְתָה יְהוּדָה לְקָדְשׁוֹ, |
| Yisra·el mam-sh'lotav. | יִשְׂרָאֵל מַמְשְׁלוֹתָיו. |
| Ha-yam ra·ah va-yanos, | הַיָּם רָאָה וַיָּנֹס, |
| ha-Yarden yisov l'aḥor. | הַיַּרְדֵּן יִסֹּב לְאָחוֹר. |
| He-harim rak'du kh'eilim, | הֶהָרִים רָקְדוּ כְאֵילִים, |
| g'va·ot kiv'nei tzon. | גְּבָעוֹת כִּבְנֵי צֹאן. |
| Mah l'kha ha-yam | מַה לְּךָ הַיָּם |
| ki tanus, | כִּי תָנוּס, |
| ha-Yardein tisov l'aḥor. | הַיַּרְדֵּן תִּסֹּב לְאָחוֹר. |
| He-harim tirk'du kh'ei-lim, | הֶהָרִים תִּרְקְדוּ כְאֵילִים, |
| g'va·ot kiv'nei tzon. | גְּבָעוֹת כִּבְנֵי צֹאן. |
| Mi-lifnei Adon ḥuli aretz, | מִלִּפְנֵי אָדוֹן חוּלִי אָרֶץ, |
| mi-lifnei Eloha Ya·akov. | מִלִּפְנֵי אֱלוֹהַּ יַעֲקֹב. |
| Ha-ḥofkhi ha-tzur | הַהֹפְכִי הַצּוּר |
| agam mayim, | אֲגַם מָיִם, |
| ḥalamish l'ma'y'no mayim. | חַלָּמִישׁ לְמַעְיְנוֹ מָיִם. |

## PSALM 115

*This section is not said on Rosh Ḥodesh or the last 6 days of Pesaḥ.*

| | |
|---|---|
| Lo lanu Adonai, | לֹא לָנוּ, יְיָ, |
| lo lanu, | לֹא לָנוּ, |
| Ki l'shimkha tein kavod | כִּי לְשִׁמְךָ תֵּן כָּבוֹד, |
| al ḥasd'kha | עַל חַסְדְּךָ |
| al amitekha. | עַל אֲמִתֶּךָ. |
| Lamah yom'ru ha-goyim | לָמָּה יֹאמְרוּ הַגּוֹיִם, |
| ayeih na Eloheihem. | אַיֵּה נָא אֱלֹהֵיהֶם. |
| vEiloheinu va-shamayim, | וֵאלֹהֵינוּ בַשָּׁמָיִם, |
| kol asher ḥafeitz asah. | כֹּל אֲשֶׁר חָפֵץ עָשָׂה. |

## PSALM 114

When Israel went out of Egypt,
The House of Jacob from a foreign people,
Judah became God's holy people, Israel [became] God's nation.
The sea saw and turned back, the Jordan fled.
The mountains danced like rams, the hills, like lambs.
What is with you, sea, that you flee;
Jordan, that you turn back?
Mountains, that you dance like rams; hills, like lambs?
Quake, earth, before the Ruler, before the God of Jacob,
Who turns the rock into a pool of water;
Who turns flint into fountains.

## PSALM 115

*This section is not said on Rosh Ḥodesh or the last 6 days of Pesaḥ.*

Not because we deserve it, Adonai, not because we deserve it,
But for Your own reasons act gloriously,
For the sake of Your lovingkindness and Your truth.

Why should the nations say, "Where is their God?"
Our God is in heaven. God does as God pleases.

**Psalm 114** describes, in terms of Nature, the significance and the effect of the Exodus of the Israelites from Egypt on the world. Nature itself reacts to the redemption by the dancing and prancing of the sea, mountains and the earth itself.

**Psalm 115** assures the Jewish people that they need not fear the nations since the gods of the nations do not exist. In fact, the gods are mocked as the worship of mere sticks and stones.

| | |
|---|---|
| עֲצַבֵּיהֶם כֶּסֶף וְזָהָב, | Atzabeihem kesef v'zahav, |
| מַעֲשֵׂה יְדֵי אָדָם. | ma·aseih y'dei adam. |
| פֶּה לָהֶם וְלֹא יְדַבֵּרוּ, | Peh lahem v'lo yi·daberu, |
| עֵינַיִם לָהֶם וְלֹא יִרְאוּ. | Einayim lahem v'lo yir·u, |
| אָזְנַיִם לָהֶם וְלֹא יִשְׁמָעוּ, | oznayim lahem v'lo yishma·u, |
| אַף לָהֶם וְלֹא יְרִיחוּן. | af lahem v'lo y'riḥun. |
| יְדֵיהֶם וְלֹא יְמִישׁוּן, | Y'deihem v'lo y'mishun, |
| רַגְלֵיהֶם וְלֹא יְהַלֵּכוּ, | ragleihem v'lo y'haleikhu, |
| לֹא יֶהְגּוּ בִּגְרוֹנָם. | lo yehgu big'ronam. |
| כְּמוֹהֶם יִהְיוּ עֹשֵׂיהֶם, | K'mohem yih'yu oseihem, |
| כֹּל אֲשֶׁר בֹּטֵחַ בָּהֶם. | kol asher bote·aḥ bahem. |
| יִשְׂרָאֵל בְּטַח בַּייָ, | Yisra·el b'taḥ bAdonai, |
| עֶזְרָם וּמָגִנָּם הוּא. | ezram u-maginam hu. |
| בֵּית אַהֲרֹן בִּטְחוּ בַייָ, | Beit Aharon bit-ḥu vAdonai, |
| עֶזְרָם וּמָגִנָּם הוּא. | ezram u-maginam hu. |
| יִרְאֵי יְיָ בִּטְחוּ בַייָ, | Yir·ei Adonai, bit-ḥu vAdonai, |
| עֶזְרָם וּמָגִנָּם הוּא. | ezram u-maginam hu. |

*This section is always said.*

| | |
|---|---|
| יְיָ זְכָרָנוּ יְבָרֵךְ, | Adonai z'kharanu y'vareikh, |
| יְבָרֵךְ אֶת בֵּית יִשְׂרָאֵל, | Y'vareikh et beit Yisra·el, |
| יְבָרֵךְ אֶת בֵּית אַהֲרֹן. | Y'vareikh et beit Aharon. |
| יְבָרֵךְ יִרְאֵי יְיָ, | Y'vareikh yir·ei Adonai, |
| הַקְּטַנִּים עִם הַגְּדֹלִים. | hak'tanim im hag'dolim. |
| יֹסֵף יְיָ עֲלֵיכֶם, | Yosef Adonai aleikhem, |
| עֲלֵיכֶם וְעַל בְּנֵיכֶם. | aleikhem v'al b'neikhem. |
| בְּרוּכִים אַתֶּם לַייָ, | B'rukhim atem lAdonai, |
| עֹשֵׂה שָׁמַיִם וָאָרֶץ. | oseih shamayim va·aretz. |
| הַשָּׁמַיִם שָׁמַיִם לַייָ, | Ha-shamayim shamayim lAdonai, |
| וְהָאָרֶץ נָתַן לִבְנֵי אָדָם. | v'ha·aretz natan liv'nei adam. |
| לֹא הַמֵּתִים יְהַלְלוּ יָהּ, | Lo ha-meitim y'hal'lu Yah |
| וְלֹא כָּל יֹרְדֵי | v'lo kol yor'dei |
| דוּמָה. | dumah. |
| וַאֲנַחְנוּ נְבָרֵךְ יָהּ, | Va·anaḥnu n'vareikh Yah |
| מֵעַתָּה וְעַד עוֹלָם, | mei-atah v'ad olam. |
| הַלְלוּיָהּ. | Hal'luyah |

Their idols are just silver and gold, made by human hands.
They have a mouth and can't speak, eyes but can't see.

They have ears but can't hear, noses but can't smell.
Their hands can't feel, their feet can't walk,
They cannot speak with their throats.

Those who make them shall become like them –
all who trust in them.

Israel, trust in Adonai, God is our help and shield.
House of Aaron, trust in Adonai, God is our help and shield.

Everyone who respects Adonai,
trust in Adonai, God is our help and shield.

*This section is always said.*

God will remember us and bless us,
God will bless the House of Israel.
God will bless the House of Aaron.
God will bless those who revere Adonai, great and small alike.
May Adonai increase you and your children.
You are blessed by Adonai, who made heaven and earth.
The heavens belong to Adonai,
But the earth was given to human beings.
The dead do not praise God,
Nor do those that death silences.
But *we* will praise God now and forever. Halleluyah.

## PSALM 116

*This section is not said on Rosh Ḥodesh or the last 6 days of Pesaḥ.*

| | |
|---|---|
| Ahavti ki yishma Adonai | אָהַבְתִּי כִּי יִשְׁמַע יְיָ, |
| et-koli taḥanunai. | אֶת קוֹלִי תַּחֲנוּנָי. |
| Ki hitah ozno li | כִּי הִטָּה אָזְנוֹ לִי, |
| u-v'yamai ekra. | וּבְיָמַי אֶקְרָא. |
| Afafuni ḥevlei-mavet | אֲפָפוּנִי חֶבְלֵי מָוֶת, |
| U-m'tzarei sh'ol | וּמְצָרֵי שְׁאוֹל |
| m'tza·uni, | מְצָאוּנִי, |
| tzarah v'yagon emtza. | צָרָה וְיָגוֹן אֶמְצָא. |
| U-v'sheim Adonai ekra, | וּבְשֵׁם יְיָ אֶקְרָא, |
| Anah Adonai mal'tah nafshi. | אָנָּה יְיָ מַלְּטָה נַפְשִׁי. |
| Ḥanun Adonai v'tzaddik, | חַנּוּן יְיָ וְצַדִּיק, |
| vEiloheinu m'raḥeim. | וֵאלֹהֵינוּ מְרַחֵם. |
| Shomeir p'ta·yim Adonai, | שֹׁמֵר פְּתָאִים יְיָ, |
| daloti v'li y'hoshi·ah. | דַּלּוֹתִי וְלִי יְהוֹשִׁיעַ. |
| Shuvi nafshi li-m'nuḥaikhi, | שׁוּבִי נַפְשִׁי לִמְנוּחָיְכִי, |
| ki Adonai gamal alaikhi. | כִּי יְיָ גָּמַל עָלָיְכִי. |
| Ki ḥilatzta nafshi mi-mavet, | כִּי חִלַּצְתָּ נַפְשִׁי מִמָּוֶת, |
| et aini min dim·ah, | אֶת עֵינִי מִן דִּמְעָה, |
| et ragli mi-deḥi. | אֶת רַגְלִי מִדֶּחִי. |
| Et-halekh lifnei Adonai | אֶתְהַלֵּךְ לִפְנֵי יְיָ, |
| b'artzot ha-ḥayyim. | בְּאַרְצוֹת הַחַיִּים. |
| He·emanti ki adabeir, | הֶאֱמַנְתִּי כִּי אֲדַבֵּר, |
| ani aniti m'od. | אֲנִי עָנִיתִי מְאֹד. |
| Ani amarti v-ḥofzi, | אֲנִי אָמַרְתִּי בְחָפְזִי, |
| kol ha-adam kozeiv. | כָּל הָאָדָם כֹּזֵב. |

*This section is always said.*

| | |
|---|---|
| Mah ashiv lAdonai | מָה אָשִׁיב לַייָ, |
| kol tagmulohi alai. | כָּל תַּגְמוּלוֹהִי עָלָי. |
| Kos y'shu·ot esa, | כּוֹס יְשׁוּעוֹת אֶשָּׂא, |
| u-v'sheim Adonai ekra. | וּבְשֵׁם יְיָ אֶקְרָא. |
| N'darai lAdonai ashaleim | נְדָרַי לַייָ אֲשַׁלֵּם, |
| negdah na l'khol amo. | נֶגְדָה נָּא לְכָל עַמּוֹ. |

## PSALM 116

*This section is not said on Rosh Ḥodesh or the last 6 days of Pesaḥ.*

I love it that God hears my voice and my plea,
For God's ear is turned toward me on the day that I call.
The cords of death surrounded me,
The narrows of She·ol found me,
I found trouble and sorrow.
I called out in Adonai's name, "Please, Adonai, save my life!"
Gracious is Adonai, and righteous, and our God shows mercy.
Adonai protects fools; I was brought low and God saved me.
Return, my soul, to tranquility, for God has treated me well.
God has freed my soul from death,
my eyes from tears, and my feet from stumbling.
I will walk before Adonai in the lands of the living.
I trusted, even though I spoke – I was greatly afflicted – I said hastily, "All people are treacherous."

*This section is always said.*

How can I pay Adonai back for all God's gifts to me?

I will lift up the cup of deliverance,
and call out Adonai's name.

I will keep my promises to Adonai,
before the whole community.

Thank You, Adonai, for the freedom to serve You,
For you have released me from bondage.

I will publicly keep my promises to Adonai,
In the courts of Adonai's house, in the center of Jerusalem.
Halleluyah!

**Psalm 116** describes how in time of trouble, he called upon God and was redeemed. Thanking God, he comes to the Temple and offers sacrifices to God while praising God's greatness.

| | |
|---|---|
| Yakar b'einei Adonai | יָקָר בְּעֵינֵי יְיָ, |
| ha-mavtah la-ḥasidav. | הַמָּוְתָה לַחֲסִידָיו. |
| Ana Adonai | אָנָּה יְיָ |
| ki ani avd'kha | כִּי אֲנִי עַבְדֶּךָ, |
| Ani avd'kha | אֲנִי עַבְדְּךָ |
| ben amatekha, | בֶּן אֲמָתֶךָ, |
| Pitaḥta l'moseirai. | פִּתַּחְתָּ לְמוֹסֵרָי. |
| L'kha ezbaḥ zevaḥ todah, | לְךָ אֶזְבַּח זֶבַח תּוֹדָה, |
| u-v'sheim Adonai ekra. | וּבְשֵׁם יְיָ אֶקְרָא. |
| N'darai lAdonai ashaleim | נְדָרַי לַייָ אֲשַׁלֵּם, |
| negdah na l'khol amo. | נֶגְדָה נָּא לְכָל עַמּוֹ. |
| B'ḥatzrot beit adonai | בְּחַצְרוֹת בֵּית יְיָ, |
| b'tokheikhi Y'rushalayim. | בְּתוֹכֵכִי יְרוּשָׁלָיִם, |
| Hale'luyah. | הַלְלוּיָהּ. |

## PSALM 117

| | |
|---|---|
| Hal'lu et Adonai kol goyim, | הַלְלוּ אֶת יְיָ, כָּל גּוֹיִם, |
| shab'ḥuhu kol ha-umim. | שַׁבְּחוּהוּ, כָּל הָאֻמִּים. |
| Ki gavar aleinu ḥasdo, | כִּי גָבַר עָלֵינוּ חַסְדּוֹ, |
| ve-emet Adonai l'olam. | וֶאֱמֶת יְיָ לְעוֹלָם, |
| Hal'luyah. | הַלְלוּיָהּ. |

## PSALM 118

| | |
|---|---|
| Hodu lAdonai ki tov, | הוֹדוּ לַייָ כִּי טוֹב, |
| ki l'olam ḥasdo. | כִּי לְעוֹלָם חַסְדּוֹ. |
| Yomar na Yisra·el, | יֹאמַר נָא יִשְׂרָאֵל, |
| ki l'olam ḥasdo. | כִּי לְעוֹלָם חַסְדּוֹ. |
| Yom'ru na veit Aharon, | יֹאמְרוּ נָא בֵית אַהֲרֹן, |
| ki l'olam ḥasdo. | כִּי לְעוֹלָם חַסְדּוֹ. |
| Yom'ru na yir'ei Adonai, | יֹאמְרוּ נָא יִרְאֵי יְיָ, |
| ki l'olam ḥasdo. | כִּי לְעוֹלָם חַסְדּוֹ. |
| Min ha-meitzar | מִן הַמֵּצַר |
| karati Yah, | קָרָאתִי יָּהּ, |
| anani | עָנָנִי |
| va-merḥav Yah. | בַמֶּרְחָב יָהּ. |

## PSALM 117

Praise Adonai, all nations, praise God, all peoples!
God's kindness overwhelms us. Adonai's truth is forever.
Halleluyah!

## PSALM 118

Thank Adonai for being good, God's kindness lasts forever.
Let Israel say: God's kindness lasts forever.
Let the House of Aaron say: God's kindness lasts forever.
Let those who respect Adonai say: God's kindness lasts forever.
From the straits I called out to God.
God answered me in a wide place.

**Psalm 117:** This is the shortest Psalm in the Book of Psalms, and calls upon the world's nations to praise God for God's mercy and faithfulness.

**Psalm 118:** This Psalm describes circumstances of distress, tells of God's salvation and describes the act of thanksgiving that is now being performed. God's love is eternal. Having experienced God's salvation, the Psalm concludes by affording worshipers a chance to petition God (with the words "deliver us") to continue to deliver them, now and in the future.

| | |
|---|---|
| Adonai li, lo ira, | יְיָ לִי לֹא אִירָא, |
| mah ya·aseh li adam. | מַה יַּעֲשֶׂה לִי אָדָם. |
| Adonai li b'oz'rai, | יְיָ לִי בְּעֹזְרָי, |
| va-ani er·eh v'son'ai. | וַאֲנִי אֶרְאֶה בְשֹׂנְאָי. |
| Tov la-ḥasot bAdonai | טוֹב לַחֲסוֹת בַּייָ, |
| mib'to·aḥ ba-adam. | מִבְּטֹחַ בָּאָדָם. |
| Tov la-ḥasot bAdonai | טוֹב לַחֲסוֹת בַּייָ, |
| mib'to·aḥ bin'divim. | מִבְּטֹחַ בִּנְדִיבִים. |
| Kol-goyim s'vavuni, | כָּל גּוֹיִם סְבָבוּנִי, |
| b'sheim Adonai ki amilam. | בְּשֵׁם יְיָ כִּי אֲמִילַם. |
| Sabuni gam s'vavuni, | סַבּוּנִי גַם סְבָבוּנִי, |
| b'sheim Adonai ki amilam. | בְּשֵׁם יְיָ כִּי אֲמִילַם. |
| Sabuni khid'vorim, | סַבּוּנִי כִדְבֹרִים |
| do·akhu k'eish kotzim, | דֹּעֲכוּ כְּאֵשׁ קוֹצִים, |
| b'sheim Adonai ki amilam. | בְּשֵׁם יְיָ כִּי אֲמִילַם. |
| Daḥo d'ḥitani lin'pol, | דָּחֹה דְחִיתַנִי לִנְפֹּל, |
| vAdonai azarani. | וַייָ עֲזָרָנִי. |
| Ozi v'zimrat Yah, | עָזִּי וְזִמְרָת יָהּ, |
| va-y'hi li lishu·ah. | וַיְהִי לִי לִישׁוּעָה. |
| Kol rinah vishu·ah | קוֹל רִנָּה וִישׁוּעָה |
| b'ohalei tzadikim, | בְּאָהֳלֵי צַדִּיקִים, |
| y'min Adonai | יְמִין יְיָ |
| osah ḥayil. | עֹשָׂה חָיִל. |
| Y'min Adonai romeimah, | יְמִין יְיָ רוֹמֵמָה, |
| y'min Adonai osah ḥayil. | יְמִין יְיָ עֹשָׂה חָיִל. |
| Lo amut ki eḥ-yeh, | לֹא אָמוּת כִּי אֶחְיֶה, |
| va-asapeir ma·asei Yah. | וַאֲסַפֵּר מַעֲשֵׂי יָהּ. |
| Yasor yis'rani Yah, | יַסֹּר יִסְּרַנִּי יָּהּ, |
| v'la-mavet lo n'tanani. | וְלַמָּוֶת לֹא נְתָנָנִי. |

| | |
|---|---|
| Pitḥu li sha·arei tzedek, | פִּתְחוּ לִי שַׁעֲרֵי צֶדֶק, |
| avo vam | אָבֹא בָם |
| odeh Yah. | אוֹדֶה יָהּ. |
| Zeh ha-sha·ar lAdonai, | זֶה הַשַּׁעַר לַייָ, |
| tzadikim yavo·u vo. | צַדִּיקִים יָבֹאוּ בוֹ. |

Adonai is with me, I will not fear,
what can any human do to me?
God is with me to help me, and I shall see my foes defeated.
It is better to seek refuge in God than to trust in people.
It is better to seek refuge in God than to trust in leaders.
All nations surrounded me, in God's name I defeated them.
They surrounded me, they surrounded me,
In God's name I defeated them.
They surrounded me like bees,
They were extinguished like burning thorns,
In God's name I defeated them.
I was pushed down, about to fall, and Adonai helped me.
God is my strength and my might, and was my rescue.
A voice of joy and salvation in the tents of the righteous –
Adonai's right hand does valiantly.
Adonai's right hand is exalted, God's right hand does valiantly.
I shall not die, but live, and tell of God's deeds.
God rebuked me strongly, but did not hand me over to death.

The sound of joyous songs celebrating God's help
is heard in the tents of the righteous:
"Adonai's right hand succeeds greatly!
Adonai's right hand is lifted up in victory!
Adonai's right hand succeeds greatly!"
I shall not die, but live, and tell of God's deeds.
God afflicted me, but did not deliver me to death
Open the gates of righteousness for me. I will enter them to thank God. This is Adonai's gate, the righteous shall enter it.

*Each verse is repeated:*

| | |
|---|---|
| אוֹדְךָ כִּי עֲנִיתָֽנִי, | Od'kha ki anitani |
| וַתְּהִי לִי לִישׁוּעָה. | va-t'hi li lishu·ah. |
| אֶֽבֶן מָאֲסוּ הַבּוֹנִים, | Even ma·asu ha-bonim |
| הָיְתָה לְרֹאשׁ פִּנָּה. | hay'tah l'rosh pinah. |
| מֵאֵת יְיָ הָֽיְתָה זֹּאת, | Mei-eit Adonai hay'tah zot, |
| הִיא נִפְלָאת בְּעֵינֵֽינוּ. | hi niflat b'eineinu. |
| זֶה הַיּוֹם עָשָׂה יְיָ, | Zeh ha-yom asah Adonai, |
| נָגִֽילָה וְנִשְׂמְחָה בוֹ. | nagilah v'nis-m'ḥa vo. |

*Each phrase is repeated:*

| | |
|---|---|
| אָנָּא יְיָ הוֹשִֽׁיעָה נָּא. | Ana Adonai hoshi·ah na. |
| אָנָּא יְיָ הוֹשִֽׁיעָה נָּא. | Ana Adonai hoshi·ah na. |
| אָנָּא יְיָ הַצְלִיחָה נָּא. | Ana Adonai hatz-liḥah na. |
| אָנָּא יְיָ הַצְלִיחָה נָּא. | Ana Adonai hatz-liḥah na. |

*Each of the following four verses is repeated twice:*

| | |
|---|---|
| בָּרוּךְ הַבָּא | Barukh ha-ba |
| בְּשֵׁם יְיָ, | b'sheim Adonai, |
| בֵּֽרַכְנוּכֶם מִבֵּית יְיָ. | beirakhnukhem mi-beit Adonai. |
| אֵל יְיָ וַיָּֽאֶר לָֽנוּ, | Eil Adonai va-ya·eir lanu, |
| אִסְרוּ חַג בַּעֲבֹתִים | isru ḥag ba·avotim |
| עַד קַרְנוֹת הַמִּזְבֵּֽחַ. | ad karnot ha-mizbei·aḥ. |
| אֵלִי אַתָּה וְאוֹדֶֽךָּ, | Eili Atah v'odeka, |
| אֱלֹהַי אֲרוֹמְמֶֽךָּ. | Elohai arom'meka. |
| הוֹדוּ לַייָ כִּי טוֹב, | Hodu lAdonai ki tov, |
| כִּי לְעוֹלָם חַסְדּוֹ. | ki l'olam ḥasdo. |

יְהַלְלוּךָ יְיָ אֱלֹהֵינוּ כָּל מַעֲשֶֽׂיךָ, וַחֲסִידֶֽיךָ צַדִּיקִים עוֹשֵׂי רְצוֹנֶֽךָ, וְכָל עַמְּךָ בֵּית יִשְׂרָאֵל בְּרִנָּה יוֹדוּ וִיבָרְכוּ וִישַׁבְּחוּ וִיפָאֲרוּ וִירוֹמְמוּ וְיַעֲרִֽיצוּ וְיַקְדִּֽישׁוּ וְיַמְלִֽיכוּ אֶת שִׁמְךָ מַלְכֵּֽנוּ. כִּי לְךָ טוֹב לְהוֹדוֹת וּלְשִׁמְךָ נָאֶה לְזַמֵּר, כִּי מֵעוֹלָם וְעַד עוֹלָם אַתָּה אֵל. בָּרוּךְ אַתָּה יְיָ, מֶֽלֶךְ מְהֻלָּל בַּתִּשְׁבָּחוֹת.

*Each verse is repeated:*

I thank You for answering me and being my deliverer.
The stone which the builders rejected is now the cornerstone.
This is Adonai's doing. It is wonderful in our eyes.
This is the day that Adonai has made,
Let us rejoice and be glad of it.

*Each phrase is repeated:*

Please, Adonai, save us! Please, Adonai, give us success!

*Each of the following four verses is repeated twice:*

Blessed are you who come in Adonai's name
May you be blessed in Adonai's name.
Adonai is God, and shines upon us.
Bind the cords of the festival offering to the corners of the altar.
You are my God, and I praise you;
My God and I exalt you.
Praise Adonai, for God is good;
God's kindness lasts forever.

May all Your work praise You, Adonai our God, and may the pious, the righteous who do Your will, and all Your people, the House of Israel, joyously thank and bless, praise, glorify, exalt and admire, sanctify and proclaim the authority of Your name, our Ruler. For it is good to give thanks to You, it feels good to praise Your name. You are God forever and ever. Praised are You, Adonai, Ruler praised with songs of praise.

## KADDISH SHALEIM

*Leader:*

| | |
|---|---|
| Yit-gadal v'yit-kadash sh'mei rabba, | יִתְגַּדַּל וְיִתְקַדַּשׁ שְׁמֵהּ רַבָּא. |
| b'al'ma di v'ra | בְּעָלְמָא דִּי בְרָא |
| khir'utei | כִּרְעוּתֵהּ, |
| v'yam-likh malkhutei | וְיַמְלִיךְ מַלְכוּתֵהּ |
| b'ḥayeikhon u-v'yomeikhon | בְּחַיֵּיכוֹן וּבְיוֹמֵיכוֹן |
| u-v'ḥayei d'khol beit Yisra·el, | וּבְחַיֵּי דְכָל בֵּית יִשְׂרָאֵל, |
| ba·agala u-viz'man kariv, | בַּעֲגָלָא וּבִזְמַן קָרִיב, |
| v'imru, Amen. | וְאִמְרוּ אָמֵן. |

*Congregation and Leader:*

| | |
|---|---|
| Y'hei sh'mei rabba m'va-rakh, | יְהֵא שְׁמֵהּ רַבָּא מְבָרַךְ |
| l'alam ul-al'mei al'maya. | לְעָלַם וּלְעָלְמֵי עָלְמַיָּא. |

*Leader:*

| | |
|---|---|
| Yitbarakh v'yishtabaḥ | יִתְבָּרַךְ וְיִשְׁתַּבַּח |
| v'yitpa·ar v'yitromam v'yitnasei | וְיִתְפָּאַר וְיִתְרוֹמַם וְיִתְנַשֵּׂא |
| v'yithadar v'yit·aleh v'yithalal | וְיִתְהַדָּר וְיִתְעַלֶּה וְיִתְהַלָּל |
| sh'mei d'kud'sha, b'rikh Hu. | שְׁמֵהּ דְּקֻדְשָׁא בְּרִיךְ הוּא, |
| L'eila | לְעֵלָּא |
| [u-l'eila mi-kol] | (בעשי"ת לְעֵלָּא וּלְעֵלָּא מִכָּל) |
| min kol birkhata v'shirata | מִן כָּל בִּרְכָתָא וְשִׁירָתָא |
| tushb'ḥata v'neḥemata | תֻּשְׁבְּחָתָא וְנֶחֱמָתָא, |
| da·amiran b'al'ma, | דַּאֲמִירָן בְּעָלְמָא, |
| v'imru Amen. | וְאִמְרוּ אָמֵן. |
| Titkabal | תִּתְקַבַּל |
| tz'lot'hon uva-ot'hon | צְלוֹתְהוֹן וּבָעוּתְהוֹן |
| d'khol Yisra·el | דְּכָל יִשְׂרָאֵל |
| kadam avuhon di vish'maya, | קֳדָם אֲבוּהוֹן דִּי בִשְׁמַיָּא |
| v'imru Amen. | וְאִמְרוּ אָמֵן. |
| Y'hei sh'lama rabbah min shamaya | יְהֵא שְׁלָמָא רַבָּא מִן שְׁמַיָּא, |
| v'ḥayyim | וְחַיִּים |
| aleinu v'al kol Yisra·el, | עָלֵינוּ וְעַל כָּל יִשְׂרָאֵל, |
| v'imru Amen. | וְאִמְרוּ אָמֵן. |
| Oseh shalom bim'romav, | עֹשֶׂה שָׁלוֹם בִּמְרוֹמָיו, |
| Hu ya·aseh shalom | הוּא יַעֲשֶׂה שָׁלוֹם |
| aleinu v'al kol Yisra·el, | עָלֵינוּ וְעַל כָּל יִשְׂרָאֵל, |
| v'imru Amen. | וְאִמְרוּ אָמֵן. |

## KADDISH SHALEIM

*Leader:*

May God's great name be made great and holy in the world which God created according to God's will. May God establish the Divine kingdom soon, in our days, quickly and in the near future, and let us say, Amen.

*Congregation and Leader together:*

May God's great name be praised forever and ever.

Blessed, praised, glorified and raised high, honored and elevated be the name of the Holy Blessed One, far beyond all blessings and songs, praises and comforts which people can say, and let us say: Amen.

May the prayers and pleas of the entire House of Israel be accepted before their Parent in heaven. And let us say: Amen.

May there be abundant peace from heaven and life for us and for all Israel, and let us say: Amen.

May the One who makes peace in the high heavens make peace for us and for all Israel, and let us say: Amen.

# Service for Taking Out the Torah

***"When I pray, I speak to God. When I study, God speaks to me." (Louis Finkelstein)***

| | |
|---|---|
| Ein ka-mokha | אֵין כָּמֽוֹךָ |
| va-Elohim Adonai, | בָאֱלֹהִים, יְיָ, |
| v'ein k'ma·asekha. | וְאֵין כְּמַעֲשֶֽׂיךָ. |
| Malkhut'kha malkhut kol olamim, | מַלְכוּתְךָ מַלְכוּת כָּל עֹלָמִים, |
| u-mem-shalt'kha b'khol dor va-dor. | וּמֶמְשַׁלְתְּךָ בְּכָל דֹּר וָדֹר. |
| Adonai Melekh, Adonai malakh, | יְיָ מֶֽלֶךְ, יְיָ מָלָךְ, |
| Adonai yimlokh l'olam va·ed. | יְיָ יִמְלֹךְ לְעֹלָם וָעֶד. |
| Adonai oz l'amo yitein, | יְיָ עֹז לְעַמּוֹ יִתֵּן, |
| Adonai y'vareikh et amo va-shalom. | יְיָ יְבָרֵךְ אֶת עַמּוֹ בַשָּׁלוֹם. |

| | |
|---|---|
| Av ha-raḥamim, | אַב הָרַחֲמִים, |
| heitivah virtzon'kha et Tziyon, | הֵיטִֽיבָה בִרְצוֹנְךָ אֶת צִיּוֹן, |
| tivneh ḥomot Y'rushalayim. | תִּבְנֶה חוֹמוֹת יְרוּשָׁלָֽיִם. |
| Ki v'kha l'vad bataḥnu, | כִּי בְךָ לְבַד בָּטָֽחְנוּ, |
| Melekh | מֶֽלֶךְ |
| Eil | אֵל |
| ram v'nisah, Adon olamim. | רָם וְנִשָּׂא, אֲדוֹן עוֹלָמִים. |

*The Ark is opened, and we rise:*

| | |
|---|---|
| Va-y'hi binso·a ha-aron | וַיְהִי בִּנְסֹֽעַ הָאָרֹן |
| va-yomeir Moshe. | וַיֹּֽאמֶר מֹשֶׁה, |
| Kumah Adonai v'yafutzu oy'vekha, | קוּמָה, יְיָ, וְיָפֻֽצוּ אֹיְבֶֽיךָ, |
| v'yanusu m'san·ekha mi-panekha. | וְיָנֻֽסוּ מְשַׂנְאֶֽיךָ מִפָּנֶֽיךָ. |
| Ki mi-Tziyon teitzei Torah, | כִּי מִצִּיּוֹן תֵּצֵא תוֹרָה, |
| u-d'var Adonai mi-Y'rushalayim. | וּדְבַר יְיָ מִירוּשָׁלָֽיִם. |
| Barukh she-natan Torah | בָּרוּךְ שֶׁנָּתַן תּוֹרָה |
| l'amo Yisra·el bi-k'dushato. | לְעַמּוֹ יִשְׂרָאֵל בִּקְדֻשָּׁתוֹ. |

# Service for Taking Out the Torah

*"When I pray, I speak to God. When I study, God speaks to me." (Louis Finkelstein)*

There is none like You, Adonai,
And there is nothing like Your deeds.
God, You rule eternally,
Your kingdom lasts for all generations.
Adonai rules, Adonai ruled,
Adonai will rule forever and ever.
Adonai will give strength to God's people,
Adonai will bless God's people with peace.
Merciful Parent, favor Zion with Your goodness.
Rebuild the walls of Jerusalem.
For we trust only You, Ruler, God on high, Sovereign of worlds.

*The Ark is opened, and we rise:*

Whenever the Ark would travel, Moses would say, "Arise, Adonai, and scatter Your enemies; may those that hate you flee from you." For Torah shall come from Zion, the word of Adonai from Jerusalem.

Blessed is the One who in holiness gave the Torah to Israel.

Think of the Torah service as a drama. We are re-enacting *Matan Torah*, the giving of the Torah on Mt. Sinai. We begin by invoking God's presence, praising God's unique power. Then we rise as the Ark is opened, revealing the scrolls within. We prepare ourselves for taking out the Torah and carrying it through the congregation by quoting the words proclaimed when the Ark of the Covenant traveled in the midst of the Israelites: "*Va-y'hi binso•a ha-aron*". Then we take the Torah, and proclaim God's unity with the Sh'ma. We bow towards the Ark, again acknowledging God's greatness. Then the Torah moves among us, as we praise God once more. After the procession, we carefully place the scroll on the reading Table, and in blessing it, we praise God for giving us the Torah, not just long ago, but right now. God is *Notein ha-Torah*, the one who continues to give us the Torah, when we study it faithfully.

*When a Festival falls on a day that is not Shabbat:*

| | |
|---|---|
| Adonai Adonai | יְיָ, יְיָ, |
| Eil raḥum v'ḥanun, | אֵל רַחוּם וְחַנּוּן, |
| erekh apayim | אֶרֶךְ אַפַּיִם |
| v'rav ḥesed ve-emet, | וְרַב חֶסֶד וֶאֱמֶת. |
| notzeir ḥesed | נֹצֵר חֶסֶד |
| la-alafim, | לָאֲלָפִים, |
| nosei avon va-fesha v'ḥata·ah | נֹשֵׂא עָוֹן וָפֶשַׁע וְחַטָּאָה, |
| v'nakeih. | וְנַקֵּה. |
| Yi-h'yu l'ratzon | יִהְיוּ לְרָצוֹן |
| imrei fi | אִמְרֵי פִי |
| v'hegyon libi l'fanekha, | וְהֶגְיוֹן לִבִּי לְפָנֶיךָ, |
| Adonai Tzuri v'Go·ali. | יְיָ צוּרִי וְגוֹאֲלִי. |
| Va-ani | וַאֲנִי |
| t'filati l'kha Adonai | תְפִלָּתִי לְךָ יְיָ |
| eit ratzon, | עֵת רָצוֹן, |
| Elohim b'rov ḥasdekha | אֱלֹהִים בְּרָב חַסְדֶּךָ, |
| aneini be-emet yishekha. | עֲנֵנִי בֶּאֱמֶת יִשְׁעֶךָ. |

## BEI ANA RAḤITZ

| | |
|---|---|
| Bei ana raḥitz | בֵּהּ אֲנָא רָחִיץ, |
| v'lishmei kadisha yakira | וְלִשְׁמֵהּ קַדִּישָׁא יַקִּירָא |
| ana eimar tushb'ḥan. | אֲנָא אֵמַר תֻּשְׁבְּחָן. |
| Y'hei ra·avah kadamakh | יְהֵא רַעֲוָא קֳדָמָךְ |
| d'tiftaḥ lib·ai b'oraita, | דְּתִפְתַּח לִבָּאִי בְּאוֹרַיְתָא, |
| v'tashlim mishalin d'libi | וְתַשְׁלִים מִשְׁאֲלִין דְּלִבָּאִי, |
| v'liba d'khol amakh Yisra·el, | וְלִבָּא דְכָל עַמָּךְ יִשְׂרָאֵל, |
| l'tav ul'ḥayin v'lishlam. | לְטַב וּלְחַיִּין וְלִשְׁלָם. |
| Amen. | אָמֵן. |

*When a Festival falls on a day that is not Shabbat, these words are chanted three times:*

Adonai, Adonai, God gracious and kindhearted, patient, great in kindness and truth, keeping lovingkindness for a thousand generations, forgiving sin done on purpose, rebellion, and sin not done on purpose, and granting pardon. May the words of my mouth and the thoughts of my mind be acceptable to You, Adonai, my Rock and My Redeemer.

As for me, may my prayer be offered to You, Adonai, at a favorable moment. God, in Your great kindness, answer me with Your true saving.

## BEI ANA RAḤITZ

Praised be the name of the Sovereign of the Universe. Praised be Your crown and Your place. May Your love for Your people Israel last forever, and may the salvation of Your right hand be revealed to Your people in Your holy House. Grant us the goodness of Your light, and accept our prayer with mercy. May it be Your will that we be granted a long, good life, and may I be counted among the righteous, so that You will have mercy on me, and protect me and all that is mine, and all that belongs to Your people Israel. You are the One who nourishes all, and sustains all. You rule over all. You are the One Who rules over earthly rulers, and sovereignty is Yours. I am a servant of the Blessed Holy One. I bow before God and before the honor of God's Torah at all times. Not in any human do I trust, nor do I rely on any angel, but in the God of Heaven, who is the true God, and Whose Torah is true, and Whose prophets are true, and Who multiplies deeds of goodness and truth. In God do I trust, and in God's holy, honored Name I speak praises. May it be Your will that You open my heart to Torah, and completely answer my heart's desires and those of Your people Israel, for good, for life, and for peace. Amen

## SH'MA AND PROCESSION

*The Torah scroll is removed from the ark. With the Torah before us, we follow the leader of the service in proclaiming our belief in one God. The leader of the service sings each of the next two lines by him/herself and the congregation repeats them:*

| | |
|---|---|
| Sh'ma Yisra·el Adonai Eloheinu | שְׁמַע יִשְׂרָאֵל, יְיָ אֱלֹהֵינוּ, |
| Adonai eḥad. | יְיָ אֶחָד. |
| Eḥad Eloheinu, gadol Adoneinu | אֶחָד אֱלֹהֵינוּ, גָּדוֹל אֲדוֹנֵנוּ, |
| kadosh (v'nora) sh'mo. | קָדוֹשׁ (וְנוֹרָא) שְׁמוֹ. |

*The leader faces the ark, bows, and chants. The congregatin bows, too:*

| | |
|---|---|
| Gad'lu lAdonai iti, | גַּדְּלוּ לַייָ אִתִּי, |
| u-n'rom'mah sh'mo yaḥdav. | וּנְרוֹמְמָה שְׁמוֹ יַחְדָּו |

*The Torah scroll is carried around in procession:*

| | |
|---|---|
| L'kha Adonai ha-g'dulah v'ha-g'vurah | לְךָ יְיָ הַגְּדֻלָּה וְהַגְּבוּרָה |
| v'ha-tif·eret v'ha-netzaḥ v'ha-hod, | וְהַתִּפְאֶרֶת וְהַנֵּצַח וְהַהוֹד, |
| ki khol ba-shamayim uva-aretz, | כִּי כֹל בַּשָּׁמַיִם וּבָאָרֶץ, |
| l'kha Adonai ha-mamlakha | לְךָ יְיָ הַמַּמְלָכָה, |
| v'ha-mitnasei l'khol l'rosh. | וְהַמִּתְנַשֵּׂא לְכֹל לְרֹאשׁ. |
| Rom'mu Adonai Eloheinu | רוֹמְמוּ יְיָ אֱלֹהֵינוּ, |
| v'hishtaḥavu la-hadom raglav | וְהִשְׁתַּחֲווּ לַהֲדֹם רַגְלָיו, |
| kadosh Hu. | קָדוֹשׁ הוּא. |
| Rom'mu Adonai Eloheinu | רוֹמְמוּ יְיָ אֱלֹהֵינוּ, |
| v'hishtaḥavu l'har kodsho, | וְהִשְׁתַּחֲווּ לְהַר קָדְשׁוֹ, |
| ki kadosh Adonai Eloheinu. | כִּי קָדוֹשׁ יְיָ אֱלֹהֵינוּ. |

*Before the first aliyah (honor of being called to the Torah), the gabbai (person who calls people up to the Torah) chants a paragraph that begins va-ya·azor v'yagein...at the end of which the congregation responds:*

| | |
|---|---|
| V'atem had'veikim | וְאַתֶּם הַדְּבֵקִים |
| bAdonai Eloheikhem | בַּייָ אֱלֹהֵיכֶם, |
| ḥayyim kulkhem ha-yom. | חַיִּים כֻּלְּכֶם הַיּוֹם. |

## SH'MA AND PROCESSION

*The Torah scroll is removed from the ark. With the Torah before us, we follow the leader of the service in proclaiming our belief in one God. The leader of the service sings each of the next two lines by him/herself and the congregation repeats them:*

Hear O Israel, Adonai is our God, Adonai is one.
One is our God, great is our Sovereign, whose name is holy and awe-inspiring.

*The leader faces the ark, bows, and chants. The congregatin bows, too:*

Declare Adonai's greatness with me; let us praise God together.

*The Torah scroll is carried around in procession:*

Greatness, might, wonder, triumph, and majesty are Yours, Adonai – yes, all that is in heaven and on earth; to You, Adonai, belong kingship and supremacy over all. Praise Adonai and bow down to God's presence; God is holy! Praise Adonai, our God, bow to God's holy mountain. Adonai our God is holy.

*Before the first aliyah (honor of being called to the Torah), the gabbai (person who calls people up to the Torah) chants a paragraph that begins va-ya·azor v'yagein…at the end of which the congregation responds:*

And you who were loyal to Adonai your God are all alive today.

## TORAH BLESSINGS

*If you are called up to the Torah, be sure your head is covered and you are wearing a tallit. The Torah reader will point out a place in the Torah, which you will touch with the tzitzit (fringes) of the tallit and then kiss the tzitzit. You begin with:*

| | |
|---|---|
| Bar'khu et Adonai ham'vorakh. | בָּרְכוּ אֶת יְיָ הַמְבֹרָךְ. |

*The congregation responds:*

| | |
|---|---|
| Barukh Adonai ha-m'vorakh | בָּרוּךְ יְיָ הַמְבֹרָךְ |
| l'olam va·ed. | לְעוֹלָם וָעֶד. |

*You repeat:*

| | |
|---|---|
| Barukh Adonai ha-m'vorakh | בָּרוּךְ יְיָ הַמְבֹרָךְ |
| l'olam va·ed. | לְעוֹלָם וָעֶד. |

*And continue:*

| | |
|---|---|
| Barukh Atah Adonai, | בָּרוּךְ אַתָּה יְיָ |
| Eloheinu Melekh ha-olam, | אֱלֹהֵינוּ מֶלֶךְ הָעוֹלָם, |
| asher baḥar banu mi-kol ha-amim, | אֲשֶׁר בָּחַר בָּנוּ מִכָּל הָעַמִּים |
| v'natan lanu et Torato. | וְנָתַן לָנוּ אֶת תּוֹרָתוֹ. |
| Barukh Atah Adonai, | בָּרוּךְ אַתָּה יְיָ, |
| notein ha-Torah. | נוֹתֵן הַתּוֹרָה. |

*After the Torah is read, the reader will again point out a place for you to touch with your tzitzit and kiss, then chant:*

| | |
|---|---|
| Barukh Atah Adonai, | בָּרוּךְ אַתָּה יְיָ |
| Eloheinu Melekh ha-olam, | אֱלֹהֵינוּ מֶלֶךְ הָעוֹלָם, |
| asher natan lanu Torat emet | אֲשֶׁר נָתַן לָנוּ תּוֹרַת אֱמֶת, |
| v'ḥayyei olam nata b'tokheinu. | וְחַיֵּי עוֹלָם נָטַע בְּתוֹכֵנוּ. |
| Barukh Atah Adonai, | בָּרוּךְ אַתָּה יְיָ, |
| notein ha-Torah. | נוֹתֵן הַתּוֹרָה. |

## TORAH BLESSINGS

*If you are called up to the Torah, be sure your head is covered and you are wearing a tallit. The Torah reader will point out a place in the Torah, which you will touch with the tzitzit (fringes) of the tallit and then kiss the tzitzit.* You begin with:*

Praise Adonai, who is to be praised.

*The congregation responds:*

Praised be Adonai who is to be praised forever and ever.

*You repeat.*

*And continue:*

Praised are You, Adonai our God, Ruler of the universe, who chose us from all nations by giving us the Torah. Praised are You, Adonai, Giver of the Torah.

*After the Torah is read, the reader will again point out a place for you to touch with your tzitzit and kiss, then chant:*

Praised are You, Adonai our God, Ruler of the universe, who gave us a Torah of truth, and thereby planted eternal life in our midst. Praised are You, Adonai, Giver of Torah.

* Note: In some synagogues women who are called to the Torah are not required to have their heads covered or wear a tallit.

## BIRKAT HA-GOMEIL

*This blessing is recited by someone who has recovered from a serious illness, returned safely from a long journey, or who survived any kind of danger (including childbirth):*

בָּרוּךְ אַתָּה יְיָ
אֱלֹהֵינוּ מֶלֶךְ הָעוֹלָם,
הַגּוֹמֵל לְחַיָּבִים טוֹבוֹת,
שֶׁגְּמָלַנִי כָּל טוֹב.

Barukh Atah Adonai,
Eloheinu Melekh ha-olam,
ha-gomeil l'ḥayavim tovot,
she-g'malani kol tov.

*The congregation responds if the person is a man:*

מִי שֶׁגְּמָלְךָ כָּל טוֹב,
הוּא יִגְמָלְךָ כָּל טוֹב סֶלָה.

Mi she-g'mal'kha kol tov
hu yigmol'kha kol-tov selah.

*The congregation responds if the person is a woman:*

מִי שֶׁגְּמָלֵךְ כָּל טוֹב,
הוּא יִגְמָלֵךְ כָּל טוֹב סֶלָה.

Mi she-g'maleikh kol tov
hu yig'maleikh kol-tov selah.

## BIRKAT HA-GOMEIL

*This blessing is recited by someone who has recovered from a serious illness, returned safely from a long journey, or who survived any kind of danger (including childbirth):*

Praised are You, Adonai our God, Ruler of the universe, who acts kindly toward the undeserving, and has dealt kindly with me.

*The congregation responds if the person is a man:*

May the one who has bestowed goodness upon you continue to grant you every kind of goodness.

*The congregation responds if the person is a woman:*

May the one who has bestowed goodness upon you continue to grant you every kind of goodness.

## PRAYERS FOR THE RECOVERY OF THOSE IN NEED OF HEALING

*For a male who is ill:*

מִי שֶׁבֵּרַךְ אֲבוֹתֵינוּ, אַבְרָהָם יִצְחָק וְיַעֲקֹב, שָׂרָה רִבְקָה רָחֵל וְלֵאָה, הוּא יְבָרֵךְ וִירַפֵּא אֶת הַחוֹלֶה: ______ בֶּן ______. הַקָּדוֹשׁ בָּרוּךְ הוּא יִמָּלֵא רַחֲמִים עָלָיו, לְהַחֲזִיקוֹ וּלְרַפְּאתוֹ, וְיִשְׁלַח לוֹ מְהֵרָה רְפוּאָה שְׁלֵמָה לְכָל־אֵבָרָיו וְגִידָיו בְּתוֹךְ שְׁאָר חוֹלֵי יִשְׂרָאֵל, רְפוּאַת הַנֶּפֶשׁ, וּרְפוּאַת הַגּוּף (שַׁבָּת הִיא מִלִּזְעֹק / יוֹם טוֹב הוּא מִלִּזְעֹק / וּרְפוּאָה קְרוֹבָה לָבֹא) הַשְׁתָּא בַּעֲגָלָא וּבִזְמַן קָרִיב, וְנֹאמַר אָמֵן.

*For a female who is ill:*

מִי שֶׁבֵּרַךְ אֲבוֹתֵינוּ, אַבְרָהָם יִצְחָק וְיַעֲקֹב, שָׂרָה רִבְקָה רָחֵל וְלֵאָה, הוּא יְבָרֵךְ וִירַפֵּא אֶת הַחוֹלָה: ______ בַּת ______. הַקָּדוֹשׁ בָּרוּךְ הוּא יִמָּלֵא רַחֲמִים עָלֶיהָ, לְהַחֲזִיקָהּ וּלְרַפְּאתָהּ, וְיִשְׁלַח לָהּ מְהֵרָה רְפוּאָה שְׁלֵמָה לְכָל־אֵבָרֶיהָ וְגִידֶיהָ בְּתוֹךְ שְׁאָר חוֹלֵי יִשְׂרָאֵל, רְפוּאַת הַנֶּפֶשׁ, וּרְפוּאַת הַגּוּף (שַׁבָּת הִיא מִלִּזְעֹק / יוֹם טוֹב הוּא מִלִּזְעֹק / וּרְפוּאָה קְרוֹבָה לָבֹא) הַשְׁתָּא בַּעֲגָלָא וּבִזְמַן קָרִיב. וְנֹאמַר אָמֵן.

*For Both Males and Females:*

| | |
|---|---|
| El Nah r'fa na lahem | אֵל נָא רְפָא נָא לָהֶם |

## PRAYERS FOR THE RECOVERY OF THOSE IN NEED OF HEALING

*For a male who is ill:*

May the Holy Blessed One who blessed our ancestors, Abraham, Isaac, Jacob, Sarah, Rebekah, Rachel and Leah, bless and heal ______. May the Holy One give him support, courage, determination and patience of spirit. Grant ______ physical and spiritual wholeness. May God in kindness strengthen and heal him speedily, body and soul, together with others who are ill. And let us say: Amen.

*For a female who is ill:*

May the Holy Blessed One who blessed our ancestors, Abraham, Isaac, Jacob, Sarah, Rebekah, Rachel and Leah, bless and heal, May the Holy One give her support, courage, determination, and patience of spirit. Grant ______ physical and spiritual wholeness. May God in kindness strengthen and heal her speedily, body and soul, together with others who are ill. And let us say: Amen.

*For Both Males and Females:*

O God, heal them speedily

## A RESPONSIVE PRAYER FOR THOSE IN NEED OF HEALING

Hear their voice, O God, when they call,
Be gracious to them and answer them.

*In Your hand is the soul of all living things,
We turn to You now to give aid to those in distress

Grant them patience, faith and courage
Never let despair overwhelm them

*Be with them in difficult times
And help them to face their anxieties with confidence and hope.

Grant them of Your healing power,
So that in vigor of body and mind
They may return to their loved ones
For a life of blessing and sustenance.

*Restore them to health O God, and give them strength
Praised are You, God, Healer of the sick.

## HEALING KAVANAH

Take a deep breath in, and take a deep breath out. Find a comfortable position and when you are comfortable, breath slowly and deeply. Breathe in and out, and focus on your breathing. Relax, and picture your breath as a pure white light which you are breathing in and out. Now imagine all of the tensions, anxieties and fears slowly leaving your body. Continue breathing in and out. Every breath is now becoming more tranquil and relaxed. Now focus on a specific part of your body that you want to become more relaxed. Imagine the warmth of the white light surrounding that part of the body that you want to relax. As you focus on your breathing, imagine a second band of white light surrounding that same part of your body, allowing you to become even more relaxed.

Now imagine a most peaceful and tranquil place where you now want to be. Now put yourself into this place. Listen to the sweet sounds of nature in this place of comfort and security. Now focus on your breathing in this place, and feel the warmth and clarity of the air, allowing you time to nourish and cleanse your spirit.

Now look up at the blue sky and picture the word "shalom" in the form of a white cloud. "Shalom" means wellness and wholeness, and you are now feeling relaxed, tranquil and whole. Your entire body now feels totally relaxed and refreshed. You are feeling relaxed in body, mind and soul. You are feeling pure and totally renewed.

Blessed are You, Adonai, faithful and merciful Healer.

## ḤATZI KADDISH

*Leader:*

| | |
|---|---|
| Yit-gadal v'yit-kadash sh'mei rabba, | יִתְגַּדַּל וְיִתְקַדַּשׁ שְׁמֵהּ רַבָּא. |
| b'al'ma di v'ra | בְּעָלְמָא דִּי בְרָא |
| khir'utei | כִרְעוּתֵהּ, |
| v'yam-likh malkhutei | וְיַמְלִיךְ מַלְכוּתֵהּ |
| b'ḥayeikhon u-v'yomeikhon | בְּחַיֵּיכוֹן וּבְיוֹמֵיכוֹן |
| u-v'ḥayei d'khol beit Yisra·el, | וּבְחַיֵּי דְכָל בֵּית יִשְׂרָאֵל, |
| ba·agala u-viz'man kariv, | בַּעֲגָלָא וּבִזְמַן קָרִיב, |
| v'imru, Amen. | וְאִמְרוּ אָמֵן. |

*Congregation and Leader:*

| | |
|---|---|
| Y'hei sh'mei rabba m'va-rakh, | יְהֵא שְׁמֵהּ רַבָּא מְבָרַךְ |
| l'alam ul'al'mei al'maya, | לְעָלַם וּלְעָלְמֵי עָלְמַיָּא. |

*Leader:*

| | |
|---|---|
| Yitbarakh v'yishtabaḥ | יִתְבָּרַךְ וְיִשְׁתַּבַּח |
| v'yitpa·ar v'yitromam v'yitnasei | וְיִתְפָּאַר וְיִתְרוֹמַם וְיִתְנַשֵּׂא |
| v'yithadar v'yit·aleh v'yithalal | וְיִתְהַדָּר וְיִתְעַלֶּה וְיִתְהַלָּל |
| sh'mei d'kud'sha, b'rikh Hu, | שְׁמֵהּ דְּקֻדְשָׁא בְּרִיךְ הוּא, |
| L'eila [u-l'eila mi-kol] | לְעֵלָּא מִכָּל |
| min kol birkhata v'shirata | בִּרְכָתָא וְשִׁירָתָא |
| tushb'ḥata v'neḥemata | תֻּשְׁבְּחָתָא וְנֶחֱמָתָא, |
| da·amiran b'al'ma, | דַּאֲמִירָן בְּעָלְמָא, |
| v'imru Amen. | וְאִמְרוּ אָמֵן. |

## ḤATZI KADDISH

May God's great name be made great and holy in the world that God created according to God's will. May God establish the Divine kingdom soon, in our days, quickly and in the near future, and let us say, Amen.

*Congregation and Leader together:*

May God's great name be praised forever and ever.

Blessed, praised, glorified and raised high, honored and elevated be the name of the Holy Blessed One, far beyond all blessings and songs, praises and comforts, which people can say, and let us say: Amen.

## V'ZOT HA-TORAH

*When the Torah is lifted, the congregation chants:*

| | |
|---|---|
| V'zot ha-Torah asher sam Moshe | וְזֹאת הַתּוֹרָה אֲשֶׁר שָׂם מֹשֶׁה |
| lifnei B'nei Yisra·el | לִפְנֵי בְּנֵי יִשְׂרָאֵל, |
| al pi Adonai b'yad Moshe. | עַל פִּי יְיָ בְּיַד מֹשֶׁה. |

*When the Torah is lifted, it is customary to point at the scroll to emphasize that this is the Torah.Some use the little finger, some the index figure, some wrap their hands in their tzitzit.*
*While the Torah is being wrapped, the congregation may chant:*

| | |
|---|---|
| Eitz ḥayyim hi la-maḥazikim bah, | עֵץ חַיִּים הִיא לַמַּחֲזִיקִים בָּהּ, |
| v'tom'kheha m'ushar. | וְתֹמְכֶיהָ מְאֻשָּׁר. |
| D'rakheha darkhei no·am, | דְּרָכֶיהָ דַרְכֵי נֹעַם, |
| v'khol n'tivoteha shalom. | וְכָל נְתִיבוֹתֶיהָ שָׁלוֹם. |

*Blessings before the haftarah:*

| | |
|---|---|
| Barukh ata Adonai, | בָּרוּךְ אַתָּה יְיָ |
| Eloheinu Melekh ha-olam, | אֱלֹהֵינוּ מֶלֶךְ הָעוֹלָם, |
| asher baḥar bin'vi·im tovim, | אֲשֶׁר בָּחַר בִּנְבִיאִים טוֹבִים, |
| v'ratzah v'divreihem | וְרָצָה בְדִבְרֵיהֶם |
| ha-ne·emarim be-emet. | הַנֶּאֱמָרִים בֶּאֱמֶת, |
| Barukh ata Adonai | בָּרוּךְ אַתָּה יְיָ, |
| ha-boḥeir ba-Torah | הַבּוֹחֵר בַּתּוֹרָה |
| u-v'Moshe avdo | וּבְמֹשֶׁה עַבְדּוֹ, |
| u-v'Yisra·el amo | וּבְיִשְׂרָאֵל עַמּוֹ, |
| u-vin'vi·ei ha-emet vatzedek. | וּבִנְבִיאֵי הָאֱמֶת וָצֶדֶק. |

*Blessings after the haftarah:*

| | |
|---|---|
| Barukh ata Adonai, | בָּרוּךְ אַתָּה יְיָ |
| Eloheinu Melekh ha-olam, | אֱלֹהֵינוּ מֶלֶךְ הָעוֹלָם, |
| Tzur kol ha-olamim, | צוּר כָּל הָעוֹלָמִים, |
| tzadik b'khol ha-dorot, | צַדִּיק בְּכָל הַדּוֹרוֹת, |
| ha-eil ha-ne·eman | הָאֵל הַנֶּאֱמָן |
| ha-omer v'oseh, | הָאוֹמֵר וְעֹשֶׂה, |
| ha-m'dabeir u-m'kayeim, | הַמְדַבֵּר וּמְקַיֵּם, |

## V'ZOT HA-TORAH

*When the Torah is lifted, the congregation chants:*

This is the Torah which Moses set before the Israelites – as God's word, by Moses' hand.

*When the Torah is lifted, it is customary to point at the scroll to emphasize that this is the Torah. Some use the little finger, some the index figure, some wrap their hands in their tzitzit.*

*While the Torah is being wrapped, the congregation may chant:*

It is a tree of life for those who hold on to it, and those who support it are happy. Its paths are pleasant and all its ways are peaceful.

*Blessings before the haftarah:*

Praised are You, Adonai our God, Ruler of the Universe, who has chosen good prophets, and was pleased with their words that were spoken in truth. Praised are You, Adonai who chooses the Torah and Moses Your servant, and Israel Your people, and the prophets of truth and righteousness.

*Blessings after the haftarah:*

Praised are You, Adonai our God, Ruler of the Universe, Rock of all the worlds, righteous in every generation, the faithful God who says it – and it is done, Who speaks – and it is fulfilled;

שֶׁכָּל דְּבָרָיו אֱמֶת וָצֶדֶק.
נֶאֱמָן אַתָּה הוּא יְיָ אֱלֹהֵינוּ,
וְנֶאֱמָנִים דְּבָרֶיךָ,
וְדָבָר אֶחָד מִדְּבָרֶיךָ
אָחוֹר לֹא יָשׁוּב רֵיקָם,
כִּי אֵל
מֶלֶךְ נֶאֱמָן (וְרַחֲמָן) אָתָּה.
בָּרוּךְ אַתָּה יְיָ,
הָאֵל
הַנֶּאֱמָן בְּכָל דְּבָרָיו.

she-kol d'varav emet va-tzedek.
Ne·eman atah hu Adonai Eloheinu
v'ne·emanim d'varekha,
v'davar eḥad mi-d'varekha
aḥor lo yashuv reikam,
ki Eil
Melekh ne·eman v'raḥaman atah.
Barukh ata Adonai,
ha-eil
ha-ne·eman b'khol d'varav.

רַחֵם עַל צִיּוֹן
כִּי הִיא בֵּית חַיֵּינוּ,
וְלַעֲלוּבַת נֶפֶשׁ
תּוֹשִׁיעַ בִּמְהֵרָה בְיָמֵינוּ.
בָּרוּךְ אַתָּה יְיָ,
מְשַׂמֵּחַ צִיּוֹן בְּבָנֶיהָ.

Raḥeim al Tziyon
ki hi beit ḥayeinu.
v'la·aluvat nefesh
toshi·ah bim'heirah v'yameinu.
Barukh ata Adonai,
m'samei·aḥ Tziyon b'vaneha.

שַׂמְּחֵנוּ, יְיָ אֱלֹהֵינוּ,
בְּאֵלִיָּהוּ הַנָּבִיא עַבְדֶּךָ,
וּבְמַלְכוּת בֵּית דָּוִד
מְשִׁיחֶךָ,
בִּמְהֵרָה יָבֹא
וְיָגֵל לִבֵּנוּ,
עַל כִּסְאוֹ לֹא יֵשֶׁב זָר,
וְלֹא יִנְחֲלוּ עוֹד אֲחֵרִים אֶת
כְּבוֹדוֹ,
כִּי בְשֵׁם קָדְשְׁךָ נִשְׁבַּעְתָּ לּוֹ
שֶׁלֹּא יִכְבֶּה נֵרוֹ לְעוֹלָם וָעֶד.
בָּרוּךְ אַתָּה יְיָ,
מָגֵן דָּוִד.

Sam'ḥeinu Adonai Eloheinu
b'Eiliyahu ha-navi avdekha
u-v'malkhut beit David
m'shiḥekha.
Bim'heirah yavo
v'yageil libeinu,
al kis·o lo yeishev zar
v'lo yinḥalu od aḥeirim
et k'vodo,
ki v'sheim kodsh'kha nishba·ta lo
she-lo yikhbeh neiro l'olam va·ed.
Barukh ata Adonai,
magein David.

for all God's words are truth and righteousness. You are faithful, Adonai our God, and your words are trustworthy, and not one word of Yours is ever taken back unfulfilled, for You are a dependable and merciful Ruler. Praised are You, Adonai the God, who is dependable in all Your words.

Have mercy on Zion for she is our life's home. Save the humbled soul quickly in our day. Praised are You, Adonai, who causes Zion and her children to rejoice.

Cause us to rejoice, Adonai our God, with Elijah the prophet Your servant, and with the kingdom of David your anointed. May he quickly come and gladden our hearts. May no stranger sit on his throne, and may no others inherit his glory, for You vowed to him by Your holy Name, that his light would never be extinguished. Praised are You, Adonai, Shield of David.

עַל הַתּוֹרָה, וְעַל הָעֲבוֹדָה,
וְעַל הַנְּבִיאִים,
וְעַל יוֹם הַשַּׁבָּת הַזֶּה,
שֶׁנָּתַתָּ לָּנוּ, יְיָ אֱלֹהֵינוּ,
לִקְדֻשָּׁה וְלִמְנוּחָה,
לְכָבוֹד וּלְתִפְאָרֶת.
עַל הַכֹּל, יְיָ אֱלֹהֵינוּ,
אֲנַחְנוּ מוֹדִים לָךְ,
וּמְבָרְכִים אוֹתָךְ,
יִתְבָּרַךְ שִׁמְךְ
בְּפִי כָּל חַי
תָּמִיד לְעוֹלָם וָעֶד.
בָּרוּךְ אַתָּה יְיָ,
מְקַדֵּשׁ הַשַּׁבָּת.

Al ha-Torah v'al ha-avodah
v'al ha-n'vi·im
v'al yom ha-Shabbat ha-zeh
she-natata lanu Adonai Eloheinu
li-k'dushah v'lim'nuḥah,
l'khavod u-l'tif·aret.
Al ha-kol Adonai Eloheinu
anaḥnu modim lakh,
u-m'var'khim otokh.
Yitbarakh shimkha
b'fi kol ḥai
tamid l'olam va·ed.
Barukh ata Adonai,
m'kadeish ha-Shabbat.

*On Festivals and the intermediate Shabbat of Sukkot:*

עַל הַתּוֹרָה, וְעַל הָעֲבוֹדָה, וְעַל הַנְּבִיאִים, וְעַל יוֹם (לשבת: הַשַּׁבָּת הַזֶּה, וְעַל יוֹם)

חַג הַמַּצּוֹת
חַג הַשָּׁבֻעוֹת
חַג הַסֻּכּוֹת
הַשְּׁמִינִי חַג הָעֲצֶרֶת

הַזֶּה, שֶׁנָּתַתָּ לָּנוּ יְיָ אֱלֹהֵינוּ, (לשבת: לִקְדֻשָּׁה וְלִמְנוּחָה,) לְשָׂשׂוֹן וּלְשִׂמְחָה, לְכָבוֹד וּלְתִפְאָרֶת.

עַל הַכֹּל יְיָ אֱלֹהֵינוּ, אֲנַחְנוּ מוֹדִים לָךְ, וּמְבָרְכִים אוֹתָךְ, יִתְבָּרַךְ שִׁמְךְ בְּפִי כָּל חַי תָּמִיד לְעוֹלָם וָעֶד.

בָּרוּךְ אַתָּה יְיָ, מְקַדֵּשׁ (לשבת שַׁבָּת וְ)יִשְׂרָאֵל וְהַזְּמַנִּים.

For Your Torah, and for the worship, and for the prophets, and for this Shabbat day that you gave us, Adonai our God, for holiness and for rest, for glory and splendor – for all these, Adonai our God, we thank You and praise You. May your name be praised perpetually forever. Praised are You, Adonai, who sanctifies the Shabbat.

*On Festivals and the intermediate Shabbat of Sukkot:*

For Your Torah, and for the worship, and for the prophets (and for this Shabbat day), and for this:

Festival of Matzot.
Festival of Shavu·ot
Festival of Sukkot
Festival of Shemini Atzeret

That you gave us, Adonai our God (for holiness and for rest), for joy and gladness, for glory and splendor — for all these, Adonai our God, we thank You and praise You. May Your name be praised by all that live, perpetually, forever. Praised are You, Adonai, who sanctifies (the Shabbat and) Israel and the Festivals.

## A PRAYER FOR OUR COUNTRY

אֱלֹהֵינוּ וֵאלֹהֵי אֲבוֹתֵינוּ, קַבֵּל נָא בְּרַחֲמִים אֶת־תְּפִלָּתֵנוּ בְּעַד אַרְצֵנוּ וּמֶמְשַׁלְתָּהּ. הָרֵק אֶת־בִּרְכָתְךָ עַל הָאָרֶץ הַזֹּאת, עַל מַנְהִיגֶיהָ, שׁוֹפְטֶיהָ, וּפְקִידֶיהָ הָעוֹסְקִים בְּצָרְכֵי צִבּוּר בֶּאֱמוּנָה. הוֹרֵם מֵחֻקֵּי תוֹרָתֶךָ, הֲבִינֵם מִשְׁפְּטֵי צִדְקֶךָ לְמַעַן לֹא יָסְוּרוּ מֵאַרְצֵנוּ שָׁלוֹם וְשַׁלְוָה, אֹשֶׁר וָחֹפֶשׁ כָּל־הַיָּמִים. אָנָּא יהוה אֱלֹהֵי הָרוּחוֹת לְכָל־בָּשָׂר, שְׁלַח רוּחֲךָ עַל כָּל־תּוֹשְׁבֵי אַרְצֵנוּ. עֲקֹר מִלִּבָּם שִׂנְאָה וְאֵיבָה, קִנְאָה וְתַחֲרוּת, וְטַע בֵּין בְּנֵי הָאֻמּוֹת וְהָאֱמוּנוֹת הַשּׁוֹנוֹת הַשּׁוֹכְנִים בָּהּ, אַהֲבָה וְאַחֲוָה, שָׁלוֹם וְרֵעוּת.

וּבְכֵן יְהִי רָצוֹן מִלְּפָנֶיךָ שֶׁתְּהִי אַרְצֵנוּ בְּרָכָה לְכָל־יוֹשְׁבֵי תֵבֵל, וְתַשְׁרֶה בֵּינֵיהֶם רֵעוּת וְחֵרוּת, וְקַיֵּם בִּמְהֵרָה חֲזוֹן נְבִיאֶךָ: לֹא יִשָּׂא גוֹי אֶל גּוֹי חֶרֶב וְלֹא יִלְמְדוּ עוֹד מִלְחָמָה וְנֹאמַר, אָמֵן.

## A PRAYER FOR OUR COUNTRY

Our God and God of our ancestors, please accept with mercy our prayer for our land and its government. Teach our leaders the values of Your Torah, help them understand Your rules of righteousness, so that our land may never lack peace and tranquility, prosperity and freedom. Adonai, God of the spirits of all flesh, send Your spirit to all the inhabitants of our land, and plant love and brotherhood, peace and friendship among all the nationalities and faiths who dwell in it. Uproot from their hearts any hatred or enmity, jealousy or rivalry, to fulfill the yearnings of Your children who delight in its honor and who desire to see it be a light for all the nations. May it be Your will that our land will be a blessing to all the inhabitants of the world, and that friendship and freedom will reign between them, and that the vision of Your prophets will soon be fulfilled, Amen.

Jews have said prayers for their countries for centuries. This is based on a verse in Jeremiah (29:7): *Seek the welfare of the city to which I have exiled you and pray to Adonai on its behalf; for in its prosperity you shall prosper.* Even in countries where we didn't feel completely at home, we included a prayer for the government. Perhaps one basis was the teaching in Pirkei Avot (3:2): "Rabbi Chanina, an assistant of the high priest, said: Pray for the welfare of the government, for were it not for fear of it men would swallow each other alive." Oppressive governments cause many problems, but a state of total lawlessness is worse. In our time, of course, we live in freedom, so such a prayer is even more natural. The great Talmudic scholar Dr. Louis Ginzberg wrote this version. In it we ask God to guide our leaders toward wisdom and justice.

## A PRAYER FOR THE STATE OF ISRAEL

| | |
|---|---|
| Avinu she-ba-shamayim, | אָבִינוּ שֶׁבַּשָּׁמַיִם, |
| tzur Yisra·el v'go·alo, | צוּר יִשְׂרָאֵל וְגוֹאֲלוֹ, |
| bareikh et-M'dinat Yisra·el, | בָּרֵךְ אֶת מְדִינַת יִשְׂרָאֵל, |
| reishit tz'miḥat g'ulateinu. | רֵאשִׁית צְמִיחַת גְּאֻלָּתֵנוּ. |
| Hagein aleha b'evrat ḥasdekha, | הָגֵן עָלֶיהָ בְּאֶבְרַת חַסְדֶּךָ |
| u-f'ros aleha | וּפְרוֹס עָלֶיהָ |
| sukkat sh'lomekha. | סֻכַּת שְׁלוֹמֶךָ, |
| U-sh'laḥ | וּשְׁלַח |
| or'kha va-amit'kha | אוֹרְךָ וַאֲמִתְּךָ |
| l'rasheha, sareha v'yo·atzeha, | לְרָאשֶׁיהָ, שָׂרֶיהָ וְיוֹעֲצֶיהָ, |
| v'takneim | וְתַקְּנֵם |
| b'eitzah tovah mil'fanekha. | בְּעֵצָה טוֹבָה מִלְּפָנֶיךָ. |
| Ḥazeik et-y'dei | חַזֵּק אֶת יְדֵי |
| m'ginei eretz kod'sheinu, | מְגִנֵּי אֶרֶץ קָדְשֵׁנוּ, |
| v'hanḥileim Eloheinu | וְהַנְחִילֵם אֱלֹהֵינוּ |
| y'shu·ah, va-ateret nitzaḥon t'atreim. | יְשׁוּעָה, וַעֲטֶרֶת נִצָּחוֹן תְּעַטְּרֵם, |
| v'natata shalom ba-aretz | וְנָתַתָּ שָׁלוֹם בָּאָרֶץ, |
| v'simḥat olam l'yosh'veha, | וְשִׂמְחַת עוֹלָם לְיוֹשְׁבֶיהָ. |
| v'nomar Amen. | וְנֹאמַר אָמֵן. |

## A PRAYER FOR THE STATE OF ISRAEL

Our Heavenly Parent, Rock of Israel and its Redeemer, bless the State of Israel, first flowering of our redemption. Shield it under Your loving wings, and spread over it Your sukkah of peace. Send Your light and truth to its leaders, ministers and advisors, and guide them rightly with Your good advice. Strengthen the hands of the defenders of our holy land, and lead them, God, to deliverance. Crown their efforts with victory. Grant peace to the land and eternal happiness to its inhabitants, and let us say, Amen.

This prayer is adapted from one recited in Israel. We add this to our service as a way of expressing our solidarity with and commitment to Israel. Notice how both the Prayer for our Country and the Prayer for the State of Israel include prayers for peace.

# Announcing the New Month

יְהִי רָצוֹן מִלְּפָנֶיךָ, יְיָ אֱלֹהֵינוּ וֵאלֹהֵי אֲבוֹתֵינוּ, שֶׁתְּחַדֵּשׁ עָלֵינוּ אֶת הַחֹדֶשׁ הַזֶּה לְטוֹבָה וְלִבְרָכָה, וְתִתֶּן לָנוּ חַיִּים אֲרוּכִים, חַיִּים שֶׁל שָׁלוֹם, חַיִּים שֶׁל טוֹבָה, חַיִּים שֶׁל בְּרָכָה, חַיִּים שֶׁל פַּרְנָסָה, חַיִּים שֶׁל חִלּוּץ עֲצָמוֹת, חַיִּים שֶׁיֵּשׁ בָּהֶם יִרְאַת שָׁמַיִם וְיִרְאַת חֵטְא, חַיִּים שֶׁאֵין בָּהֶם בּוּשָׁה וּכְלִמָּה, חַיִּים שֶׁל עֹשֶׁר וְכָבוֹד, חַיִּים שֶׁתְּהֵא בָנוּ אַהֲבַת תּוֹרָה וְיִרְאַת שָׁמַיִם, חַיִּים שֶׁיְּמַלֵּא יְיָ מִשְׁאֲלוֹת לִבֵּנוּ לְטוֹבָה, אָמֵן סֶלָה.

| | |
|---|---|
| Mi she-asah nissim la-avoteinu, | מִי שֶׁעָשָׂה נִסִּים לַאֲבוֹתֵינוּ, |
| v'ga·al otam mei-avdut l'ḥeirut, | וְגָאַל אוֹתָם מֵעַבְדוּת לְחֵרוּת, |
| Hu yig·al otanu b'karov | הוּא יִגְאַל אוֹתָנוּ בְּקָרוֹב, |
| vikabeitz nidaḥeinu | וִיקַבֵּץ נִדָּחֵינוּ |
| mei-arba kanfot ha-aretz, | מֵאַרְבַּע כַּנְפוֹת הָאָרֶץ, |
| ḥaveirim kol-Yisra·el, | חֲבֵרִים כָּל יִשְׂרָאֵל, |
| v'nomar Amen. | וְנֹאמַר אָמֵן. |

| | |
|---|---|
| Rosh Ḥodesh ______ yih'yeh | רֹאשׁ חֹדֶשׁ (פלוני) יִהְיֶה |
| b'yom ______ ha-ba aleinu | בְּיוֹם (פלוני) הַבָּא עָלֵינוּ |
| v'al kol-Yisra·el l'tovah. | וְעַל כָּל יִשְׂרָאֵל לְטוֹבָה. |

*There are congregational responses of "Amen" in the last paragraph of the prayer:*

| | |
|---|---|
| L'ḥayyim u-l'shalom Amen! | לְחַיִּים וּלְשָׁלוֹם אָמֵן! |
| L'sason u-l'simḥah Amen! | לְשָׂשׂוֹן וּלְשִׂמְחָה אָמֵן! |
| Lishu·ah u-l'neḥamah, | לִישׁוּעָה וּלְנֶחָמָה, |
| v'nomar Amen! | וְנֹאמַר אָמֵן! |

# Announcing the New Month

May it be Your will, Adonai our God and God of our ancestors, to renew this month for us for good and for blessing. Grant us long life, a life of peace, a life of goodness, a life of blessing, a life of good livelihood, a life of physical strength, a life in which we will have reverence for God and revulsion for sin, a life which is free of shame or reproach, a life of wealth and honor, a life in which we will have love of Torah and love of God, a life in which our worthy heart's desires will be fulfilled, Amen, Selah.

*The Leader holds the Sefer Torah and continues:*

May the One Who worked miracles for our ancestors and redeemed them from slavery to freedom soon redeem us, and gather our exiles from the four corners of the earth. All Israel are friends, and let us say, Amen.
The new month of ______ will begin on ______ to come. May it bring goodness for us and for all the people Israel.

*The congregation repeats the previous paragraph, and then continues:*

May the Blessed Holy One renew it for us and for all God's people, the House of Israel,
For life and peace. Amen,
For joy and gladness. Amen.
For redemption and consolation. And let us say, Amen.
Amen!

## ASHREI

*Congregation sings the parts marked with **

| | |
|---|---|
| Ashrei yosh'vei | אַשְׁרֵי יוֹשְׁבֵי |
| veitekha, | בֵיתֶךָ, |
| od y'hal'lukha selah. | עוֹד יְהַלְלְוּךָ סֶּלָה. |
| *Ashrei ha-am she-kakha lo, | *אַשְׁרֵי הָעָם שֶׁכָּכָה לּוֹ, |
| ashrei ha-am | אַשְׁרֵי הָעָם |
| she-Adonai Elohav. | שֶׁיְיָ אֱלֹהָיו. |
| T'hilah l'David | תְּהִלָּה לְדָוִד, |
| Aromim'kha Elohai ha-Melekh, | אֲרוֹמִמְךָ אֱלוֹהַי הַמֶּלֶךְ, |
| va-avarkha shimkha l'olam va·ed. | וַאֲבָרְכָה שִׁמְךָ לְעוֹלָם וָעֶד. |
| *B'khol yom avar'kheka, | *בְּכָל יוֹם אֲבָרְכֶךָּ, |
| va·ahal'lah shimkha l'olam va·ed. | וַאֲהַלְלָה שִׁמְךָ לְעוֹלָם וָעֶד. |
| Gadol Adonai u-m'hulal m'od, | גָּדוֹל יְיָ וּמְהֻלָּל מְאֹד, |
| v'lig'dulato ein ḥeiker. | וְלִגְדֻלָּתוֹ אֵין חֵקֶר. |
| *Dor l'dor | *דּוֹר לְדוֹר |
| y'shabaḥ ma·asekha, | יְשַׁבַּח מַעֲשֶׂיךָ, |
| u-g'vurotekha yagidu. | וּגְבוּרֹתֶיךָ יַגִּידוּ. |
| Hadar k'vod hodekha, | הֲדַר כְּבוֹד הוֹדֶךָ, |
| v'divrei nifl'otekha asiḥah. | וְדִבְרֵי נִפְלְאֹתֶיךָ אָשִׂיחָה. |
| *Ve-ezuz nor'otekha yo·meiru, | *וֶעֱזוּז נוֹרְאוֹתֶיךָ יֹאמֵרוּ, |
| u-g'dulat'kha asap'renah. | וּגְדֻלָּתְךָ אֲסַפְּרֶנָּה. |
| Zekher rav tuv'kha yabi·u, | זֵכֶר רַב טוּבְךָ יַבִּיעוּ, |
| v'tzidkat'kha y'raneinu. | וְצִדְקָתְךָ יְרַנֵּנוּ. |
| *Ḥanun v'raḥum Adonai, | *חַנּוּן וְרַחוּם יְיָ, |
| erekh apayim ug'dol ḥased. | אֶרֶךְ אַפַּיִם וּגְדָל חָסֶד. |
| Tov Adonai lakol, | טוֹב יְיָ לַכֹּל, |
| v'raḥamav al kol ma·asav. | וְרַחֲמָיו עַל כָּל מַעֲשָׂיו. |
| *Yodukha Adonai kol ma·asekha, | *יוֹדוּךָ יְיָ כָּל מַעֲשֶׂיךָ, |
| va-ḥasidekha y'var'khukha. | וַחֲסִידֶיךָ יְבָרְכוּכָה. |
| K'vod malkhut'kha yo·meiru, | כְּבוֹד מַלְכוּתְךָ יֹאמֵרוּ, |
| u-g'vurat'kha y'dabeiru | וּגְבוּרָתְךָ יְדַבֵּרוּ. |
| *L'hodi·a livnei ha-adam g'vurotav, | לְהוֹדִיעַ לִבְנֵי הָאָדָם גְּבוּרֹתָיו, |
| u-kh'vod hadar malkhuto | וּכְבוֹד הֲדַר מַלְכוּתוֹ. |

## ASHREI

*Congregation sings the parts marked with **

Happy are they who live in Your house;
They shall continue to praise You. (Psalm 84:5)

Happy are the people for whom this is so;
Happy are the people whose God is Adonai. (Psalm 144:15)

A Psalm of David.
א I will honor you, my God and Ruler,
I will praise Your name forever and ever.

ב Every day I will praise You,
And sing praises to Your name forever and ever.

ג Great is Adonai and greatly praised;
There is no limit to God's greatness.

ד One generation shall praise Your deeds to another,
And tell about Your mighty deeds.

ה I will speak about Your splendor and glory,
And Your wonderful deeds.

ו They will talk about the power of Your mighty acts;
And I will tell of Your greatness.

ז They recall Your great goodness,
And sing of Your righteousness.

ח Adonai is gracious and caring,
patient and very kind.

ט Adonai is good to all,
And merciful to everything God made.

י All Your works shall praise You, Adonai,
And Your faithful ones shall bless You.

כ They shall speak of the glory of Your rule,
And talk of Your might,

| | |
|---|---|
| Malkhut'kha malkhut kol olamim, | מַלְכוּתְךָ מַלְכוּת כָּל עוֹלָמִים, |
| u-memshalt'kha b'khol dor va-dor | וּמֶמְשַׁלְתְּךָ בְּכָל דֹּר וָדֹר. |
| *Someikh Adonai l'khol ha-nf'lim, | *סוֹמֵךְ יְיָ לְכָל הַנֹּפְלִים, |
| v'zokeif l'khol hak'fufim. | וְזוֹקֵף לְכָל הַכְּפוּפִים. |
| Einei khol eilekha y'sabeiru, | עֵינֵי כֹל אֵלֶיךָ יְשַׂבֵּרוּ, |
| v'Atah notein lahem | וְאַתָּה נוֹתֵן לָהֶם |
| et okhlam b'ito. | אֶת אָכְלָם בְּעִתּוֹ. |
| *Pote·aḥ et yadekha, | *פּוֹתֵחַ אֶת יָדֶךָ, |
| u-masbi·a l'khol ḥai ratzon. | וּמַשְׂבִּיעַ לְכָל חַי רָצוֹן. |
| Tzadik Adonai b'khol d'rakhav, | צַדִּיק יְיָ בְּכָל דְּרָכָיו, |
| v'ḥasid b'khol ma·asav. | וְחָסִיד בְּכָל מַעֲשָׂיו. |
| *Karov Adonai l'khol kor'av, | *קָרוֹב יְיָ לְכָל קֹרְאָיו, |
| l'khol asher yikra·uhu ve-emet. | לְכֹל אֲשֶׁר יִקְרָאֻהוּ בֶאֱמֶת. |
| R'tzon y'rei·av ya·aseh, | רְצוֹן יְרֵאָיו יַעֲשֶׂה, |
| v'et shav·atam yishmah v'yoshi·eim. | וְאֶת שַׁוְעָתָם יִשְׁמַע וְיוֹשִׁיעֵם. |
| *Shomeir Adonai et kol ohavav | *שׁוֹמֵר יְיָ אֶת כָּל אֹהֲבָיו, |
| v'et kol har'sha·im yashmid | וְאֵת כָּל הָרְשָׁעִים יַשְׁמִיד. |
| T'hilat Adonai y'daber pi, | תְּהִלַּת יְיָ יְדַבֶּר פִּי, |
| Vi-varekh kol basar | וִיבָרֵךְ כָּל בָּשָׂר |
| sheim kodsho l'olam va·ed. | שֵׁם קָדְשׁוֹ לְעוֹלָם וָעֶד. |
| *Va-anaḥnu n'vareikh Yah, | *וַאֲנַחְנוּ נְבָרֵךְ יָהּ, |
| mei-atah v'ad olam. | מֵעַתָּה וְעַד עוֹלָם, |
| Hal'luyah. | הַלְלוּיָהּ. |

*We rise to return the Sefer Torah to the Ark.*

| | |
|---|---|
| Y'hal'lu et sheim Adonai | יְהַלְלוּ אֶת שֵׁם יְיָ, |
| ki nisgav sh'mo l'vado. | כִּי נִשְׂגָּב שְׁמוֹ לְבַדּוֹ. |
| Hodo al eretz v'shamayim, | הוֹדוֹ עַל אֶרֶץ וְשָׁמָיִם. |
| va-yarem keren l'amo, | וַיָּרֶם קֶרֶן לְעַמּוֹ, |
| T'hilah l'khol ḥasidav, | תְּהִלָּה לְכָל חֲסִידָיו, |
| liv'nei Yisra·el am k'rovo. | לִבְנֵי יִשְׂרָאֵל עַם קְרוֹבוֹ, |
| Hal'luyah. | הַלְלוּיָהּ. |

ל To announce to humanity God's greatness,
The splendor and glory of God's rule.

מ God, You rule forever,
Your kingdom is for all generations.

ס God holds up all who fall,
And helps all who are bent over stand straight.

ע The eyes of all look to You with hope,
And You give them their food at the right time.

פ You open Your hand,
And feed everything that lives to its heart's content.

צ Adonai is good in every way,
And kind in every deed.

ק Adonai is near to all who call,
To all who call to God sincerely.

ר God does the wishes of those who respect God,
God hears their cry and saves them.

ש Adonai protects all who love God,
But God will destroy the wicked.

ת My mouth shall speak praises of God,
And all beings shall bless God's holy name
Forever and ever. (Psalm 145)

We shall praise God,
Now and forever. Halleluyah. (Psalm 115:18)

*We rise to return the Sefer Torah to the Ark.*

Praise God's name, for God's name is uniquely exalted.
God's glory is above heaven and earth,
God has exalted God's people's might,
given praise to the pious ones,
the people of Israel, who are close to God.
Halleluyah.

## MIZMOR L'DAVID

*On Shabbat, the congregation sings parts marked with **

| | |
|---|---|
| Mizmor l'David. | מִזְמוֹר לְדָוִד, |
| *Havu lAdonai b'nei eilim, | הָבוּ לַייָ בְּנֵי אֵלִים, |
| havu lAdonai kavod va-oz. | הָבוּ לַייָ כָּבוֹד וָעֹז. |
| Havu lAdonai k'vod sh'mo, | הָבוּ לַייָ כְּבוֹד שְׁמוֹ, |
| hishtaḥavu lAdonai | הִשְׁתַּחֲווּ לַייָ |
| b'hadrat kodesh. | בְּהַדְרַת קֹדֶשׁ. |
| Kol Adonai al ha-mayim, | קוֹל יְיָ עַל הַמָּיִם, |
| Eil ha-kavod hir·im, | אֵל הַכָּבוֹד הִרְעִים, |
| Adonai al mayim rabim. | יְיָ עַל מַיִם רַבִּים. |
| *Kol Adonai ba-ko·aḥ, | קוֹל יְיָ בַּכֹּחַ, |
| kol Adonai be-hadar. | קוֹל יְיָ בֶּהָדָר. |
| Kol Adonai shoveir arazim | קוֹל יְיָ שֹׁבֵר אֲרָזִים, |
| vay'shabeir Adonai | וַיְשַׁבֵּר יְיָ |
| et arzei hal'vanon. | אֶת אַרְזֵי הַלְּבָנוֹן. |
| Va-yarkideim k'mo eigel, | וַיַּרְקִידֵם כְּמוֹ עֵגֶל, |
| l'vanon v'siryon k'mo ven r'eimim. | לְבָנוֹן וְשִׂרְיוֹן כְּמוֹ בֶן רְאֵמִים. |
| *Kol Adonai ḥotzeiv la-havot eish, | קוֹל יְיָ חֹצֵב לַהֲבוֹת אֵשׁ. |
| kol Adonai yaḥil midbar, | קוֹל יְיָ יָחִיל מִדְבָּר, |
| yaḥil Adonai midbar kadeish. | יָחִיל יְיָ מִדְבַּר קָדֵשׁ. |
| Kol Adonai y'ḥolel ayalot. | קוֹל יְיָ יְחוֹלֵל אַיָּלוֹת |
| Va-yeḥesof y'arot, | וַיֶּחֱשֹׂף יְעָרוֹת, |
| u-v'heikhalo | וּבְהֵיכָלוֹ |
| kulo omeir kavod. | כֻּלּוֹ אֹמֵר כָּבוֹד. |
| *Adonai lamabul yashav, | יְיָ לַמַּבּוּל יָשָׁב, |
| vayeishev Adonai Melekh l'olam. | וַיֵּשֶׁב יְיָ מֶלֶךְ לְעוֹלָם. |
| Adonai oz l'amo yitein, | יְיָ עֹז לְעַמּוֹ יִתֵּן, |
| Adonai y'vareikh et amo va-shalom. | יְיָ יְבָרֵךְ אֶת עַמּוֹ בַשָּׁלוֹם. |

## MIZMOR L'DAVID

A Psalm of David:
Attribute to Adonai, mighty ones, attribute to God glory and strength.
Attribute to Adonai the glory of God's Name,
Bow before Adonai in the beauty of holiness.
Adonai's voice is over the waters, the God of glory thunders
Adonai is over the many waters.
Adonai's voice sounds with power,
Adonai's voice sounds with beauty.
Adonai's voice breaks cedars,
Adonai shatters the cedars of Lebanon.
God makes them leap like a calf,
Lebanon and Sirion like a wild ox.
Adonai's voice carves out flames of fire.
Adonai's voice makes the desert quake.
Adonai makes the desert of Kadesh quake.
Adonai's voice causes deer to give birth,
And strips the forests bare.
In God's sanctuary, all speak of God's glory.
Adonai sat enthroned at the Flood,
Adonai is enthroned as Ruler forever.
Adonai will give strength to God's people;
Adonai will bless God's people with peace.

**Mizmor L'David:** Have you ever experienced a summer storm? At first, you hear the pitter-patter of the rain drops on the rooftop, and soon see the incredible lightning bolts and sounds of rumbling thunder. Close your eyes and see whether you can return to such a place. Such is the kind of place in which King David may have found himself when he composed Psalm 29, often known as "The majesty of God in the storm" The Hebrew word "kol" appears seven times in the Psalm, alluding to the Sabbath as God's seventh day of creation. Even the angels on High proclaim God's glory. Try to picture God's angels. Imagine what they look like. Listen to the sound of their voice and clap your hands along with their song. Feel God's blessing of peace at the end of Psalm 29. May it help you feel whole again.

*On weekdays:*

| | |
|---|---|
| לְדָוִד מִזְמוֹר, | L'David mizmor. |
| לַייָ הָאָרֶץ וּמְלוֹאָהּ, | Ladonai ha-aretz um'lo·ah, |
| תֵּבֵל וְיֹשְׁבֵי בָהּ. | teiveil v'yosh'vei va. |
| כִּי הוּא עַל יַמִּים יְסָדָהּ, | Ki Hu al yamim y'sadah, |
| וְעַל נְהָרוֹת יְכוֹנְנֶהָ. | v'al n'harot y'khon'neha. |
| מִי יַעֲלֶה בְהַר יְיָ, | Mi ya·aleh v'har Adonai, |
| וּמִי יָקוּם בִּמְקוֹם קָדְשׁוֹ. | u-mi yakum bim'kom kodsho. |
| נְקִי כַפַּיִם וּבַר לֵבָב, | N'ki khapayim u-var leivav, |
| אֲשֶׁר לֹא נָשָׂא לַשָּׁוְא נַפְשִׁי, | asher lo nasa la-shav nafshi, |
| וְלֹא נִשְׁבַּע לְמִרְמָה. | v'lo nishba l'mirmah. |
| יִשָּׂא בְרָכָה מֵאֵת יְיָ, | Yisa v'rakha mei·eit Adonai, |
| וּצְדָקָה | u-tz'dakah |
| מֵאֱלֹהֵי יִשְׁעוֹ. | mei-Elohei yis·o. |
| זֶה דּוֹר דּוֹרְשָׁיו, | Zeh dor dorshav, |
| מְבַקְשֵׁי פָנֶיךָ | m'vakshei faneikha |
| יַעֲקֹב סֶלָה. | Ya·akov, selah. |
| שְׂאוּ שְׁעָרִים רָאשֵׁיכֶם, | S'u sḥarim rasheikhem, |
| וְהִנָּשְׂאוּ פִּתְחֵי עוֹלָם, | v'hinas'u pitḥei olam, |
| וְיָבוֹא מֶלֶךְ הַכָּבוֹד. | v'yavo Melekh ha-kavod. |
| מִי זֶה מֶלֶךְ הַכָּבוֹד, | Mi zeh Melekh ha-kavod, |
| יְיָ עִזּוּז וְגִבּוֹר, | Adonai izuz v'gibor, |
| יְיָ גִּבּוֹר מִלְחָמָה. | Adonai gibor milḥamah. |
| שְׂאוּ שְׁעָרִים רָאשֵׁיכֶם, | S'u sh'arim rasheikhem, |
| וּשְׂאוּ פִּתְחֵי עוֹלָם, | u-s'u pitḥei olam, |
| וְיָבֹא מֶלֶךְ הַכָּבוֹד. | v'yavo Melekh ha-kavod. |
| מִי הוּא זֶה מֶלֶךְ הַכָּבוֹד, | Mi Hu zeh Melekh ha-kavod, |
| יְיָ צְבָאוֹת, | Adonai tz'va·ot |
| הוּא מֶלֶךְ הַכָּבוֹד סֶלָה. | Hu Melekh ha-kavod. Selah. |

*On weekdays:*

A Psalm of David:
The earth is Adonai's and all it contains,
The world and all who dwell in it.
For God founded it on the seas,
And set it in place upon rivers.
Who may go up on Adonai's mountain,
And who may stand in the place of God's holiness?
One who has clean hands and a pure heart,
Who has not taken My name in vain,
And who has not sworn falsely.
He will carry Adonai's blessing,
And just reward from God who saves him.
This is the generation of those who seek God;
Jacob's descendents who pursue God's presence.
Lift up your heads, O gates;
Be lifted up, entrances to eternity,
So that the glorious Ruler may enter.
Who is the glorious Ruler,
Adonai, strong and mighty;
Adonai, mighty in battle.
Lift up your heads, O gates;
Be lifted up, entrances to eternity,
So that the glorious Ruler may enter.
Who is the glorious Ruler?
*Adonai Tzevàot* is the glorious Ruler.

Think of this Psalm as a song for entering the Temple. Scholars think that the first part celebrates the entrance of pilgrims into the Temple. The words beginning "Who may go up on Adonai's mountain" are a kind of prayer asking that they may be worthy of standing in such a holy place. In the second part. The Ark of the Covenant enters. The phrase "Lift up your heads, O gates," gives us an image of the gates of the Temple joyously welcoming the Ark, and therefore also God's presence. The connection with returning the Torah to the Ark today is easy to see. As the Torah moves in procession, we worshippers seek to engage with the Torah by kissing it as it passes by.

## UV'NUḤO YOMAR

***We praise the Torah as a wonderful gift from God.***

*The ark is closed.*

| | |
|---|---|
| Uv'nuḥo yomar: | וּבְנֻחֹה יֹאמַר, |
| Shuvah Adonai | שׁוּבָה, יְיָ, |
| riv'vot alfei Yisra·el. | רִבְבוֹת אַלְפֵי יִשְׂרָאֵל. |
| Kumah Adonai lim'nuḥatekha, | קוּמָה יְיָ לִמְנוּחָתֶךָ, |
| Atah va-aron uzekha. | אַתָּה וַאֲרוֹן עֻזֶּךָ. |
| Kohanekha | כֹּהֲנֶיךָ |
| yilb'shu tzedek, | יִלְבְּשׁוּ צֶדֶק, |
| va-ḥasidekha y'raneinu. | וַחֲסִידֶיךָ יְרַנֵּנוּ. |
| Ba·avur David avdekha, | בַּעֲבוּר דָּוִד עַבְדֶּךָ, |
| al tasheiv p'nei m'shiḥekha. | אַל תָּשֵׁב פְּנֵי מְשִׁיחֶךָ. |
| Ki lekaḥ tov natati lakhem, | כִּי לֶקַח טוֹב נָתַתִּי לָכֶם, |
| Torati al ta·azovu. | תּוֹרָתִי אַל תַּעֲזֹבוּ. |
| Eitz ḥayim hi la-maḥazikim bah, | עֵץ חַיִּים הִיא לַמַּחֲזִיקִים בָּהּ, |
| v'tom'kheha m'ushar. | וְתֹמְכֶיהָ מְאֻשָּׁר. |
| D'rakheha darkhei no-am, | דְּרָכֶיהָ דַרְכֵי נֹעַם, |
| v'khol n'tivoteha shalom. | וְכָל נְתִיבוֹתֶיהָ שָׁלוֹם. |
| Ha-shiveinu Adonai eilekha v'nashuvah, | הֲשִׁיבֵנוּ יְיָ אֵלֶיךָ וְנָשׁוּבָה, |
| ḥadesh yameinu k'kedem. | חַדֵּשׁ יָמֵינוּ כְּקֶדֶם. |

## UV'NUḤO YOMAR

***We praise the Torah as a wonderful gift from God.***

When the Ark rested, Moses would say:
Return, Adonai to the millions of Israel. (Numbers 10:36)
Rise up, Adonai to Your resting place, the Temple,
You and the Ark of Your strength.
May Your priests be clothed in righteousness,
And your faithful sing with joy.
For the sake of David, Your servant,
Do not reject Your anointed one.
I have given you good teaching,
do not leave My Torah.
It is a tree of life for those who hold on to it,
and those who support it are happy.
Its paths are pleasant
and all its ways are peaceful.
Return us to You, Adonai, and we shall return.
Renew our days as in days of old.

## ḤATZI KADDISH

*Leader:*

| | |
|---|---|
| Yit-gadal v'yit-kadash sh'mei rabba, | יִתְגַּדַּל וְיִתְקַדַּשׁ שְׁמֵהּ רַבָּא. |
| b'a'lma di v'ra | בְּעָלְמָא דִּי בְרָא |
| khir'utei | כִרְעוּתֵהּ, |
| v'yam-likh malkhutei | וְיַמְלִיךְ מַלְכוּתֵהּ |
| b'ḥayeikhon u-v'yomeikhon | בְּחַיֵּיכוֹן וּבְיוֹמֵיכוֹן |
| u-v'ḥayei d'khol beit Yisra·el, | וּבְחַיֵּי דְכָל בֵּית יִשְׂרָאֵל, |
| ba·agala u-viz'man kariv, | בַּעֲגָלָא וּבִזְמַן קָרִיב, |
| v'imru, Amen. | וְאִמְרוּ אָמֵן. |

*Congregation and Leader:*

| | |
|---|---|
| Y'hei sh'mei rabba m'va-rakh, | יְהֵא שְׁמֵהּ רַבָּא מְבָרַךְ |
| l'alam ul'al'mei al'maya, | לְעָלַם וּלְעָלְמֵי עָלְמַיָּא. |

*Leader:*

| | |
|---|---|
| Yitbarakh v'yishtabaḥ | יִתְבָּרַךְ וְיִשְׁתַּבַּח |
| v'yitpa·ar v'yitromam v'yitnasei | וְיִתְפָּאַר וְיִתְרוֹמַם וְיִתְנַשֵּׂא |
| v'yit-hadar v'yit·aleh v'yit-halal | וְיִתְהַדָּר וְיִתְעַלֶּה וְיִתְהַלָּל |
| sh'mei d'kud'sha, b'rikh Hu, | שְׁמֵהּ דְּקֻדְשָׁא בְּרִיךְ הוּא, |
| L'eila [u-l'eila mi-kol] | לְעֵלָּא (וּלְעֵלָּא מִכָּל) |
| min kol birkhata v'shirata | מִן כָּל בִּרְכָתָא וְשִׁירָתָא |
| tushb'ḥata v'neḥemata | תֻּשְׁבְּחָתָא וְנֶחֱמָתָא, |
| da·amiran b'al'ma, | דַּאֲמִירָן בְּעָלְמָא, |
| v'imru Amen. | וְאִמְרוּ אָמֵן. |

## ḤATZI KADDISH

May God's great name be made great and holy in the world that God created according to God's will. May God establish the Divine kingdom soon, in our days, quickly and in the near future, and let us say, Amen.

*Congregation and Leader together:*

May God's great name be praised for ever and ever.

Blessed, praised, glorified and raised high, honored and elevated be the name of the Holy Blessed One, far beyond all blessings and songs, praises and comforts which people can say, and let us say: Amen.

# Musaf Amidah

***An additional service, where we recall the added sacrifice for Shabbat in the Temple of old.***

*Before starting, we take three steps backward, leaving our earthly realm, and three steps forward, entering the Presence of God. As we recite the words Adonai, s'fatai tiftaḥ "Adonai, open my lips," we walk three steps forward to enter God's presence. Then at the beginning and end of the first blessing, bend your knees at "Barukh," bend over from your waist at "atah," and straighten up at "Adonai."*

| | |
|---|---|
| Ki sheim Adonai ekra, | כִּי שֵׁם יְיָ אֶקְרָא, |
| havu godel lEiloheinu. | הָבוּ גֹדֶל לֵאלֹהֵינוּ. |
| Adonai, s'fatai tiftaḥ, | אֲדֹנָי שְׂפָתַי תִּפְתָּח |
| u-fi yagid tihilatekha. | וּפִי יַגִּיד תְּהִלָּתֶךָ |

## AVOT

*God of our Ancestors*

| | |
|---|---|
| Barukh Atah Adonai | בָּרוּךְ אַתָּה יְיָ |
| Eloheinu vEilohei avoteinu, | אֱלֹהֵינוּ וֵאלֹהֵי אֲבוֹתֵינוּ, |
| Elohei Avraham, | אֱלֹהֵי אַבְרָהָם, |
| Elohei Yitzhak | אֱלֹהֵי יִצְחָק, |
| vEilohei Ya'akov, | וֵאלֹהֵי יַעֲקֹב, |
| [Elohei Sarah, Elohei Rivkah, | (אֱלֹהֵי שָׂרָה, אֱלֹהֵי רִבְקָה, |
| Elohei Raḥel vEilohei Le·ah] | אֱלֹהֵי רָחֵל, וֵאלֹהֵי לֵאָה,) |
| ha-Eil ha-gadol ha-gibor v'ha-nora | הָאֵל הַגָּדוֹל הַגִּבּוֹר וְהַנּוֹרָא, |
| Eil elyon, | אֵל עֶלְיוֹן, |
| gomeil ḥasadim tovim | גּוֹמֵל חֲסָדִים טוֹבִים, |
| v'koneih hakol | וְקֹנֵה הַכֹּל, |
| v'zokheir ḥasdei avot, | וְזוֹכֵר חַסְדֵי אָבוֹת, |
| u-meivi go·eil | וּמֵבִיא גוֹאֵל |
| liv'nei v'neihem | לִבְנֵי בְנֵיהֶם, |
| l'ma·an sh'mo b'ahavah. | לְמַעַן שְׁמוֹ בְּאַהֲבָה. |

*On Shabbat Shuvah, the Shabbat between Rosh Hashanah and Yom Kippur:*

| | |
|---|---|
| Zokhreinu l'ḥayyim, melekh ḥafeitz | זָכְרֵנוּ לְחַיִּים, מֶלֶךְ חָפֵץ |
| ba-ḥayyim, | בַּחַיִּים, |
| v'khotveinu b'seifer ha-ḥayyim, | וְכָתְבֵנוּ בְּסֵפֶר הַחַיִּים, |
| l'ma·ankha Elohim ḥayyim. | לְמַעַנְךָ אֱלֹהִים חַיִּים. |

# Musaf Amidah

## *An additional service, where we recall the added sacrifice for Shabbat in the Temple of old.*

*Before starting, we take three steps backward, leaving our earthly realm, and three steps forward, entering the Presence of God. As we recite the words Adonai, s'fatai tiftaḥ "Adonai, open my lips," we walk three steps forward to enter God's presence. Then at the beginning and end of the first blessing, bend your knees at "Barukh," bend over from your waist at "atah," and straighten up at "Adonai."*

When I call God's name, acknowledge our God's greatness. God, open my lips so that my mouth may speak your praise.

### AVOT

### *God of our Ancestors*

Praised are You, Adonai our God and God of our ancestors, God of Abraham, God of Isaac, and God of Jacob, [God of Sarah, God of Rebecca, God of Rachel and God of Leah], the great, strong and awe-inspiring God, God on high. You act with lovingkindness and create everything. God remembers the loving deeds of our ancestors, and will bring a redeemer to their children's children because that is God's loving nature.

*On Shabbat Shuvah, the Shabbat between Rosh Hashanah and Yom Kippur:*

Remember us for life, Ruler who wants life, and write us in the Book of Life, for Your sake, living God.

> Although the Musaf Amidah is different for Shabbat, Festivals, and Rosh Ḥodesh, the parts we chant out loud are virtually the same. The only difference is two lines added to the K'dushah on the Pilgrimage Festivals.

| | |
|---|---|
| Melekh ozeir u-moshi·a u-magein. | מֶלֶךְ עוֹזֵר וּמוֹשִׁיעַ וּמָגֵן. |
| Barukh Atah Adonai | בָּרוּךְ אַתָּה יְיָ, |
| magein Avraham [u-fokeid Sarah]. | מָגֵן אַבְרָהָם. (וּפֹקֵד שָׂרָה) |

## G'VUROT

### *God's benevolent power*

| | |
|---|---|
| Atah gibor l'olam Adonai, | אַתָּה גִּבּוֹר לְעוֹלָם אֲדֹנָי, |
| m'ḥayeih meitim Atah, | מְחַיֵּה מֵתִים אַתָּה, |
| rav l'hoshi·a. | רַב לְהוֹשִׁיעַ. |

*From Sh'mini Atzeret until Pesaḥ, we pray for rain:*

| | |
|---|---|
| mashiv haru·aḥ u-morid ha-gashem | מַשִּׁיב הָרוּחַ וּמוֹרִיד הַגֶּשֶׁם. |

| | |
|---|---|
| M'khalkeil ḥayim b'ḥesed, | מְכַלְכֵּל חַיִּים בְּחֶסֶד, |
| m'ḥayei meitim b'raḥamim rabim, | מְחַיֵּה מֵתִים בְּרַחֲמִים רַבִּים, |
| someikh nof'lim | סוֹמֵךְ נוֹפְלִים, |
| v'rofei ḥolim | וְרוֹפֵא חוֹלִים, |
| u-matir asurim, | וּמַתִּיר אֲסוּרִים, |
| um'kayeim emunato | וּמְקַיֵּם אֱמוּנָתוֹ |
| lisheinei afar. | לִישֵׁנֵי עָפָר, |
| Mi khamokha, ba·al g'vurot | מִי כָמְוֹךָ בַּעַל גְּבוּרוֹת |
| u-mi domeh lakh, | וּמִי דּוֹמֶה לָּךְ, |
| Melekh meimit um'ḥayeih | מֶלֶךְ מֵמִית וּמְחַיֶּה |
| u-matzmi·aḥ y'shu·a. | וּמַצְמְיחַ יְשׁוּעָה. |

*On Shabbat Shuvah, the Shabbat between Rosh Hashanah and Yom Kippur:*

| | |
|---|---|
| Mi khamokha Av ha-rahamim, | מִי כָמְוֹךָ אַב הָרַחֲמִים, |
| zokeir y'tzurav l'hayyim b'rachamim. | זוֹכֵר יְצוּרָיו לְחַיִּים בְּרַחֲמִים. |

| | |
|---|---|
| v'ne·eman Atah | וְנֶאֱמָן אַתָּה |
| l'haḥayot meitim. | לְהַחֲיוֹת מֵתִים. |
| Barukh Atah Adonai, | בָּרוּךְ אַתָּה יְיָ, |
| m'ḥayeih ha-meitim. | מְחַיֵּה הַמֵּתִים. |

You are a helping, saving and shielding Ruler. Praised are You, Adonai, Shield of Abraham.

## G'VUROT

***God's benevolent power***

You are mighty forever, Adonai, giving life to the dead with Your great saving power.

*From Sh'mini Atzeret until Pesaḥ, we pray for rain:*

You cause the wind to blow and the rain to fall.

You support the living with kindness, you give life to the dead with great mercy. You support the fallen, heal the sick and set free those in prison. You keep faith with those who sleep in the dust. Who is like You, Sovereign of mighty deeds, and who can compare to You, Ruler of life and death who causes salvation to bloom.

*On Shabbat Shuvah, the Shabbat between Rosh Hashanah and Yom Kippur:*

Who is like you, Merciful Parent? You remember those You created with the merciful gift of life.

You are trustworthy in giving life to the dead. Praised are You, who gives life to the dead.

## K'DUSHAH

נַעֲרִיצְךָ וְנַקְדִּישְׁךָ,
כְּסוֹד שִׂיחַ
שַׂרְפֵי קֹדֶשׁ
הַמַּקְדִּישִׁים שִׁמְךָ בַּקֹּדֶשׁ,
כַּכָּתוּב עַל יַד נְבִיאֶךָ,
וְקָרָא זֶה אֶל זֶה וְאָמַר:

Na·aritz'kha v'nakdish'kha
k'sod si·aḥ
sarfei kodesh
hamakdishim shimkha ba-kodesh,
kakatuv al yad n'vi·ekha,
v'kara zeh el zeh v'amar.

*קָדוֹשׁ, קָדוֹשׁ, קָדוֹשׁ,
יְיָ צְבָאוֹת,
מְלֹא כָל הָאָרֶץ כְּבוֹדוֹ.

*Kadosh kadosh kadosh
Adonai tz'va·ot,
m'lo khol ha-aretz k'vodo.

כְּבוֹדוֹ מָלֵא עוֹלָם,
מְשָׁרְתָיו שׁוֹאֲלִים זֶה לָזֶה,
אַיֵּה מְקוֹם כְּבוֹדוֹ,
לְעֻמָּתָם בָּרוּךְ יֹאמֵרוּ:

K'vodo malei olam,
m'shar'tav sho·alim zeh lazeh,
ayeih m'kom k'vodo.
L'umatam barukh yo·meiru.

*בָּרוּךְ כְּבוֹד יְיָ מִמְּקוֹמוֹ.
מִמְּקוֹמוֹ הוּא יִפֶן בְּרַחֲמִים,
וְיָחֹן עַם
הַמְיַחֲדִים שְׁמוֹ
עֶרֶב וָבֹקֶר בְּכָל יוֹם תָּמִיד,
פַּעֲמַיִם בְּאַהֲבָה שְׁמַע אוֹמְרִים:

*Barukh k'vod Adonai mim'komo.
Mimkomo Hu yifen b'raḥamim,
v'yaḥon am
ha-m'yaḥadim sh'mo
erev va-voker b'khol-yom tamid
pa·amayim b'ahavah sh'ma omrim.

*שְׁמַע יִשְׂרָאֵל,
יְיָ אֱלֹהֵינוּ, יְיָ אֶחָד.

*Sh'ma Yisra·el
Adonai Eloheinu Adonai eḥad.

## K'DUSHAH

We revere and sanctify You on earth using the mystic speech of the holy seraphim who sanctify Your name in the Sanctuary. As is written by Your prophet, "They called one to another, saying:

Holy, Holy, Holy, Adonai of the heavenly Hosts, the whole world is filled with God's glorious presence."

God's glorious presence fills the world, his servants ask each other, "Where is the place of God's glory?" Those facing them say, "Blessed":

"Blessed is Adonai's glory from its place."

From God's place God will turn with mercy, and deal graciously with the people who proclaim the Oneness of the Name, evening and morning, twice every day, perpetually reciting the Shema with love:

Listen, O Israel, Adonai is your God, Adonai is One.

**K'dushah Kavanah:** The great Rav Abraham Isaac Kook once taught: It is really holiness when you are able to lift yourself to the point where all of your efforts are no longer directed at your own needs, but toward the glory of God.

**K'dushah Kavanah:** What evidence do you see of God's bringing redemption? You might consider two hopeful events in your own or the world's life which suggest that redemption could be on the way. (*On Wings of Light*, Richard Levy)

***K'dushah:*** In this version of the Kedushah, the mystical, visionary element is very clear. It is rich in imagery of heavenly beings: angels and seraphim. Seraphim are mentioned in the Bible as part of Isaiah's vision in the Temple. The idea is that there is a heavenly chorus above, singing God's praises. We below also raise our voices in praise of God. The effect is of a "cast of thousands," above and below, united in song. We are taught that God prefers our efforts, because angels are "programmed" to praise God, while we have a choice. Even if you don't believe in angels, think of this moment as one of great holiness, where we are trying to raise our consciousness toward God. We express that yearning to experience God's *kavod*, God's glorious presence, by rising up on our toes for each "Kadosh."

| | |
|---|---|
| Hu Eloheinu Hu Avinu | הוּא אֱלֹהֵינוּ, הוּא אָבִינוּ, |
| Hu Malkeinu Hu Moshi·einu, | הוּא מַלְכֵּנוּ, הוּא מוֹשִׁיעֵנוּ, |
| v'Hu yashmi·einu b'raḥamav | וְהוּא יַשְׁמִיעֵנוּ בְּרַחֲמָיו |
| sheinit l'einei kol ḥai, | שֵׁנִית לְעֵינֵי כָּל חָי, |
| lih'yot lakhem leilohim. | לִהְיוֹת לָכֶם לֵאלֹהִים, |
| *Ani Adonai Eloheikhem. | *אֲנִי יְיָ אֱלֹהֵיכֶם. |
| *Festivals only:* Adir adireinu | אַדִּיר אַדִּירֵנוּ, |
| Adonai Adoneinu, | יְיָ אֲדֹנֵינוּ, |
| ma adir shimkha b'khol ha-aretz. | מָה אַדִּיר שִׁמְךָ בְּכָל הָאָרֶץ. |
| v'hayah Adonai | וְהָיָה יְיָ |
| l'Melekh al kol ha-aretz, | לְמֶלֶךְ עַל כָּל הָאָרֶץ, |
| ba-yom hahu | בַּיּוֹם הַהוּא |
| yih'yeh Adonai eḥad | יִהְיֶה יְיָ אֶחָד |
| u-sh'mo eḥad. | וּשְׁמוֹ אֶחָד. |
| Uv'divrei kodsh'kha katuv leimor: | וּבְדִבְרֵי קָדְשְׁךָ כָּתוּב לֵאמֹר: |
| *Yimlokh Adonai l'olam, | *יִמְלוֹךְ יְיָ לְעוֹלָם, |
| Elohayikh tziyon | אֱלֹהַיִךְ צִיּוֹן, |
| l'dor va-dor. Hal'luyah. | לְדֹר וָדֹר, הַלְלוּיָהּ. |
| L'dor va-dor nagid godlekha | לְדוֹר וָדוֹר נַגִּיד גָּדְלֶךָ, |
| u-l'netzaḥ n'tzaḥim | וּלְנֵצַח נְצָחִים |
| k'dushat'kha nakdish. | קְדֻשָּׁתְךָ נַקְדִּישׁ, |
| v'shivḥa'kha Eloheinu | וְשִׁבְחֲךָ, אֱלֹהֵינוּ, |
| mi-pinu lo yamush | מִפִּינוּ לֹא יָמוּשׁ |
| l'olam va·ed. | לְעוֹלָם וָעֶד, |
| Ki Eil | כִּי אֵל |
| Melekh gadol v'kadosh Atah. | מֶלֶךְ גָּדוֹל וְקָדוֹשׁ אָתָּה. |
| Barukh Atah Adonai, | בָּרוּךְ אַתָּה יְיָ, |
| he-Eil ha-kadosh. | הָאֵל הַקָּדוֹשׁ. |

*Between Rosh Hashanah and Yom Kippur:*

| | |
|---|---|
| Barukh atah Adonai, | בָּרוּךְ אַתָּה יְיָ, |
| ha-Melekh ha-kadosh. | הַמֶּלֶךְ הַקָּדוֹשׁ. |

*On Shabbat, continue on the next page. On Festivals, including those that fall on Shabbat, continue on page 148.*

This is our God, our Parent, our Ruler, our Redeemer, the One who will cause us to hear again in the presence of all who live, God's commitment to be our God:

"I am Adonai your God!"

And in Your holy words it is written:

May God rule forever, your God, O Zion, for all generations to come.

For all generations to come we will tell of Your greatness, and forever and ever we will sanctify You, and praise of You, our God, will never depart from our mouths forever and ever, for You are a sovereign, great and holy God. Praised are You Adonai, the holy God.

*Between Rosh Hashanah and Yom Kippur:*

Praised are You, Adonai, the holy Ruler.

*On Shabbat, continue on the next page. On Festivals, including those that fall on Shabbat, continue on page 149.*

## K'DUSHAT HAYOM

### *Sanctification of the Day*

תִּכַּֽנְתָּ שַׁבָּת, רָצִֽיתָ קָרְבְּנוֹתֶֽיהָ, צִוִּֽיתָ פֵּרוּשֶֽׁיהָ עִם סִדּוּרֵי נְסָכֶֽיהָ.

מְעַנְּגֶֽיהָ לְעוֹלָם כָּבוֹד יִנְחָֽלוּ, טוֹעֲמֶֽיהָ חַיִּים זָכוּ, וְגַם הָאוֹהֲבִים דְּבָרֶֽיהָ גְּדֻלָּה בָּחָֽרוּ, אָז מִסִּינַי נִצְטַוּוּ עָלֶֽיהָ.

וַתְּצַוֵּֽנוּ, יְיָ אֱלֹהֵֽינוּ, לְהַקְרִיב בָּהּ קָרְבַּן מוּסַף שַׁבָּת כָּרָאוּי. יְהִי רָצוֹן מִלְּפָנֶֽיךָ, יְיָ אֱלֹהֵֽינוּ וֵאלֹהֵי אֲבוֹתֵֽינוּ, שֶׁתַּעֲלֵֽנוּ בְשִׂמְחָה לְאַרְצֵֽנוּ, וְתִטָּעֵֽנוּ בִּגְבוּלֵֽנוּ, וְשָׁם נַעֲשֶׂה לְפָנֶֽיךָ אֶת קָרְבְּנוֹת חוֹבוֹתֵֽינוּ, תְּמִידִים כְּסִדְרָם וּמוּסָפִים כְּהִלְכָתָם.

וְאֶת מוּסַף יוֹם הַשַּׁבָּת הַזֶּה, נַעֲשֶׂה וְנַקְרִיב לְפָנֶֽיךָ בְּאַהֲבָה, כְּמִצְוַת רְצוֹנֶֽךָ, כְּמוֹ שֶׁכָּתַֽבְתָּ עָלֵֽינוּ בְּתוֹרָתֶֽךָ, עַל יְדֵי מֹשֶׁה עַבְדֶּֽךָ, מִפִּי כְבוֹדֶֽךָ, כָּאָמוּר:

*Some congregations leave these words out, because they deal with the details of the sacrifices:*

וּבְיוֹם הַשַּׁבָּת, שְׁנֵי כְבָשִׂים בְּנֵי שָׁנָה תְּמִימִם, וּשְׁנֵי עֶשְׂרֹנִים סֹלֶת מִנְחָה בְּלוּלָה בַשֶּֽׁמֶן וְנִסְכּוֹ. עֹלַת שַׁבַּת בְּשַׁבַּתּוֹ, עַל עֹלַת הַתָּמִיד וְנִסְכָּהּ.

## K'DUSHAT HAYOM

### *Sanctification of the Day*

You established the Shabbat, accepted its sacrifices, commanded its special duties with its offerings. Those who delight in the Shabbat will always be honored. Those who taste Shabbat will merit life. Those who love its teachings have chosen greatness. At Sinai our ancestors were commanded about Shabbat, and You told them, Adonai our God, to offer an additional sacrifice on Shabbat. May it be Your will, Adonai our God and God of our ancestors, that you will return Your children to the borders of their land, bringing us up with joy to our land and planting us within our borders. For it was there that our ancestors presented the sacrifices to You: the daily offerings in proper order and the additional sacrifices as the law requires. There we will worship You with love and awe as in the days of old in former times. This additional sacrifice for Shabbat they offered to You with love, according to Your mitzvah, as is written in Your Torah, by Moses Your servant according to Your glory, saying:

*Some congregations leave these words out, because they deal with the details of the sacrifices:*

On the Shabbat day, two perfect year-old lambs, and two-tenths of an ephah of fine flour mixed with oil, and the proper drink-offering. A burnt-offering for the Shabbat in addition to the daily burnt-offering and its drink-offering. (Numbers 28:9–10)

> We tend not to think much about the sacrifices, and many people find them distasteful, but remember one thing: in Bible times, flocks and herds were an important measure of wealth. Our ancestors brought to the altar the finest of their possessions. What do we bring of ourselves to our worship? What does it mean to dedicate the best we have to God? What are we willing to sacrifice to make Shabbat a part of our lives?

| | |
|---|---|
| Melech rachaman | מֶֽלֶךְ רַחֲמָן רַחֵם עָלֵֽינוּ |
| | |
| Yism'ḥu b'mal'khut'kha | יִשְׂמְחוּ בְמַלְכוּתְךָ |
| shomrei Shabbat v'kor·ei oneg, | שׁוֹמְרֵי שַׁבָּת וְקוֹרְאֵי עֹֽנֶג, |
| am m'kad'shei sh'vi·i, | עַם מְקַדְּשֵׁי שְׁבִיעִי, |
| kulam yisb'u | כֻּלָּם יִשְׂבְּעוּ |
| v'yitangu mi-tuvekha, | וְיִתְעַנְּגוּ מִטּוּבֶֽךָ, |
| u-vash'vi·i ratzita bo, | וּבַשְּׁבִיעִי רָצִֽיתָ בּוֹ |
| v'kidashto, | וְקִדַּשְׁתּוֹ, |
| ḥemdat yamim oto karata, | חֶמְדַּת יָמִים אוֹתוֹ קָרָֽאתָ, |
| zeikher l'ma·asei v'reishit. | זֵֽכֶר לְמַעֲשֵׂה בְרֵאשִׁית. |
| | |
| Eloheinu vEilohei avoteinu, | אֱלֹהֵֽינוּ וֵאלֹהֵי אֲבוֹתֵֽינוּ, |
| r'tzei vim'nuḥateinu. | רְצֵה בִמְנוּחָתֵֽנוּ, |
| Kad'sheinu b'mitz-votekha | קַדְּשֵֽׁנוּ בְּמִצְוֹתֶֽיךָ, |
| v'tein ḥelkeinu b'Toratekha, | וְתֵן חֶלְקֵֽנוּ בְּתוֹרָתֶֽךָ, |
| sab'einu mi-tuvekha | שַׂבְּעֵֽנוּ מִטּוּבֶֽךָ, |
| v'samḥeinu bishu·atekha, | וְשַׂמְּחֵֽנוּ בִּישׁוּעָתֶֽךָ, |
| v'taheir libeinu l'ov-d'kha be·emet. | וְטַהֵר לִבֵּֽנוּ לְעָבְדְּךָ בֶּאֱמֶת, |
| v'hanḥileinu | וְהַנְחִילֵֽנוּ |
| Adonai Eloheinu | יְיָ אֱלֹהֵֽינוּ |
| b'ahavah uv'ratzon | בְּאַהֲבָה וּבְרָצוֹן |
| Shabbat kod-shekha. | שַׁבַּת קָדְשֶֽׁךָ, |
| v'yanuḥu vo Yisra·el | וְיָנֽוּחוּ בוֹ יִשְׂרָאֵל |
| m'kad'shei sh'mekha. | מְקַדְּשֵׁי שְׁמֶֽךָ. |
| Barukh Atah Adonai, | בָּרוּךְ אַתָּה יְיָ, |
| m'kadeish ha-Shabbat. | מְקַדֵּשׁ הַשַּׁבָּת. |

*Continue with Avodah on page 150.*

Merciful Ruler, accept with mercy the prayer of Your people Israel wherever they live.

Those who keep the Shabbat will be happy with Your rule, calling it a delight. The people who make the seventh day holy, will all be satisfied and delighted with Your goodness. For You were pleased with the seventh day and made it holy, calling it the most delightful of days, a reminder of Creation.

Our God and God of our ancestors, be pleased with our Shabbat rest, make us holy with Your mitzvot and let us share in Your Torah. Satisfy us with Your goodness and make us happy with Your help. Purify our hearts so that we can serve you truly. Adonai our God, let us receive Your holy Shabbat with love and favor, so that Your people Israel who make Your name holy will rest on it. Praised are You Adonai, who makes the Shabbat holy.

*Continue with Avodah on page 151.*

# Musaf Amidah for Festivals

## K'DUSHAT HAYOM

*Sanctification of the Day*

אַתָּה בְחַרְתָּנוּ מִכָּל הָעַמִּים, אָהַבְתָּ אוֹתָנוּ וְרָצִיתָ בָּנוּ, וְרוֹמַמְתָּנוּ מִכָּל הַלְּשׁוֹנוֹת, וְקִדַּשְׁתָּנוּ בְּמִצְוֹתֶיךָ, וְקֵרַבְתָּנוּ מַלְכֵּנוּ לַעֲבוֹדָתֶךָ, וְשִׁמְךָ הַגָּדוֹל וְהַקָּדוֹשׁ עָלֵינוּ קָרָאתָ.

וַתִּתֶּן לָנוּ יְיָ אֱלֹהֵינוּ בְּאַהֲבָה (שַׁבָּתוֹת לִמְנוּחָה וּ) מוֹעֲדִים לְשִׂמְחָה, חַגִּים וּזְמַנִּים לְשָׂשׂוֹן, אֶת יוֹם (הַשַּׁבָּת הַזֶּה וְאֶת יוֹם)

*On Pesaḥ:*

חַג הַמַּצּוֹת הַזֶּה, זְמַן חֵרוּתֵנוּ

*On Shavuot:*

חַג הַשָּׁבֻעוֹת הַזֶּה,זְמַן מַתַּן תּוֹרָתֵנוּ

*On Sukkot:*

חַג הַסֻּכּוֹת הַזֶּה, זְמַן שִׂמְחָתֵנוּ

*On Sh'mini Atzeret and Simchat Torah:*

הַשְּׁמִינִי חַג הָעֲצֶרֶת הַזֶּה, זְמַן זְמַן שִׂמְחָתֵנוּ
(בְּאַהֲבָה) מִקְרָא קֹדֶשׁ, זֵכֶר לִיצִיאַת מִצְרָיִם.

*On Shabbat add:*

| | |
|---|---|
| Yism'ḥu b'mal'khut'kha | יִשְׂמְחוּ בְמַלְכוּתְךָ |
| shom'rei Shabbat v'kor·ei oneg, | שׁוֹמְרֵי שַׁבָּת וְקוֹרְאֵי עֹנֶג, |
| am m'kad'shei she'vi·i, | עַם מְקַדְּשֵׁי שְׁבִיעִי, |
| kulam yisb'u | כֻּלָּם יִשְׂבְּעוּ |
| v'yitangu mi-tuvekha, | וְיִתְעַנְּגוּ מִטּוּבֶךָ, |
| u-vash'vi·i ratzi bo, v'kidashto, | וּבַשְּׁבִיעִי רָצִיתָ בּוֹ וְקִדַּשְׁתּוֹ, |
| ḥemdat yamim oto karata, | חֶמְדַּת יָמִים אוֹתוֹ קָרָאתָ, |
| zekher l'ma·asei v'reishit. | זֵכֶר לְמַעֲשֵׂה בְרֵאשִׁית. |

וְהַשִּׂיאֵנוּ, יְיָ אֱלֹהֵינוּ, אֶת בִּרְכַּת מוֹעֲדֶיךָ, לְחַיִּים וּלְשָׁלוֹם, לְשִׂמְחָה וּלְשָׂשׂוֹן, כַּאֲשֶׁר רָצִיתָ וְאָמַרְתָּ לְבָרְכֵנוּ. (לשבת אֱלֹהֵינוּ וֵאלֹהֵי אֲבוֹתֵינוּ, רְצֵה

# Musaf Amidah for Festivals

## K'DUSHAT HAYOM

*Sanctification of the Day*

You chose us from all the nations. You loved us and were pleased with us, and you lifted us up from among all peoples by making us holy with Your mitzvot and by bringing us close to You to serve You. We are called by Your great and holy Name. Adonai our God, You lovingly gave us [Shabbatot for rest, and] holidays for joy, festivals and special times for rejoicing, this [Shabbat and this]

*On Pesaḥ:*
Festival of Matzot, the time when we became free,

*On Shavuot:*
Festival of Shavuot Festival of Shavuot, the time of the giving of the Torah,

*On Sukkot:*
Festival of Sukkot, our time to rejoice

*On Sh'mini Atzeret and Simchat Torah:*
Festival of Sh'mini Atzeret, our time to rejoice,
a holy day, a reminder of the Exodus from Egypt.

*On Shabbat add:*

Those who keep the Shabbat will be happy with Your rule, calling it a delight. The people who make the seventh day holy will all be satisfied and delighted with Your goodness. For You were pleased with the seventh day and made it holy, calling it the most delightful of days, a reminder of Creation.

Adonai our God, give us the blessing of Your Festivals for life and peace, for joy and happiness, as You have promised us You would bless us. Our God and God of our ancestors, [be pleased with our Shabbat rest,] make us holy with Your mitzvot and

בִּמְנוּחָתֵֽנוּ,) קַדְּשֵֽׁנוּ בְּמִצְוֹתֶֽיךָ, וְתֵן חֶלְקֵֽנוּ בְּתוֹרָתֶֽךָ, שַׂבְּעֵֽנוּ מִטּוּבֶֽךָ, וְשַׂמְּחֵֽנוּ בִּישׁוּעָתֶֽךָ, וְטַהֵר לִבֵּֽנוּ לְעָבְדְּךָ בֶּאֱמֶת, וְהַנְחִילֵֽנוּ יְיָ אֱלֹהֵֽינוּ (לשבת בְּאַהֲבָה וּבְרָצוֹן) בְּשִׂמְחָה וּבְשָׂשׂוֹן (לשבת שַׁבָּת וּ)מוֹעֲדֵי קָדְשֶֽׁךָ, וְיִשְׂמְחוּ בְךָ יִשְׂרָאֵל מְקַדְּשֵׁי שְׁמֶֽךָ. בָּרוּךְ אַתָּה יְיָ, מְקַדֵּשׁ (לשבת הַשַּׁבָּת וְ)יִשְׂרָאֵל וְהַזְּמַנִּים.

## AVODAH

### *Accept our Prayer*

| | |
|---|---|
| R'tzeih Adonai Eloheinu | רְצֵה, יְיָ אֱלֹהֵֽינוּ, |
| b'amkha Yisra·el u-vit'filatam, | בְּעַמְּךָ יִשְׂרָאֵל וּבִתְפִלָּתָם, |
| v'hasheiv et ha-avodah | וְהָשֵׁב אֶת הָעֲבוֹדָה |
| li-d'vir beitekha, | לִדְבִיר בֵּיתֶֽךָ, |
| v'ishai Yisra·el | וְאִשֵּׁי יִשְׂרָאֵל, |
| u-t'filatam b'ahavah | וּתְפִלָּתָם בְּאַהֲבָה |
| t'kabeil b'ratzon. | תְקַבֵּל בְּרָצוֹן, |
| U-t'hi l'ratzon tamid | וּתְהִי לְרָצוֹן תָּמִיד |
| avodat Yisra·el amekha. | עֲבוֹדַת יִשְׂרָאֵל עַמֶּֽךָ. |
| v'teḥezenah eineinu | וְתֶחֱזֶֽינָה עֵינֵֽינוּ |
| b'shuv'kha l'Tziyon b'raḥamim. | בְּשׁוּבְךָ לְצִיּוֹן בְּרַחֲמִים. |
| Barukh Atah Adonai | בָּרוּךְ אַתָּה יְיָ, |
| ha-maḥazir sh'khinato l'Tziyon. | הַמַּחֲזִיר שְׁכִינָתוֹ לְצִיּוֹן. |

## MODIM

### *Thank You, God.*

*We bow, bending the knee at "modim," bowing from the waist at "anaḥnu," and standing straight again at "lakh."*

מוֹדִים אֲנַֽחְנוּ לָךְ, שָׁאַתָּה הוּא, יְיָ אֱלֹהֵֽינוּ וֵאלֹהֵי אֲבוֹתֵֽינוּ, לְעוֹלָם וָעֶד, צוּר חַיֵּֽינוּ, מָגֵן יִשְׁעֵֽנוּ, אַתָּה הוּא לְדוֹר וָדוֹר, נוֹדֶה לְּךָ וּנְסַפֵּר תְּהִלָּתֶֽךָ, עַל חַיֵּֽינוּ הַמְּסוּרִים בְּיָדֶֽךָ, וְעַל נִשְׁמוֹתֵֽינוּ הַפְּקוּדוֹת לָךְ, וְעַל נִסֶּֽיךָ שֶׁבְּכָל יוֹם עִמָּֽנוּ, וְעַל נִפְלְאוֹתֶֽיךָ וְטוֹבוֹתֶֽיךָ שֶׁבְּכָל עֵת, עֶֽרֶב וָבֹֽקֶר וְצָהֳרָֽיִם, הַטּוֹב, כִּי לֹא כָלוּ רַחֲמֶֽיךָ, וְהַמְרַחֵם, כִּי לֹא תַֽמּוּ חֲסָדֶֽיךָ, מֵעוֹלָם קִוִּֽינוּ לָךְ

וְעַל כֻּלָּם יִתְבָּרַךְ וְיִתְרוֹמַם שִׁמְךָ מַלְכֵּֽנוּ תָּמִיד לְעוֹלָם וָעֶד.

let Torah be Your gift to us, fill us up with Your goodness and make us happy by saving us. Make our hearts pure so that we can truly serve You. Adonai our God, [lovingly and willingly,] joyfully and happily give us Your gift of [Shabbat and] your holy days, so that Israel who treats Your Name as holy will always rejoice in You. Praised are You, Adonai, who makes [the Shabbat and] Israel and the special times holy.

## AVODAH

### *Accept our Prayer.*

Adonai, be pleased with Your people Israel and with their prayer. Restore worship to Your Temple. May the prayer of Your people Israel always be accepted with love and favor. May we see Your merciful return to Zion. Praised are You, Adonai, who restores Your presence to Zion.

## MODIM

### *Thank You, God.*

*We bow, bending the knee at modim, bowing from the waist at anaḥnu, and standing straight again at lakh.*

We thank You for being our God and God of our ancestors for ever and ever. You are the Rock of our lives and our saving Shield. In every generation we will thank and praise You for our lives which are in Your power, for our souls which are in Your keeping, for Your miracles which are with us every day, and for your wonders and good things that are with us at all times, evening, morning and noon. O Good One, Your mercies have never stopped. O Merciful One, your kindness has never stopped. We have always placed our hope in You.

For all these things, our Ruler, may Your name be blessed and honored forever.

*On Shabbat Shuvah, the Shabbat between Rosh Hashanah and Yom Kippur, add:*

וּכְתוֹב לְחַיִּים טוֹבִים כָּל בְּנֵי בְרִיתֶךָ.

וְכֹל הַחַיִּים יוֹדְוּךָ סֶּלָה, וִיהַלְלוּ אֶת שִׁמְךָ בֶּאֱמֶת, הָאֵל יְשׁוּעָתֵנוּ וְעֶזְרָתֵנוּ סֶלָה.

*We bow again, bending the knee at barukh, bowing from the waist at atah, and standing straight again at Adonai.*

בָּרוּךְ אַתָּה יְיָ, הַטּוֹב שִׁמְךָ וּלְךָ נָאֶה לְהוֹדוֹת.

*When the Amidah is recited aloud. Leader:*

אֱלֹהֵינוּ וֵאלֹהֵי אֲבוֹתֵינוּ, בָּרְכֵנוּ בַבְּרָכָה הַמְשֻׁלֶּשֶׁת בַּתּוֹרָה הַכְּתוּבָה עַל יְדֵי מֹשֶׁה עַבְדֶּךָ, הָאֲמוּרָה מִפִּי אַהֲרֹן וּבָנָיו כֹּהֲנִים, עַם קְדוֹשֶׁךָ, כָּאָמוּר

יְבָרֶכְךָ יְיָ וְיִשְׁמְרֶךָ. (כֵּן יְהִי רָצוֹן)
Y'varekh'kha Adonai v'Yishm'rekha (Kein y'hi ratzon)

יָאֵר יְיָ פָּנָיו אֵלֶיךָ וִיחֻנֶּךָּ. (כֵּן יְהִי רָצוֹן)
Ya·eir Adonai panav eilekha vikhuneka. (Kein y'hi ratzon)

יִשָּׂא יְיָ פָּנָיו אֵלֶיךָ וְיָשֵׂם לְךָ שָׁלוֹם. (כֵּן יְהִי רָצוֹן)
Yisa Adonai panav eilekha v'yaseim l'kha shalom. (Kein y'hi ratzon)

*On Shabbat Shuvah, the Shabbat between Rosh Hashanah and Yom Kippur, add:*

Write us down for a good life.

May every living thing thank You and praise You sincerely, O God, our rescue and help.

*We bow again, bending the knee at barukh, bowing from the waist at atah, and standing straight again at Adonai.*

Praised are You, Your Name is "the Good One," and it is good to thank You.

*When the Amidah is recited aloud. Leader:*

Our God and God of our ancestors, bless us with the three part blessing of the Torah, written by Your servant Moses, spoken by Aaron and his sons the Kohanim, and Your holy people, as it is said:

| *Leader:* | *Congregation:* |
|---|---|
| May Adonai bless You and protect You. | So may it be God's will. |
| May Adonai show you favor and be gracious to you. | So may it be God's will. |
| May Adonai show you kindness and grant you peace | So may it be God's will. |

## BIRKAT SHALOM

### *The Blessing for Peace*

| | |
|---|---|
| Sim shalom ba-olam, | שִׂים שָׁלוֹם בָּעוֹלָם, |
| tovah uv'rakha, | טוֹבָה וּבְרָכָה, |
| ḥein va-ḥesed v'raḥamim | חֵן וָחֶסֶד וְרַחֲמִים, |
| aleinu v'al kol Yisra·el amekha. | עָלֵינוּ וְעַל כָּל יִשְׂרָאֵל עַמֶּךָ. |
| Bar'kheinu Avinu kulanu k'eḥad | בָּרְכֵנוּ, אָבִינוּ, כֻּלָּנוּ כְּאֶחָד |
| b'or panekha, | בְּאוֹר פָּנֶיךָ, |
| ki v'or panekha | כִּי בְאוֹר פָּנֶיךָ |
| natata lanu, Adonai Eloheinu, | נָתַתָּ לָּנוּ, יְיָ אֱלֹהֵינוּ, |
| Torat ḥayim v'ahavat ḥesed, | תּוֹרַת חַיִּים וְאַהֲבַת חֶסֶד, |
| u-tz'dakah uv'rakha v'raḥamim | וּצְדָקָה וּבְרָכָה וְרַחֲמִים |
| v'ḥayim v'shalom. | וְחַיִּים וְשָׁלוֹם, |
| v'tov b'einekha | וְטוֹב בְּעֵינֶיךָ |
| l'varekh et am'kha Yisra·el | לְבָרֵךְ אֶת עַמְּךָ יִשְׂרָאֵל |
| b'khol eit uv'khol sha·ah | בְּכָל עֵת וּבְכָל שָׁעָה |
| bish'lo-mekha. | בִּשְׁלוֹמֶךָ. |

*On Shabbat Shuvah, the Shabbat between Rosh Hashanah and Yom Kippur, say these words instead of the next paragraph:*

| | |
|---|---|
| B'seifer ḥayyim, b'rakhah v'shalom, | בְּסֵפֶר חַיִּים, בְּרָכָה וְשָׁלוֹם, |
| u-farnasah tovah, n'zakheir | וּפַרְנָסָה טוֹבָה, נִזָּכֵר |
| v'nikateiv l'fanekha, | וְנִכָּתֵב לְפָנֶיךָ, |
| anaḥnu v'khol amkha beit Yisra·el. | אֲנַחְנוּ וְכָל עַמְּךָ בֵּית יִשְׂרָאֵל, |
| L'ḥayyim tovim u-l'shalom. | לְחַיִּים טוֹבִים וּלְשָׁלוֹם. |
| Barukh atah Adonai | בָּרוּךְ אַתָּה יְיָ, |
| oseh ha-shalom. | עוֹשֵׂה הַשָּׁלוֹם. |

| | |
|---|---|
| Barukh Atah Adonai | בָּרוּךְ אַתָּה יְיָ, |
| ha-m'vareikh et amo Yisra·el | הַמְבָרֵךְ אֶת עַמּוֹ יִשְׂרָאֵל |
| ba-shalom. | בַּשָּׁלוֹם. |

## BIRKAT SHALOM

### *The Blessing for Peace*

Make peace in the world, with goodness, blessing, grace, lovingkindness and mercy for us and for all Your people Israel. Bless us, our Parent, all of us together, with Your light, by which You taught us Your Torah of life, love and kindness, justice and mercy, life and peace. May it be good in Your sight to bless Your people Israel at all times with peace.

*On Shabbat Shuvah, the Shabbat between Rosh Hashanah and Yom Kippur, say these words instead of the next paragraph:*

Remember us and write us down in the Book of life, blessing, peace, and support, along with the entire Jewish people, for a good life and for peace. Praised are You, Adonai, who makes peace.

Praised are You, Adonai, who blesses God's people Israel with peace.

**Sim Shalom:** Our Rabbis taught that no prayer is complete without asking for peace, so we end the Amidah, the Kaddish, and the Birkat Ha-mazon with a prayer for peace, which means not only a lack of conflict, but the positive experience of well-being and contentment.

## ELOHAI N'TZOR

***A prayer for self-mastery and purification.***

אֱלֹהַי, נְצוֹר לְשׁוֹנִי מֵרָע, וּשְׂפָתַי מִדַּבֵּר מִרְמָה, וְלִמְקַלְלַי נַפְשִׁי תִדֹּם, וְנַפְשִׁי כֶּעָפָר לַכֹּל תִּהְיֶה. פְּתַח לִבִּי בְּתוֹרָתֶךָ, וּבְמִצְוֹתֶיךָ תִּרְדּוֹף נַפְשִׁי. וְכָל הַחוֹשְׁבִים עָלַי רָעָה, מְהֵרָה הָפֵר עֲצָתָם וְקַלְקֵל מַחֲשַׁבְתָּם. עֲשֵׂה לְמַעַן שְׁמֶךָ, עֲשֵׂה לְמַעַן יְמִינֶךָ, עֲשֵׂה לְמַעַן קְדֻשָּׁתֶךָ, עֲשֵׂה לְמַעַן תּוֹרָתֶךָ. לְמַעַן יֵחָלְצוּן יְדִידֶיךָ, הוֹשִׁיעָה יְמִינְךָ וַעֲנֵנִי. יִהְיוּ לְרָצוֹן אִמְרֵי פִי וְהֶגְיוֹן לִבִּי לְפָנֶיךָ, יְיָ צוּרִי וְגוֹאֲלִי.

*Take three steps back and bow to the left at the word "oseh", to the right at "hu", and to the center at "aleinu".*

| | |
|---|---|
| Oseh shalom bimromav, | עֹשֶׂה שָׁלוֹם בִּמְרוֹמָיו, |
| Hu ya·aseh shalom aleinu | הוּא יַעֲשֶׂה שָׁלוֹם עָלֵינוּ, |
| v'al kol Yisra·el, | וְעַל כָּל יִשְׂרָאֵל, |
| v'imru Amen. | וְאִמְרוּ אָמֵן. |

## ELOHAI N'TZOR

*A prayer for self-mastery and purification.*

My God, help me not to say bad things or to tell lies. Help me to ignore people who say bad things about me. Open my heart to Your Torah, so that I can do Your mitzvot. If anyone wants to do me harm, quickly stop their ideas and spoil their plans. Do this because of Your love, Your holiness, and Your Torah: so that those You love will be free. May the words of my mouth and the thoughts of my heart find favor with You, my Rock and my Savior. May the One who makes peace up above give peace to us and to all the people of Israel. Amen.

## KADDISH SHALEIM

*Leader:*

| | |
|---|---|
| Yit-gadal v'yit-kadash sh'mei rabba, | יִתְגַּדַּל וְיִתְקַדַּשׁ שְׁמֵהּ רַבָּא. |
| b'al'ma di v'ra | בְּעָלְמָא דִּי בְרָא |
| khir'utei | כִרְעוּתֵהּ, |
| v'yam-likh malkhutei | וְיַמְלִיךְ מַלְכוּתֵהּ |
| b'ḥayeikhon u-v'yomeikhon | בְּחַיֵּיכוֹן וּבְיוֹמֵיכוֹן |
| u-v'ḥayei d'khol Yisra·el, | וּבְחַיֵּי דְכָל יִשְׂרָאֵל, |
| ba·agala u-viz'man kariv, | בַּעֲגָלָא וּבִזְמַן קָרִיב, |
| v'imru, Amen. | וְאִמְרוּ אָמֵן. |

*Congregation and Leader:*

| | |
|---|---|
| Y'hei sh'mei rabba m'va-rakh, | יְהֵא שְׁמֵהּ רַבָּא מְבָרַךְ |
| l'alam ul'al'mei al'maya. | לְעָלַם וּלְעָלְמֵי עָלְמַיָּא. |

*Leader:*

| | |
|---|---|
| Yitbarakh v'yishtabaḥ | יִתְבָּרַךְ וְיִשְׁתַּבַּח |
| v'yitpa·ar v'yitromam v'yitnasei | וְיִתְפָּאַר וְיִתְרוֹמַם וְיִתְנַשֵּׂא |
| v'yithadar v'yit·aleh v'yithalal | וְיִתְהַדָּר וְיִתְעַלֶּה וְיִתְהַלָּל |
| sh'mei d'kud'sha, b'rikh Hu. | שְׁמֵהּ דְּקֻדְשָׁא בְּרִיךְ הוּא, |
| L'eila [u-l'eila mi-kol] | לְעֵלָּא (בעשי"ת לְעֵלָּא וּלְעֵלָּא מִכָּל) |
| min kol birkhata v'shirata | מִן כָּל בִּרְכָתָא וְשִׁירָתָא |
| tushb'ḥata v'neḥemata | תֻּשְׁבְּחָתָא וְנֶחֱמָתָא, |
| da·amiran b'al'ma, | דַּאֲמִירָן בְּעָלְמָא, |
| v'imru Amen. | וְאִמְרוּ אָמֵן. |
| Titkabel | תִּתְקַבֵּל |
| tz'lot'hon uva-ut'hon | צְלוֹתְהוֹן וּבָעוּתְהוֹן |
| d'khol Yisra·el | דְּכָל יִשְׂרָאֵל |
| kadam avuhon di vish'maya, | קֳדָם אֲבוּהוֹן דִּי בִשְׁמַיָּא |
| v'imru Amen. | וְאִמְרוּ אָמֵן. |
| Y'hei sh'lama rabbah min shamaya | יְהֵא שְׁלָמָא רַבָּא מִן שְׁמַיָּא, |
| v'ḥayyim | וְחַיִּים |
| aleinu v'al kol Yisra·el, | עָלֵינוּ וְעַל כָּל יִשְׂרָאֵל, |
| v'imru Amen. | וְאִמְרוּ אָמֵן. |

*Take three steps back and bow to the left at the word "oseh", to the right at "hu", and to the center at "aleinu".*

| | |
|---|---|
| Oseh shalom bimromav, | עֹשֶׂה שָׁלוֹם בִּמְרוֹמָיו, |
| Hu ya·aseh shalom | הוּא יַעֲשֶׂה שָׁלוֹם |
| aleinu v'al kol Yisra·el, | עָלֵינוּ וְעַל כָּל יִשְׂרָאֵל, |
| v'imru Amen. | וְאִמְרוּ אָמֵן. |

## KADDISH SHALEIM

*Leader:*

May God's great name be made great and holy in the world which God created according to God's will. May God establish the Divine kingdom soon, in our days, quickly and in the near future, and let us say, Amen.

*Congregation and Leader together:*

May God's great name be praised forever and ever.

Blessed, praised, glorified and raised high, honored and elevated be the name of the Holy Blessed One, far beyond all blessings and songs, praises and comforts which people can say, and let us say: Amen.

May the prayers and pleas of the entire House of Israel be accepted before their Parent in heaven. And let us say: Amen.

May there be abundant peace from heaven and life for us and for all Israel, and let us say: Amen.

May the One who makes peace in the high heavens make peace for us and for all Israel, and let us say: Amen.

## EIN KELOHEINU

***A piyyut (poetic prayer) praising God's uniqueness.***

| | |
|---|---|
| Ein kEiloheinu, | אֵין כֵּאלֹהֵינוּ, |
| ein kAdoneinu, | אֵין כַּאדוֹנֵינוּ, |
| ein k'Malkeinu, | אֵין כְּמַלְכֵּנוּ, |
| ein k'Moshi·einu. | אֵין כְּמוֹשִׁיעֵנוּ. |
| Mi khEiloheinu, | מִי כֵאלֹהֵינוּ, |
| mi khAdoneinu, | מִי כַאדוֹנֵינוּ, |
| mi kh'Malkeinu, | מִי כְמַלְכֵּנוּ, |
| mi kh'Moshi·einu. | מִי כְמוֹשִׁיעֵנוּ. |
| Nodeh lEiloheinu, | נוֹדֶה לֵאלֹהֵינוּ, |
| nodeh lAdoneinu, | נוֹדֶה לַאדוֹנֵינוּ, |
| nodeh l'Malkeinu, | נוֹדֶה לְמַלְכֵּנוּ, |
| nodeh l'moshieinu. | נוֹדֶה לְמוֹשִׁיעֵנוּ. |
| Barukh Eloheinu, | בָּרוּךְ אֱלֹהֵינוּ, |
| barukh Adoneinu, | בָּרוּךְ אֲדוֹנֵינוּ, |
| barukh Malkeinu, | בָּרוּךְ מַלְכֵּנוּ, |
| barukh Moshi·einu. | בָּרוּךְ מוֹשִׁיעֵנוּ. |
| Atah Hu Eloheinu, | אַתָּה הוּא אֱלֹהֵינוּ, |
| Atah Hu Adoneinu, | אַתָּה הוּא אֲדוֹנֵינוּ, |
| Atah Hu Malkeinu, | אַתָּה הוּא מַלְכֵּנוּ, |
| Atah Hu Moshi·einu. | אַתָּה הוּא מוֹשִׁיעֵנוּ. |
| Atah hu | אַתָּה הוּא |
| she-hiktiru avoteinu l'fanekha | שֶׁהִקְטִירוּ אֲבוֹתֵינוּ לְפָנֶיךָ |
| et k'toret ha-samim. | אֶת קְטֹֽרֶת הַסַּמִּים. |

## EIN KELOHEINU

***A piyyut (poetic prayer) praising God's uniqueness.***

There is none like our God, there is none like our Sovereign, there is none like our Ruler, there is none like our Deliverer.

Who is like our God, Who is like our Sovereign, Who is like our Ruler, Who is like our Deliverer?

Let us thank our God, Let us thank our Sovereign, Let us thank our Ruler, Let us thank our Deliverer.

Blessed is our God, Blessed is our Sovereign, Blessed is our Ruler, Blessed is our Deliverer.

You are our God, You are our Sovereign, You are our Ruler, You are our Deliverer.

You are the One to whom our ancestors offered the incense offering.

Originally this poem began with Mi khEloheinu, "who is like our God?" Then someone rearranged the verses so that the first letters of the verses spell out Amen.

## ALEINU

***Praise and hope; the particular blessings of being a Jew and universal hopes for all mankind.***

| | |
|---|---|
| Aleinu l'shabei·aḥ | עָלֵינוּ לְשַׁבֵּחַ |
| la-Adon hakol, | לַאֲדוֹן הַכֹּל, |
| lateit g'dulah | לָתֵת גְּדֻלָּה |
| l'yotzeir b'reishit. | לְיוֹצֵר בְּרֵאשִׁית, |
| Shelo asanu | שֶׁלֹּא עָשָׂנוּ |
| k'goyei ha-aratzot | כְּגוֹיֵי הָאֲרָצוֹת, |
| v'lo samanu | וְלֹא שָׂמָנוּ |
| k'mishp'ḥot ha-adamah, | כְּמִשְׁפְּחוֹת הָאֲדָמָה, |
| shelo sam | שֶׁלֹּא שָׂם |
| ḥelkeinu kahem | חֶלְקֵנוּ כָּהֶם, |
| v'goraleinu k'khol hamonam. | וְגֹרָלֵנוּ כְּכָל הֲמוֹנָם, |
| Va-anaḥnu kor'im u-mishtaḥavim | וַאֲנַחְנוּ כּוֹרְעִים וּמִשְׁתַּחֲוִים |
| u-modim | וּמוֹדִים, |
| lifnei Melekh malkhei ham'lakhim | לִפְנֵי מֶלֶךְ מַלְכֵי הַמְּלָכִים, |
| Hakadosh Barukh Hu. | הַקָּדוֹשׁ בָּרוּךְ הוּא. |
| She-hu noteh shamayim | שֶׁהוּא נוֹטֶה שָׁמַיִם |
| v'yoseid aretz, | וְיֹסֵד אָרֶץ, |
| u-moshav y'karo | וּמוֹשַׁב יְקָרוֹ |
| ba-shamayim mima·al | בַּשָּׁמַיִם מִמַּעַל, |
| ush'khinat uzo | וּשְׁכִינַת עֻזּוֹ |
| b'govhei m'romim. | בְּגָבְהֵי מְרוֹמִים, |
| Hu Eloheinu ein od. | הוּא אֱלֹהֵינוּ אֵין עוֹד. |
| Emet Malkeinu | אֱמֶת מַלְכֵּנוּ, |
| efes zulato | אֶפֶס זוּלָתוֹ, |
| kakatuv b'Torato: | כַּכָּתוּב בְּתוֹרָתוֹ: |
| v'yada·ta hayom | וְיָדַעְתָּ הַיּוֹם |
| vahashevotah el l'vavekha, | וַהֲשֵׁבֹתָ אֶל לְבָבֶךָ, |
| ki Adonai Hu ha-Elohim | כִּי יְיָ הוּא הָאֱלֹהִים |
| ba-shamayim mima·al | בַּשָּׁמַיִם מִמַּעַל, |
| v'al ha-aretz mitaḥat | וְעַל הָאָרֶץ מִתָּחַת, |
| ein od. | אֵין עוֹד. |

## ALEINU

***Praise and hope; the particular blessings of being a Jew and universal hopes for all mankind.***

We should praise the Ruler of all, tell the greatness of the Creator, for not making us like the other peoples and families of the earth, nor giving us the same destiny. We bend the knee and bow and give thanks to the Ruler of all earthly rulers, the Blessed Holy One. God spread out the heavens and built the earth's foundations, and lives in glory in the heavens. God's mighty presence is high above. God is our God – no one else. Our Ruler is true, there is nothing besides God, as it is written in His Torah: "You shall know, therefore, this day and keep in mind that Adonai alone is God in heaven above and on earth below; there is no other." (Deuteronomy 4:39)

**Aleinu:** The Aleinu is a blend of the particular and the universal. In its two paragraphs it expresses the twin polarities of loyalty to one's own people, together with deep concern for the welfare of a redeemed world in which all humanity will recognize God's sovereignty. Imagine what the world might look like when all on earth will acknowledge the one Creator of all and abide by all of God's expectations. Close your eyes and picture all the people in the world holding hands around the equator and being at peace, one with the other. Will this ever be possible? Such is the vision of Zechariah 14:9 whose words conclude the Aleinu prayer: "On that day Adonai will be One, and Adonai's Name One."

| | |
|---|---|
| Al kein n'kaveh l'kha | עַל כֵּן נְקַוֶּה לְּךָ |
| Adonai Eloheinu | יְיָ אֱלֹהֵינוּ, |
| lir'ot m'heirah b'tif·eret uzekha, | לִרְאוֹת מְהֵרָה בְּתִפְאֶרֶת עֻזֶּךָ, |
| l'ha·avir gilulim min ha-aretz | לְהַעֲבִיר גִּלּוּלִים מִן הָאָרֶץ, |
| v'ha-elilim karot yikareitun, | וְהָאֱלִילִים כָּרוֹת יִכָּרֵתוּן, |
| l'takein olam | לְתַקֵּן עוֹלָם |
| b'malkhut Shadai | בְּמַלְכוּת שַׁדַּי, |
| v'khol b'nei vasar yikr'u vi-Sh'mekha, | וְכָל בְּנֵי בָשָׂר יִקְרְאוּ בִשְׁמֶךָ, |
| l'hafnot eilekha | לְהַפְנוֹת אֵלֶיךָ |
| kol risḥ·ei aretz. | כָּל רִשְׁעֵי אָרֶץ. |
| Yakiru v'yeid'u | יַכִּירוּ וְיֵדְעוּ |
| kol yoshvei teiveil | כָּל יוֹשְׁבֵי תֵבֵל, |
| ki l'kha tikhra kol berekh | כִּי לְךָ תִּכְרַע כָּל בֶּרֶךְ, |
| tishava kol lashon. | תִּשָּׁבַע כָּל לָשׁוֹן. |
| L'fanekha Adonai Eloheinu | לְפָנֶיךָ יְיָ אֱלֹהֵינוּ |
| yikhr'u v'yipolu. | יִכְרְעוּ וְיִפֹּלוּ, |
| v'likh'vod shimkha y'kar yiteinu, | וְלִכְבוֹד שִׁמְךָ יְקָר יִתֵּנוּ, |
| vikab'lu khulam | וִיקַבְּלוּ כֻלָּם |
| et ol malkhutekha | אֶת עוֹל מַלְכוּתֶךָ, |
| v'timlokh aleihem m'heirah | וְתִמְלֹךְ עֲלֵיהֶם מְהֵרָה |
| l'olam va·ed, | לְעוֹלָם וָעֶד. |
| ki ha-malkhut shel'kha hi | כִּי הַמַּלְכוּת שֶׁלְּךָ הִיא, |
| u-l'ol'mei ad timlokh b'khavod, | וּלְעוֹלְמֵי עַד תִּמְלוֹךְ בְּכָבוֹד, |
| kakatuv b'Toratekha: | כַּכָּתוּב בְּתוֹרָתֶךָ, |
| Adonai yimlokh l'olam va·ed. | יְיָ יִמְלֹךְ לְעוֹלָם וָעֶד. |
| v'ne·emar: | וְנֶאֱמַר, |
| v'hayah Adonai l'Melekh | וְהָיָה יְיָ לְמֶלֶךְ |
| al kol ha-aretz, | עַל כָּל הָאָרֶץ, |
| ba-yom ha-hu yih'yeh Adonai eḥad | בַּיּוֹם הַהוּא יִהְיֶה יְיָ אֶחָד, |
| ush'mo eḥad. | וּשְׁמוֹ אֶחָד. |

And so we hope in You, Adonai our God, soon to see the glory of Your might, removing idols from the earth, and banishing false gods, fixing the brokenness of the world so that it will be God's kingdom. All humanity will call Your name, and all the wicked of the earth will turn toward You. All who live in the world will know and understand that every knee must bend to You and every tongue must promise loyalty. They will bow to You, Adonai our God, honoring the glory of Your Name. All will accept Your authority, and the time will come soon when You will rule over them forever. For the world is Your kingdom, and you will always rule over it in glory. As it is written in the Torah: "The Ruler shall rule forever and ever." (Exodus 15:18) And the Prophet Zechariah said: "Then God will be Ruler over all the earth. On that day God will be One and God's name will be One." (Zechariah 14:9)

## KADDISH YATOM (MOURNER'S KADDISH)

***We remember the dead by praising God***

*Leader:*

| | |
|---|---|
| Yit-gadal v'yit-kadash sh'mei rabba, | יִתְגַּדַּל וְיִתְקַדַּשׁ שְׁמֵהּ רַבָּא. |
| b'al'ma di v'ra | בְּעָלְמָא דִּי בְרָא |
| khir'utei | כִרְעוּתֵהּ, |
| v'yam-likh malkhutei | וְיַמְלִיךְ מַלְכוּתֵהּ |
| b'ḥayeikhon u-v'yomeikhon | בְּחַיֵּיכוֹן וּבְיוֹמֵיכוֹן |
| u-v'ḥayei d'khol beit Yisra·el, | וּבְחַיֵּי דְכָל בֵּית יִשְׂרָאֵל, |
| ba·agala u-viz'man kariv, | בַּעֲגָלָא וּבִזְמַן קָרִיב, |
| v'imru, Amen. | וְאִמְרוּ אָמֵן. |

*Congregation and Leader:*

| | |
|---|---|
| Y'hei sh'mei rabba m'va-rakh, | יְהֵא שְׁמֵהּ רַבָּא מְבָרַךְ |
| l'alam ul'al'mei al'maya, | לְעָלַם וּלְעָלְמֵי עָלְמַיָּא. |

*Leader:*

| | |
|---|---|
| Yitbarakh v'yishtabaḥ | יִתְבָּרַךְ וְיִשְׁתַּבַּח |
| v'yitpa·ar v'yitromam v'yitnasei | וְיִתְפָּאַר וְיִתְרוֹמַם וְיִתְנַשֵּׂא |
| v'yithadar v'yit·aleh v'yithalal | וְיִתְהַדָּר וְיִתְעַלֶּה וְיִתְהַלָּל |
| sh'mei d'kud'sha, b'rikh Hu. | שְׁמֵהּ דְּקֻדְשָׁא בְּרִיךְ הוּא, |
| L'eila [u-l'eila mi-kol] | לְעֵלָּא (לְעֵלָּא וּלְעֵלָּא מִכָּל) |
| min kol birkhata v'shirata | מִן כָּל בִּרְכָתָא וְשִׁירָתָא |
| tushb'ḥata v'neḥemata | תֻּשְׁבְּחָתָא וְנֶחֱמָתָא, |
| da·amiran b'al'ma, | דַּאֲמִירָן בְּעָלְמָא, |
| v'imru Amen. | וְאִמְרוּ אָמֵן. |
| Y'hei sh'lama rabba min shamaya | יְהֵא שְׁלָמָא רַבָּא מִן שְׁמַיָּא, |
| v'ḥayyim aleinu | וְחַיִּים עָלֵינוּ |
| v'al kol Yisra·el, | וְעַל כָּל יִשְׂרָאֵל, |
| v'imru Amen. | וְאִמְרוּ אָמֵן. |
| Oseh shalom bim'romav, | עֹשֶׂה שָׁלוֹם בִּמְרוֹמָיו, |
| hu ya·aseh shalom | הוּא יַעֲשֶׂה שָׁלוֹם |
| aleinu v'al kol Yisra·el, | עָלֵינוּ וְעַל כָּל יִשְׂרָאֵל, |
| v'imru Amen. | וְאִמְרוּ אָמֵן. |

## KADDISH YATOM (MOURNER'S KADDISH)

*We remember the dead by praising God.*

May God's great name be made great and holy in the world that God created according to God's will. May God establish the Divine kingdom soon, in our days, quickly and in the near future, and let us say, Amen.

*Congregation and Leader together:*

May God's great name be praised forever and ever.

Blessed, praised, glorified and raised high, honored and elevated be the name of the Holy Blessed One, far beyond all blessings and songs, praises and comforts which people can say, and let us say: Amen.

May there be abundant peace from heaven and life for us and for all Israel, and let us say: Amen.

May the One who makes peace in the high heavens make peace for us and for all Israel, and let us say: Amen.

**Kaddish Yatom:** The Kaddish recited by mourners is one of a number of different forms of the Kaddish, the prayer that sanctifies God, praising God's Name. Originally recited at the conclusion of a biblical discourse, it became connected to death and mourning when the custom began of giving honor of reciting the prayer to the bereaved at the end of worship services. The custom seems to have been connected to the ancient belief that the souls of those who died who were being punished are released on the Sabbath. The prayer then recited by the mourner could thereby earn merit for the deceased by showing how loyal their children were to God's mitzvot.

If you have recently lost someone you love, if today is the yahrzeit of someone you love, or if this moment stirs memories of someone you love, try to bring your memories into the room with you. What Shabbat recollections does this person evoke? In what ways has s/he become part of you? Try to be aware of that part of you.

On Shabbat, when all the desires of our hearts are meant to be fulfilled, try to feel some thankfulness that your desire for the presence of this person whom you miss is partially fulfilled in the manner in which you have woven some of what s/he was into your being. (Richard Levy, *On Wings of Light*)

## ADON OLAM

*We praise God as eternal Ruler of the world.*

| | |
|---|---|
| Adon olam asher malakh | אֲדוֹן עוֹלָם אֲשֶׁר מָלַךְ, |
| b'terem kol y'tzir nivra | בְּטֶרֶם כָּל יְצִיר נִבְרָא. |
| L'eit na·asah v'ḥeftzo kol | לְעֵת נַעֲשָׂה בְחֶפְצוֹ כֹּל, |
| azai Melekh sh'mo nikra. | אֲזַי מֶלֶךְ שְׁמוֹ נִקְרָא. |
| v'aḥarei kikh'lot ha-kol | וְאַחֲרֵי כִּכְלוֹת הַכֹּל, |
| l'vado yimlokh norah | לְבַדּוֹ יִמְלוֹךְ נוֹרָא. |
| v'hu hayah v'hu hoveh | וְהוּא הָיָה, וְהוּא הֹוֶה, |
| v'hu yih'yeh b'tif·arah | וְהוּא יִהְיֶה, בְּתִפְאָרָה. |
| v'hu eḥad v'ein sheini | וְהוּא אֶחָד וְאֵין שֵׁנִי, |
| l'hamshil lo l'haḥbirah | לְהַמְשִׁיל לוֹ לְהַחְבִּירָה. |
| B'li reishit b'li takhlit | בְּלִי רֵאשִׁית בְּלִי תַכְלִית, |
| v'lo ha·oz v'hamisrah | וְלוֹ הָעֹז וְהַמִּשְׂרָה. |
| v'hu Eili v'ḥai go·ali | וְהוּא אֵלִי וְחַי גֹּאֲלִי, |
| v'tzur ḥevli b'eit tzarah | וְצוּר חֶבְלִי בְּעֵת צָרָה. |
| v'hu nisi u-manos li | וְהוּא נִסִּי וּמָנוֹס לִי, |
| m'nat kosi b'yom ekra | מְנָת כּוֹסִי בְּיוֹם אֶקְרָא. |
| B'yado afkid ruḥi | בְּיָדוֹ אַפְקִיד רוּחִי, |
| b'eit ishan v'a·irah | בְּעֵת אִישַׁן וְאָעִירָה. |
| v'im ruḥi g'viyati | וְעִם רוּחִי גְּוִיָּתִי, |
| Adonai li v'lo ira. | יְיָ לִי וְלֹא אִירָא. |

## ADON OLAM

***We praise God as eternal Ruler of the world.***

Sovereign of the universe who ruled before anything was created,
When all was made by God's will then was God known as Ruler.
When everything ends at the end of time,
God will still reign alone.
God was, God is, God will be – in splendor.
God is one, there is no other being that compares.
Without beginning, without end, power and authority are God's.
My God and living Redeemer, my sheltering Rock in times of trouble,
God is my banner and my shelter, filling my cup on the day I call.
Into God's hand I place my spirit, when I sleep and when I awake,
and with my spirit, my body too. Adonai is with me, I shall not fear.

**Adon Olam:** Try to extend the mood of your prayer into this closing song, attributed to the great Spanish poet Solomon ibn Gabirol. Try to form the words on your lips into a closing offering to God.

When the service ends, try to take some of the singing and words along with you for the rest of Shabbat. Reflect on some insights that came to you during the service, that you want to keep and hold onto for the duration of Shabbat. Finally, imagine that each person to whom you are about to wish a "Shabbat Shalom" is the Sabbath Bride or some other aspect of Shabbat personified–its restfulness, its peace, its beauty–and that you and the Shabbat Bride are leaving the service hand in hand.

# Shabbat Minḥah Service

## מנחה

### ASHREI

*The joy of praising God.*

| | |
|---|---|
| Ashrei yosh'vei | אַשְׁרֵי יוֹשְׁבֵי |
| veitekha, | בֵיתֶךָ, |
| od y'hal'lukha selah. | עוֹד יְהַלְלוּךָ סֶּלָה. |
| *Ashrei ha-am she-kakha lo, | *אַשְׁרֵי הָעָם שֶׁכָּכָה לּוֹ, |
| ashrei ha-am | אַשְׁרֵי הָעָם |
| she-Adonai Elohav. | שֶׁיְיָ אֱלֹהָיו. |
| T'hilah l'David | תְּהִלָּה לְדָוִד, |
| Aromimkha Elohai ha-Melekh, | אֲרוֹמִמְךָ אֱלוֹהַי הַמֶּלֶךְ, |
| va-avar'kha shimkha l'olam va·ed. | וַאֲבָרְכָה שִׁמְךָ לְעוֹלָם וָעֶד. |
| *B'khol yom avar'kheka, | *בְּכָל יוֹם אֲבָרְכֶךָּ, |
| va·ahal'lah shimkha l'olam va·ed. | וַאֲהַלְלָה שִׁמְךָ לְעוֹלָם וָעֶד. |
| Gadol Adonai u-m'hulal m'od, | גָּדוֹל יְיָ וּמְהֻלָּל מְאֹד, |
| v'lig'dulato ein ḥeiker. | וְלִגְדֻלָּתוֹ אֵין חֵקֶר. |
| *Dor l'dor | *דּוֹר לְדוֹר |
| y'shabaḥ ma·asekha, | יְשַׁבַּח מַעֲשֶׂיךָ, |
| u-g'vurotekha yagidu. | וּגְבוּרֹתֶיךָ יַגִּידוּ. |
| Hadar k'vod hodekha, | הֲדַר כְּבוֹד הוֹדֶךָ, |
| v'divrei nifl'otekha asiḥah. | וְדִבְרֵי נִפְלְאֹתֶיךָ אָשִׂיחָה. |
| *Ve-ezuz nor'otekha yo·meiru, | *וֶעֱזוּז נוֹרְאוֹתֶיךָ יֹאמֵרוּ, |
| u-g'dulat'kha asap'renah. | וּגְדֻלָּתְךָ אֲסַפְּרֶנָּה. |
| Zekher rav tuv'kha yabi·u, | זֵכֶר רַב טוּבְךָ יַבִּיעוּ, |
| v'tzidkat'kha y'raneinu. | וְצִדְקָתְךָ יְרַנֵּנוּ. |
| *Ḥanun v'raḥum Adonai, | *חַנּוּן וְרַחוּם יְיָ, |
| erekh apayim ug'dol ḥased. | אֶרֶךְ אַפַּיִם וּגְדָל חָסֶד. |
| Tov Adonai lakol, | טוֹב יְיָ לַכֹּל, |
| v'raḥamav al kol ma·asav. | וְרַחֲמָיו עַל כָּל מַעֲשָׂיו. |
| *Yodukha Adonai kol ma·asekha, | *יוֹדוּךָ יְיָ כָּל מַעֲשֶׂיךָ, |
| va-ḥasidekha y'var'khukha. | וַחֲסִידֶיךָ יְבָרְכוּכָה. |
| K'vod malkhut'kha yo·meiru, | כְּבוֹד מַלְכוּתְךָ יֹאמֵרוּ, |
| u-g'vurat'kha y'dabeiru | וּגְבוּרָתְךָ יְדַבֵּרוּ. |

# Shabbat Minḥah Service

## ASHREI

*The joy of praising God.*

Happy are they who live in Your house;
They shall continue to praise You. (Psalm 84:5)
Happy are the people for whom this is so;
Happy are the people whose God is Adonai. (Psalm 144:15)

A Psalm of David.
א I will honor you, my God and Ruler,
I will praise Your Name forever and ever.
ב Every day I will praise You,
And sing praises to Your Name forever and ever.
ג Great is Adonai and greatly praised;
There is no limit to God's greatness.
ד One generation shall praise Your deeds to another,
And tell about Your mighty deeds.
ה I will speak about Your splendor and glory,
And Your wonderful deeds.
ו They will talk about the power of Your mighty acts;
And I will tell of Your greatness.
ז They recall Your great goodness,
And sing of Your righteousness.
ח Adonai is gracious and caring, patient and very kind.
ט Adonai is good to all,
And merciful to everything God made.
י All Your works shall praise You, Adonai,
And Your faithful ones shall bless You.
כ They shall speak of the glory of Your rule,
And talk of Your might,

| | |
|---|---|
| *L'hodi·a liv'nei ha-adam g'vurotav, | *לְהוֹדִיעַ לִבְנֵי הָאָדָם גְּבוּרֹתָיו, |
| u-kh'vod hadar malkhuto | וּכְבוֹד הֲדַר מַלְכוּתוֹ. |
| Malkhut'kha malkhut kol olamim, | מַלְכוּתְךָ מַלְכוּת כָּל עֹלָמִים, |
| u-memshalt'kha b'khol dor va-dor | וּמֶמְשַׁלְתְּךָ בְּכָל דֹּר וָדֹר. |
| *Someikh Adonai l'khol ha-nof'lim, | *סוֹמֵךְ יְיָ לְכָל הַנֹּפְלִים, |
| v'zokeif l'khol hak'fufim. | וְזוֹקֵף לְכָל הַכְּפוּפִים. |
| Einei khol eilekha y'sabeiru, | עֵינֵי כֹל אֵלֶיךָ יְשַׂבֵּרוּ, |
| v'Atah notein lahem | וְאַתָּה נוֹתֵן לָהֶם |
| et okhlam b'ito. | אֶת אָכְלָם בְּעִתּוֹ. |
| *Pote·aḥ et yadekha, | *פּוֹתֵחַ אֶת יָדֶךָ, |
| u-masbi·a l'khol ḥai ratzon. | וּמַשְׂבִּיעַ לְכָל חַי רָצוֹן. |
| Tzadik Adonai b'khol d'rakhav, | צַדִּיק יְיָ בְּכָל דְּרָכָיו, |
| v'ḥasid b'khol ma·asav. | וְחָסִיד בְּכָל מַעֲשָׂיו. |
| *Karov Adonai l'khol kor'av, | *קָרוֹב יְיָ לְכָל קֹרְאָיו, |
| l'khol asher yikra·uhu ve-emet. | לְכֹל אֲשֶׁר יִקְרָאֻהוּ בֶאֱמֶת. |
| R'tzon y'rei·av ya·aseh, | רְצוֹן יְרֵאָיו יַעֲשֶׂה, |
| v'et shav·atam yishma v'yoshi·eim. | וְאֶת שַׁוְעָתָם יִשְׁמַע וְיוֹשִׁיעֵם. |
| *Shomeir Adonai et kol ohavav | *שׁוֹמֵר יְיָ אֶת כָּל אֹהֲבָיו, |
| v'et kol har'sha·im yashmid | וְאֵת כָּל הָרְשָׁעִים יַשְׁמִיד. |
| T'hilat Adonai y'daber pi, | תְּהִלַּת יְיָ יְדַבֶּר פִּי, |
| Vi-varekh kol basar | וִיבָרֵךְ כָּל בָּשָׂר |
| sheim kodsho l'olam va·ed. | שֵׁם קָדְשׁוֹ לְעוֹלָם וָעֶד. |
| *Va-anaḥnu n'vareikh Yah, | *וַאֲנַחְנוּ נְבָרֵךְ יָהּ, |
| mei-atah v'ad olam. | מֵעַתָּה וְעַד עוֹלָם, |
| Hal'luyah. | הַלְלוּיָהּ. |

ל To announce to humanity God's greatness,
The splendor and glory of God's rule.
מ God, You rule forever,
Your kingdom is for all generations.
ס God holds up all who fall,
And helps all who are bent over stand straight.
ע The eyes of all look to You with hope,
And You give them their food at the right time.
פ You open Your hand,
And feed everything that lives to its heart's content.
צ Adonai is good in every way,
And kind in every deed.
ק Adonai is near to all who call,
To all who call to God sincerely.
ר God does the wishes of those who respect God,
God hears their cry and saves them.
ש Adonai protects all who love God,
But God will destroy the wicked.
ת My mouth shall speak praises of God,
And all beings shall bless God's holy name
Forever and ever. (Psalm 145)

We shall praise God,
now and forever. Halleluyah. (Psalm 115:18)

## K'DUSHAH D'SIDRA

וּבָא לְצִיּוֹן גּוֹאֵל, וּלְשָׁבֵי פֶשַׁע בְּיַעֲקֹב, נְאֻם יְיָ.

וַאֲנִי זֹאת בְּרִיתִי אוֹתָם, אָמַר יְיָ, רוּחִי אֲשֶׁר עָלֶיךָ, וּדְבָרַי אֲשֶׁר שַׂמְתִּי בְּפִיךָ, לֹא יָמוּשׁוּ מִפִּיךָ, וּמִפִּי זַרְעֲךָ, וּמִפִּי זֶרַע זַרְעֲךָ, אָמַר יְיָ, מֵעַתָּה וְעַד עוֹלָם.

וְאַתָּה קָדוֹשׁ, יוֹשֵׁב תְּהִלּוֹת יִשְׂרָאֵל.

וְקָרָא זֶה אֶל זֶה וְאָמַר, קָדוֹשׁ קָדוֹשׁ קָדוֹשׁ יְיָ צְבָאוֹת, מְלֹא כָל הָאָרֶץ כְּבוֹדוֹ.

וּמְקַבְּלִין דֵּין מִן דֵּין, וְאָמְרִין, קַדִּישׁ בִּשְׁמֵי מְרוֹמָא עִלָּאָה בֵּית שְׁכִינְתֵּהּ, קַדִּישׁ עַל אַרְעָא עוֹבַד גְּבוּרְתֵּהּ, קַדִּישׁ לְעָלַם וּלְעָלְמֵי עָלְמַיָּא, יְיָ צְבָאוֹת, מַלְיָא כָל אַרְעָא זִיו יְקָרֵהּ.

וַתִּשָּׂאֵנִי רוּחַ, וָאֶשְׁמַע אַחֲרַי קוֹל רַעַשׁ גָּדוֹל, בָּרוּךְ כְּבוֹד יְיָ מִמְּקוֹמוֹ.

וּנְטָלַתְנִי רוּחָא, וְשִׁמְעֵת בַּתְרַי קָל זִיעַ סַגִּיא, דִּמְשַׁבְּחִין וְאָמְרִין, בְּרִיךְ יְקָרָא דַייָ מֵאֲתַר בֵּית שְׁכִינְתֵּהּ.

יְיָ יִמְלֹךְ לְעֹלָם וָעֶד. יְיָ מַלְכוּתֵהּ קָאֵם לְעָלַם וּלְעָלְמֵי עָלְמַיָּא.

יְיָ אֱלֹהֵי אַבְרָהָם יִצְחָק וְיִשְׂרָאֵל אֲבוֹתֵינוּ, שָׁמְרָה זֹּאת לְעוֹלָם, לְיֵצֶר מַחְשְׁבוֹת לְבַב עַמֶּךָ, וְהָכֵן לְבָבָם אֵלֶיךָ.

וְהוּא רַחוּם, יְכַפֵּר עָוֹן וְלֹא יַשְׁחִית, וְהִרְבָּה לְהָשִׁיב אַפּוֹ, וְלֹא יָעִיר כָּל חֲמָתוֹ. כִּי אַתָּה אֲדֹנָי טוֹב וְסַלָּח, וְרַב חֶסֶד לְכָל קֹרְאֶיךָ.

צִדְקָתְךָ צֶדֶק לְעוֹלָם, וְתוֹרָתְךָ אֱמֶת. תִּתֵּן אֱמֶת לְיַעֲקֹב, חֶסֶד לְאַבְרָהָם, אֲשֶׁר נִשְׁבַּעְתָּ לַאֲבוֹתֵינוּ מִימֵי קֶדֶם.

בָּרוּךְ אֲדֹנָי, יוֹם | יוֹם יַעֲמָס לָנוּ, הָאֵל יְשׁוּעָתֵנוּ סֶלָה.

## K'DUSHAH D'SIDRA

*This prayer is a compilation of Bible verses, some of them translated into Aramaic. The themes are comfort, holiness (you will recognize verses found in the K'dushah blessing of the Amidah), and God's forgiveness. The prayer then concludes with a blessing.*

*Shabbat afternoon is a time of holiness and well-being, a taste of the world to come. So our thoughts turn to the future redemption, when the promise of Shabbat will be fulfilled, and we will experience God's presence every day.*

To Jacob's descendents who turn away from sin.

God tells us, I have a covenant with you:
My spirit is within you, and my words which are in your mouths,
Will never leave you or your children – ever.

We envision the Holy One seated on a throne made from our praises,

As the angels call to each other, saying,
"Holy, holy, holy, *Adonai Tz'va·ot*",
The whole world is filled with God's glory.

God, you are holy above, You are holy here on earth.
We remember Ezekiel's words,

"Praised is God's glory from the place where God dwells."
Adonai will rule forever and ever.

Adonai, God of Abraham, Isaac and Jacob
(Sarah, Rebeca, Rachel and Leah), our ancestors,
Keep forever in our hearts; focus our minds on this:

God is merciful, forgiving sin, not destroying,
Generously controlling anger, quenching fires of wrath.
God, my Sovereign, you are good and forgiving,
Great in lovingkindness to all who call upon you.
Your righteousness is eternal and Your Torah is truth.
You will give truth to Jacob, lovingkindess to Abraham,
Just as You promised our ancestors long ago.
Blessed is God every day.

יְיָ צְבָאוֹת עִמָּנוּ, מִשְׂגָּב לָנוּ אֱלֹהֵי יַעֲקֹב סֶלָה.

יְיָ צְבָאוֹת, אַשְׁרֵי אָדָם בֹּטֵחַ בָּךְ.

יְיָ הוֹשִׁיעָה, הַמֶּלֶךְ יַעֲנֵנוּ בְיוֹם קָרְאֵנוּ.

בָּרוּךְ אֱלֹהֵינוּ, שֶׁבְּרָאָנוּ לִכְבוֹדוֹ, וְהִבְדִּילָנוּ מִן הַתּוֹעִים, וְנָתַן לָנוּ תּוֹרַת אֱמֶת, וְחַיֵּי עוֹלָם נָטַע בְּתוֹכֵנוּ, הוּא יִפְתַּח לִבֵּנוּ בְּתוֹרָתוֹ וְיָשֵׂם בְּלִבֵּנוּ אַהֲבָתוֹ וְיִרְאָתוֹ, וְלַעֲשׂוֹת רְצוֹנוֹ וּלְעָבְדוֹ בְּלֵבָב שָׁלֵם, לְמַעַן לֹא נִיגַע לָרִיק, וְלֹא נֵלֵד לַבֶּהָלָה.

יְהִי רָצוֹן מִלְּפָנֶיךָ, יְיָ אֱלֹהֵינוּ וֵאלֹהֵי אֲבוֹתֵינוּ, שֶׁנִּשְׁמֹר חֻקֶּיךָ בָּעוֹלָם הַזֶּה, וְנִזְכֶּה וְנִחְיֶה וְנִרְאֶה, וְנִירַשׁ טוֹבָה וּבְרָכָה, לִשְׁנֵי יְמוֹת הַמָּשִׁיחַ, וּלְחַיֵּי הָעוֹלָם הַבָּא.

לְמַעַן יְזַמֶּרְךָ כָבוֹד וְלֹא יִדֹּם, יְיָ אֱלֹהַי לְעוֹלָם אוֹדֶךָּ.

בָּרוּךְ הַגֶּבֶר אֲשֶׁר יִבְטַח בַּייָ, וְהָיָה יְיָ מִבְטַחוֹ.

בִּטְחוּ בַייָ עֲדֵי עַד, כִּי בְּיָהּ יְיָ צוּר עוֹלָמִים.

וְיִבְטְחוּ בְךָ יוֹדְעֵי שְׁמֶךָ, כִּי לֹא עָזַבְתָּ דֹרְשֶׁיךָ יְיָ.

יְיָ חָפֵץ לְמַעַן צִדְקוֹ, יַגְדִּיל תּוֹרָה וְיַאְדִּיר.

*Adonai Tz'va·ot* is with us, Jacob's God is our shelter.

*Adonai Tz'va·ot,* happy is the one who trusts in You.

Deliver us, Adonai, the Ruler will answer us when we call.

Blessed is God
Who created us for glory,
Who distinguished us from those who stray,
Who gave us the Torah of truth,
And who planted eternal life within us.
God, open our hearts to Your Torah,
Place in our hearts love and reverence for You
So that we can do Your will and serve You whole-heartedly.

May it be Your will, Adonai our God and God of our ancestors,
That we keep Your laws in this world, and thus merit
Living to see and inherit the goodness and blessings
Of messianic times and the life of the World to Come.

So that my soul will sing to You and not be mute,
Adonai my God, I will thank You forever.

Blessed is the One who trusts in Adonai,
So that Adonai is his security.

Trust in Adonai until the end of time,
For God is the eternal Rock, foundation of our lives.

Those who know Your nature trust in You,
For You have never abandoned those who seek You, Adonai.

Adonai desired, because of God's essential righteousness,
To make the Torah great and glorious.

## ḤATZI KADDISH

*Leader:*

Yit-gadal v'yit-kadash sh'mei rabba,
b'al'ma di v'ra
khir'utei
v'yam-likh malkhutei
b'ḥayeikhon u-v'yomeikhon
u-v'ḥayei d'khol beit Yisra·el,
ba·agala u-viz'man kariv,
v'imru, Amen.

יִתְגַּדַּל וְיִתְקַדַּשׁ שְׁמֵהּ רַבָּא.
בְּעָלְמָא דִּי בְרָא
כִרְעוּתֵהּ,
וְיַמְלִיךְ מַלְכוּתֵהּ
בְּחַיֵּיכוֹן וּבְיוֹמֵיכוֹן
וּבְחַיֵּי דְכָל בֵּית יִשְׂרָאֵל,
בַּעֲגָלָא וּבִזְמַן קָרִיב,
וְאִמְרוּ אָמֵן.

*Congregation and Leader:*

Y'hei sh'mei rabba m'va-rakh,
l'alam ul'almei al'maya.

יְהֵא שְׁמֵהּ רַבָּא מְבָרַךְ
לְעָלַם וּלְעָלְמֵי עָלְמַיָּא.

*Leader:*

Yitbarakh v'yishtabaḥ
v'yitpa·ar v'yitromam v'yitnasei
v'yithadar v'yit·aleh v'yithalal
sh'mei d'kud'sha, b'rikh Hu,
L'eila [u-l'eila mi-kol]
min kol birkhata v'shirata
tushb'ḥata v'neḥemata
da·amiran b'al'ma,
v'imru Amen.

יִתְבָּרַךְ וְיִשְׁתַּבַּח
וְיִתְפָּאַר וְיִתְרוֹמַם וְיִתְנַשֵּׂא
וְיִתְהַדָּר וְיִתְעַלֶּה וְיִתְהַלָּל
שְׁמֵהּ דְּקֻדְשָׁא בְּרִיךְ הוּא,
לְעֵלָּא מִן כָּל (וּלְעֵלָּא מִכָּל)
בִּרְכָתָא וְשִׁירָתָא
תֻּשְׁבְּחָתָא וְנֶחֱמָתָא,
דַּאֲמִירָן בְּעָלְמָא,
וְאִמְרוּ אָמֵן.

## ḤATZI KADDISH

May God's great Name be made great and holy in the world that God created according to God's will. May God establish the Divine kingdom soon, in our days, quickly and in the near future, and let us say, Amen.

*Congregation and Leader together:*

May God's great Name be praised forever and ever.

Blessed, praised, glorified and raised high, honored and elevated be the Name of the Holy Blessed One, far beyond all blessings and songs, praises and comforts which people can say, and let us say: Amen.

## TORAH SERVICE

| | |
|---|---|
| Va-ani t'filati l'kha Adonai eit ratzon, | וַאֲנִי תְפִלָּתִי לְךָ יְיָ עֵת רָצוֹן, |
| Elohim b'rov ḥasdekha, | אֱלֹהִים בְּרָב חַסְדֶּךָ, |
| aneini be-met yish·ekha. | עֲנֵנִי בֶּאֱמֶת יִשְׁעֶךָ. |

*We rise as the ark is opened.*

| | |
|---|---|
| Va-y'hi binso·a ha-aron | וַיְהִי בִּנְסֹעַ הָאָרֹן |
| va-yo·meir Moshe, Kumah Adonai | וַיֹּאמֶר מֹשֶׁה, קוּמָה, יְיָ, |
| v'yafutzu oy'vekha, | וְיָפֻצוּ אֹיְבֶיךָ, |
| v'yanusu m'san·ekha mi-panekha. | וְיָנֻסוּ מְשַׂנְאֶיךָ מִפָּנֶיךָ. |
| Ki mi-Tziyon teitzei Torah, | כִּי מִצִּיּוֹן תֵּצֵא תוֹרָה, |
| u-d'var Adonai mi-Y'rushalayim. | וּדְבַר יְיָ מִירוּשָׁלָיִם. |
| Barukh she-natan Torah | בָּרוּךְ שֶׁנָּתַן תּוֹרָה |
| l'amo Yisra·el bi-k'dushato. | לְעַמּוֹ יִשְׂרָאֵל בִּקְדֻשָּׁתוֹ. |

*The Torah scroll is taken from the Ark. The leader faces the ark, bows, and chants:*

| | |
|---|---|
| Gadl'u lAdonai iti, | גַּדְּלוּ לַייָ אִתִּי, |
| u-n'rom'mah sh'mo yaḥdav. | וּנְרוֹמְמָה שְׁמוֹ יַחְדָּו. |

*The Torah scrolls are carried around in procession:*

| | |
|---|---|
| L'kha Adonai ha-g'dulah v'ha-g'vurah | לְךָ יְיָ הַגְּדֻלָּה וְהַגְּבוּרָה |
| v'ha-tif·eret v'ha-netzaḥ v'ha-hod, | וְהַתִּפְאֶרֶת וְהַנֵּצַח וְהַהוֹד, |
| ki khol ba-shamayim uva-aretz, | כִּי כֹל בַּשָּׁמַיִם וּבָאָרֶץ, |
| l'kha Adonai ha-mamlakhah | לְךָ יְיָ הַמַּמְלָכָה, |
| v'ha-mitnasei l'khol l'rosh. | וְהַמִּתְנַשֵּׂא לְכֹל לְרֹאשׁ. |
| Rom'mu Adonai Eloheinu | רוֹמְמוּ יְיָ אֱלֹהֵינוּ, |
| v'hishtaḥavu la-hadom raglav | וְהִשְׁתַּחֲווּ לַהֲדֹם רַגְלָיו, |
| kadosh Hu. | קָדוֹשׁ הוּא. |
| Rom'mu Adonai Eloheinu | רוֹמְמוּ יְיָ אֱלֹהֵינוּ, |
| v'hishtaḥavu l'har kodsho, | וְהִשְׁתַּחֲווּ לְהַר קָדְשׁוֹ, |
| ki kadosh Adonai Eloheinu. | כִּי קָדוֹשׁ יְיָ אֱלֹהֵינוּ. |

*Before the first aliyah (honor of being called to the Torah), the gabbai (person who calls people up to the Torah) chants a paragraph that begins v'tigaleh v'teira·eh...at the end of which the congregation responds:*

| | |
|---|---|
| v'atem had'veikim bAdonai | וְאַתֶּם הַדְּבֵקִים בַּייָ |
| Eloheikhem | אֱלֹהֵיכֶם, |
| ḥayyim kul'khem ha-yom. | חַיִּים כֻּלְּכֶם הַיּוֹם. |

## TORAH SERVICE

But as for me, may my prayer come before You at a favorable time. God, in your great lovingkindness, answer me with Your saving truth.

*We rise as the ark is opened.*

Whenever the Ark would travel, Moses would say, "Arise, Adonai, and scatter Your enemies; may those that hate you flee from you."
For Torah shall come from Zion, the word of Adonai from Jerusalem.
Blessed is the One who in holiness gave the Torah to Israel.

*The Torah scroll is taken from the Ark. The leader faces the ark, bows, and chants:*

Declare Adonai's greatness with me; let us praise God together.

*The Torah scrolls are carried around in procession:*

Greatness, might, wonder, triumph, and majesty are Yours, Adonai – yes, all that is in heaven and on earth; to You, Adonai, belong kingship and supremacy over all.

Praise Adonai and bow down to God's presence; God is holy! Praise Adonai, our God, bow to God's holy mountain. Adonai our God is holy.

*Before the first aliyah (honor of being called to the Torah), the gabbai (person who calls people up to the Torah) chants a paragraph that begins v'tigaleh v'teiràeh...at the end of which the congregation responds:*

And you who were loyal to Adonai your God are alive today.

## TORAH BLESSINGS

*[If you are called up to the Torah, be sure your head is covered and you are wearing a tallit. The Torah reader will point out a place in the Torah, which you will touch with the tzitzit (fringes) of the tallit and then kiss the tzitzit. You begin with:*

| | |
|---|---|
| Bar'khu et Adonai ham'vorakh. | בָּרְכוּ אֶת יְיָ הַמְבֹרָךְ. |

*The congregation responds:*

| | |
|---|---|
| Barukh Adonai ha-m'vorakh | בָּרוּךְ יְיָ הַמְבֹרָךְ |
| l'olam va·ed. | לְעוֹלָם וָעֶד. |

*You repeat:*

| | |
|---|---|
| Barukh Adonai ha-m'vorakh | בָּרוּךְ יְיָ הַמְבֹרָךְ |
| l'olam va·ed. | לְעוֹלָם וָעֶד. |

*And continue:*

| | |
|---|---|
| Barukh Atah Adonai, | בָּרוּךְ אַתָּה יְיָ |
| Eloheinu Melekh ha-olam, | אֱלֹהֵינוּ מֶלֶךְ הָעוֹלָם, |
| asher baḥar banu mi-kol ha-amim, | אֲשֶׁר בָּחַר בָּנוּ מִכָּל הָעַמִּים |
| v'natan lanu et Torato. | וְנָתַן לָנוּ אֶת תּוֹרָתוֹ. |
| Barukh Atah Adonai, | בָּרוּךְ אַתָּה יְיָ, |
| notein ha-Torah. | נוֹתֵן הַתּוֹרָה. |

*After the Torah is read, the reader will again point out a place for you to touch with your tzitzit and kiss, then chant:*

| | |
|---|---|
| Barukh Atah Adonai, | בָּרוּךְ אַתָּה יְיָ |
| Eloheinu Melekh ha-olam, | אֱלֹהֵינוּ מֶלֶךְ הָעוֹלָם, |
| asher natan lanu Torat emet | אֲשֶׁר נָתַן לָנוּ תּוֹרַת אֱמֶת, |
| v'ḥayei olam nata b'tokheinu. | וְחַיֵּי עוֹלָם נָטַע בְּתוֹכֵנוּ. |
| Barukh Atah Adonai, | בָּרוּךְ אַתָּה יְיָ, |
| notein ha-Torah. | נוֹתֵן הַתּוֹרָה. |

## TORAH BLESSINGS

*If you are called up to the Torah, be sure your head is covered and you are wearing a tallit. The Torah reader will point out a place in the Torah, which you will touch with the tzitzit (fringes) of the tallit and then kiss the tzitzit. You begin with:*

Praise Adonai, who is to be praised.

*The congregation responds:*

Praised be Adonai who is to be praised forever and ever.

*You repeat.*

*And continue:*

Praised are You, Adonai our God, Ruler of the universe, who chose us from all nations by giving us the Torah. Praised are You, Adonai, Giver of the Torah.

*After the Torah is read, the reader will again point out a place for you to touch with your tzitzit and kiss, then chant:*

Praised are You, Adonai our God, Ruler of the universe, who gave us a Torah of truth, and thereby planted eternal life in our midst. Praised are You, Adonai, Giver of the Torah.

## V'ZOT HA-TORAH

*When the Torah is lifted, the congregation chants:*

| | |
|---|---|
| V'zot ha-Torah asher sam Moshe | וְזֹאת הַתּוֹרָה אֲשֶׁר שָׂם מֹשֶׁה |
| lifnei B'nei Yisra·el | לִפְנֵי בְּנֵי יִשְׂרָאֵל, |
| al pi Adonai b'yad Moshe. | עַל פִּי יְיָ בְּיַד מֹשֶׁה. |

*While the Torah is being wrapped, the congregation chants:*

| | |
|---|---|
| Eitz ḥayyim hi | עֵץ חַיִּים הִיא |
| la-maḥazikim bah, | לַמַּחֲזִיקִים בָּהּ, |
| v'tom'kheha m'ushar. | וְתֹמְכֶיהָ מְאֻשָּׁר. |
| D'rakheha darkhei no·am, | דְּרָכֶיהָ דַרְכֵי נֹעַם, |
| v'khol n'tivoteha shalom. | וְכָל נְתִיבוֹתֶיהָ שָׁלוֹם. |

*We rise to return the Sefer Torah to the Ark.*

| | |
|---|---|
| Y'hal'lu et sheim Adonai | יְהַלְלוּ אֶת שֵׁם יְיָ, |
| ki nisgav sh'mo l'vado. | כִּי נִשְׂגָּב שְׁמוֹ לְבַדּוֹ. |
| Hodo al eretz v'shamayim, | הוֹדוֹ עַל אֶרֶץ וְשָׁמָיִם. |
| va-yarem keren l'amo, | וַיָּרֶם קֶרֶן לְעַמּוֹ, |
| T'hilah l'khol ḥasidav, | תְּהִלָּה לְכָל חֲסִידָיו, |
| liv'nei Yisra·el am k'rovo. | לִבְנֵי יִשְׂרָאֵל עַם קְרוֹבוֹ, |
| Hal'luyah. | הַלְלוּיָהּ. |

| | |
|---|---|
| L'David mizmor. | לְדָוִד מִזְמוֹר, |
| LAdonai ha-aretz um'lo·ah, | לַייָ הָאָרֶץ וּמְלוֹאָהּ, |
| teiveil v'yosh'vei va. | תֵּבֵל וְיֹשְׁבֵי בָהּ. |
| Ki Hu al yamim y'sadah, | כִּי הוּא עַל יַמִּים יְסָדָהּ, |
| v'al n'harot y'khon'neha. | וְעַל נְהָרוֹת יְכוֹנְנֶהָ. |
| Mi ya·aleh v'har Adonai, | מִי יַעֲלֶה בְהַר יְיָ, |
| u-mi yakum bim'kom kodsho. | וּמִי יָקוּם בִּמְקוֹם קָדְשׁוֹ. |
| N'ki khapayim u-var leivav, | נְקִי כַפַּיִם וּבַר לֵבָב, |
| ashser lo nasa la-shav nafshi, | אֲשֶׁר לֹא נָשָׂא לַשָּׁוְא נַפְשִׁי, |
| v'lo nishba l'mirmah. | וְלֹא נִשְׁבַּע לְמִרְמָה. |
| Yisa v'rakha mei·eit Adonai, | יִשָּׂא בְרָכָה מֵאֵת יְיָ, |
| u-tz'dakah mei-Elohei yis·o. | וּצְדָקָה מֵאֱלֹהֵי יִשְׁעוֹ. |
| Zeh dor dorshav, | זֶה דּוֹר דֹּרְשָׁיו, |
| m'vakshei faneikha Ya·akov, selah. | מְבַקְשֵׁי פָנֶיךָ יַעֲקֹב סֶלָה. |

## V'ZOT HA-TORAH

*When the Torah is lifted, the congregation chants:*

This is the Torah which Moses placed before the people of Israel; from God's mouth, by Moses' hand.

*While the Torah is being wrapped, the congregation chants:*

It is a tree of life for those who hold on to it,
and those who support it are happy.
Its paths are pleasant
and all its ways are peaceful.

*We rise to return the Sefer Torah to the Ark.*

Praise God's name, for God's name is uniquely exalted.
God's glory is above heaven and earth,
God has exalted God's people's might,
given praise to the pious ones,
the people of Israel, who are close to God.
Halleluyah.

A Psalm of David:
The earth is Adonai's and all it contains,
The world and all who dwell in it.
For God founded it on the seas,
And set it in place upon rivers.
Who may go up on Adonai's mountain,
And who may stand in the place of God's holiness?
One who has clean hands and a pure heart,
Who has not taken My name in vain,
And who has not sworn falsely.
He will carry Adonai's blessing,
And just reward from God who saves him.
This is the generation of those who seek God;
Jacob's descendents who pursue God's presence.

| | |
|---|---|
| S'u sh'arim rasheikhem, | שְׂאוּ שְׁעָרִים רָאשֵׁיכֶם, |
| v'hinas'u pitḥei olam, | וְהִנָּשְׂאוּ פִּתְחֵי עוֹלָם, |
| v'yavo Melekh ha-kavod. | וְיָבוֹא מֶלֶךְ הַכָּבוֹד. |
| Mi zeh Melekh ha-kavod, | מִי זֶה מֶלֶךְ הַכָּבוֹד, |
| Adonai izuz v'gibor, | יְיָ עִזּוּז וְגִבּוֹר, |
| Adonai gibor milḥamah. | יְיָ גִּבּוֹר מִלְחָמָה. |
| S'u sh'arim rasheikhem, | שְׂאוּ שְׁעָרִים רָאשֵׁיכֶם, |
| u-s'u pitḥei olam, | וּשְׂאוּ פִּתְחֵי עוֹלָם, |
| v'yavo Melekh ha-kavod. | וְיָבֹא מֶלֶךְ הַכָּבוֹד. |
| Mi Hu zeh Melekh ha-kavod, | מִי הוּא זֶה מֶלֶךְ הַכָּבוֹד, |
| Adonai tz'va·ot | יְיָ צְבָאוֹת, |
| Hu Melekh ha-kavod. Selah. | הוּא מֶלֶךְ הַכָּבוֹד סֶלָה. |

## UV'NUḤO YO·MAR

***We praise the Torah as a wonderful gift from God.***

| | |
|---|---|
| Uv'nuḥo yo·mar: | וּבְנֻחֹה יֹאמַר, |
| Shuvah Adonai | שׁוּבָה, יְיָ, |
| riv'vot alfei Yisra·el. | רִבְבוֹת אַלְפֵי יִשְׂרָאֵל. |
| Kumah Adonai lim'nuḥatekha, | קוּמָה יְיָ לִמְנוּחָתֶךָ, |
| Atah va-aron uzekha. | אַתָּה וַאֲרוֹן עֻזֶּךָ. |
| Kohanekha | כֹּהֲנֶיךָ |
| yilb'shu tzedek, | יִלְבְּשׁוּ צֶדֶק, |
| va-ḥasidekha y'raneinu. | וַחֲסִידֶיךָ יְרַנֵּנוּ. |
| Ba·avur David avdekha, | בַּעֲבוּר דָּוִד עַבְדֶּךָ, |
| al tasheiv p'nei m'shiḥekha. | אַל תָּשֵׁב פְּנֵי מְשִׁיחֶךָ. |
| Ki lekaḥ tov natati lakhem, | כִּי לֶקַח טוֹב נָתַתִּי לָכֶם, |
| Torati al ta·azovu. | תּוֹרָתִי אַל תַּעֲזֹבוּ. |
| Eitz ḥayim hi la-maḥazikim bah, | עֵץ חַיִּים הִיא לַמַּחֲזִיקִים בָּהּ, |
| v'tom'kheha m'ushar. | וְתֹמְכֶיהָ מְאֻשָּׁר. |
| D'rakheha darkhei no·am, | דְּרָכֶיהָ דַרְכֵי נֹעַם, |
| v'khol n'tivoteha shalom. | וְכָל נְתִיבוֹתֶיהָ שָׁלוֹם. |
| Hashiveinu Adonai eilekha | הֲשִׁיבֵנוּ יְיָ אֵלֶיךָ |
| v'nashuvah, | וְנָשׁוּבָה, |
| ḥadesh yameinu k'kedem. | חַדֵּשׁ יָמֵינוּ כְּקֶדֶם. |

Lift up your heads, O gates;
Be lifted up, entrances to eternity,
So that the glorious Ruler may enter.
Who is the glorious Ruler,
Adonai, strong and mighty;
Adonai, mighty in battle.
Lift up your heads, O gates;
Be lifted up, entrances to eternity,
So that the glorious Ruler may enter.
Who is the glorious Ruler?
Adonai Tzevàot is the glorious Ruler.

## UV'NUḤO YO·MAR

***We praise the Torah as a wonderful gift from God.***

When the Ark rested, Moses would say:
Return, Adonai to the millions of Israel.
Rise up, Adonai to Your resting place, the Temple,
You and the Ark of Your strength.
May Your priests be clothed in righteousness,
And your faithful sing with joy.
For the sake of David, Your servant,
Do not reject Your anointed one.
I have given you good teaching,
do not leave My Torah.
It is a tree of life for those who hold on to it,
and those who support it are happy.
Its paths are pleasant
and all its ways are peaceful.
Return us to You, Adonai, and we shall return.
Renew our days as in days of old.

## ḤATZI KADDISH

*Leader:*

| | |
|---|---|
| Yit-gadal v'yit-kadash sh'mei rabba, | יִתְגַּדַּל וְיִתְקַדַּשׁ שְׁמֵהּ רַבָּא. |
| b'al'ma di v'ra | בְּעָלְמָא דִּי בְרָא |
| khir'utei | כִרְעוּתֵהּ, |
| v'yam-likh malkhutei | וְיַמְלִיךְ מַלְכוּתֵהּ |
| b'ḥayeikhon u-v'yomeikhon | בְּחַיֵּיכוֹן וּבְיוֹמֵיכוֹן |
| u-v'ḥayei d'khol beit Yisra·el, | וּבְחַיֵּי דְכָל בֵּית יִשְׂרָאֵל, |
| ba·agala u-viz'man kariv, | בַּעֲגָלָא וּבִזְמַן קָרִיב, |
| v'imru, Amen. | וְאִמְרוּ אָמֵן. |

*Congregation and Leader:*

| | |
|---|---|
| Y'hei sh'mei rabba m'va-rakh, | יְהֵא שְׁמֵהּ רַבָּא מְבָרַךְ |
| l'alam ul'al'mei al'maya, | לְעָלַם וּלְעָלְמֵי עָלְמַיָּא. |
| Yit-ba-rakh. | יִתְבָּרַךְ |

*Leader:*

| | |
|---|---|
| Yitbarakh v'yishtabaḥ | יִתְבָּרַךְ וְיִשְׁתַּבַּח |
| v'yitpa·ar v'yitromam v'yitnasei | וְיִתְפָּאַר וְיִתְרוֹמַם וְיִתְנַשֵּׂא |
| v'yithadar v'yit·aleh v'yithalal | וְיִתְהַדַּר וְיִתְעַלֶּה וְיִתְהַלָּל |
| sh'mei d'kud'sha, b'rikh Hu, | שְׁמֵהּ דְּקֻדְשָׁא בְּרִיךְ הוּא, |
| L'eila [u-l'eila mi-kol] | לְעֵלָּא (וּלְעֵלָּא מִן כָּל) |
| min kol birkhata v'shirata | בִּרְכָתָא וְשִׁירָתָא |
| tushb'ḥata v'neḥemata | תֻּשְׁבְּחָתָא וְנֶחֱמָתָא, |
| da·amiran b'al'ma, | דַּאֲמִירָן בְּעָלְמָא, |
| v'imru Amen. | וְאִמְרוּ אָמֵן. |

## ḤATZI KADDISH

May God's great name be made great and holy in the world that God created according to God's will. May God establish the Divine kingdom soon, in our days, quickly and in the near future, and let us say, Amen.

*Congregation and Leader together:*

May God's great Name be praised forever and ever.

Blessed, praised, glorified and raised high, honored and elevated be the Name of the Holy Blessed One, far beyond all blessings and songs, praises and comforts which people can say, and let us say: Amen.

# Amidah for Shabbat Minḥah

## AVOT

### *God of our Ancestors*

Barukh Atah Adonai
Eloheinu vEilohei avoteinu,
Elohei Avraham,
Elohei Yitzḥak
vEilohei Ya'akov,
[Elohei Sarah, Elohei Rivkah,
Elohei Raḥel vEilohei Le·ah]
ha-Eil
ha-gadol ha-gibor v'ha-nora
Eil elyon,
gomeil ḥasadim tovim
v'koneih hakol
v'zokheir ḥasdei avot,
u-meivi go·eil
liv'nei v'neihem
l'ma·an sh'mo b'ahavah.

בָּרוּךְ אַתָּה יְיָ
אֱלֹהֵינוּ וֵאלֹהֵי אֲבוֹתֵינוּ,
אֱלֹהֵי אַבְרָהָם,
אֱלֹהֵי יִצְחָק,
וֵאלֹהֵי יַעֲקֹב,
(אֱלֹהֵי שָׂרָה, אֱלֹהֵי רִבְקָה,
אֱלֹהֵי רָחֵל, וֵאלֹהֵי לֵאָה,)
הָאֵל
הַגָּדוֹל הַגִּבּוֹר וְהַנּוֹרָא,
אֵל עֶלְיוֹן,
גּוֹמֵל חֲסָדִים טוֹבִים,
וְקֹנֵה הַכֹּל,
וְזוֹכֵר חַסְדֵי אָבוֹת,
וּמֵבִיא גוֹאֵל
לִבְנֵי בְנֵיהֶם,
לְמַעַן שְׁמוֹ בְּאַהֲבָה.

*On Shabbat Shuvah, the Shabbat between Rosh Hashanah and Yom Kippur:*

Zokhreinu l'ḥayyim,
melekh ḥafeitz ba-ḥayyim,
v'khotveinu b'seifer ha-ḥayyim,
l'ma·ankha Elohim ḥayyim.

זָכְרֵנוּ לְחַיִּים,
מֶלֶךְ חָפֵץ בַּחַיִּים,
וְכָתְבֵנוּ בְּסֵפֶר הַחַיִּים,
לְמַעַנְךָ אֱלֹהִים חַיִּים.

Melekh ozeir u-moshi·a u-magein.
Barukh Atah Adonai
magein Avraham [u-fokeid Sarah].

מֶלֶךְ עוֹזֵר וּמוֹשִׁיעַ וּמָגֵן.
בָּרוּךְ אַתָּה יְיָ,
מָגֵן אַבְרָהָם (וּפֹקֵד שָׂרָה).

# Amidah for Shabbat Minḥah

## AVOT

### *God of our Ancestors*

Praised are You, Adonai our God and God of our ancestors, God of Abraham, God of Isaac, and God of Jacob, [God of Sarah, God of Rebecca, God of Rachel and God of Leah], the great, strong and awe-inspiring God, God on high. You act with lovingkindness and create everything. God remembers the loving deeds of our ancestors, and will bring a redeemer to their children's children because that is God's loving nature.

*On Shabbat Shuvah, the Shabbat between Rosh Hashanah and Yom Kippur:*

Remember us for life, Ruler who wants life, and write us in the Book of Life, for Your sake, living God.

You are a helping, saving and shielding Ruler. Praised are You, Adonai, Shield of Abraham and Guardian of Sarah.

## G'VUROT

### *God's benevolent power*

| | |
|---|---|
| Atah gibor l'olam Adonai, | אַתָּה גִּבּוֹר לְעוֹלָם אֲדֹנָי, |
| m'ḥayeih meitim Atah, | מְחַיֵּה מֵתִים אַתָּה, |
| rav l'hoshi·a. | רַב לְהוֹשִׁיעַ. |
| (mashiv haru·aḥ | (מַשִּׁיב הָרוּחַ |
| u-morid ha-gashem) | וּמוֹרִיד הַגֶּשֶׁם). |
| M'khalkeil ḥayim b'ḥesed, | מְכַלְכֵּל חַיִּים בְּחֶסֶד, |
| m'ḥayei meitim b'raḥamim | מְחַיֵּה מֵתִים בְּרַחֲמִים רַבִּים, |
| rabim, someikh nof'lim | סוֹמֵךְ נוֹפְלִים, |
| v'rofei ḥolim | וְרוֹפֵא חוֹלִים, |
| u-matir asurim, | וּמַתִּיר אֲסוּרִים, |
| um'kayeim emunato | וּמְקַיֵּם אֱמוּנָתוֹ |
| lisheinei afar. | לִישֵׁנֵי עָפָר, |
| Mi khamokha, | מִי כָמוֹךָ |
| ba·al g'vurot | בַּעַל גְּבוּרוֹת |
| u-mi domeh lakh, | וּמִי דּוֹמֶה לָּךְ, |
| Melekh meimit um'ḥayeih | מֶלֶךְ מֵמִית וּמְחַיֶּה |
| u-matzmi·aḥ y'shu·a. | וּמַצְמִיחַ יְשׁוּעָה. |

*On Shabbat Shuvah, the Shabbat between Rosh Hashanah and Yom Kippur:*

| | |
|---|---|
| Mi khamokha Av ha-raḥamim | מִי כָמוֹךָ אַב הָרַחֲמִים, |
| Zokeir y'tsurav l'ḥayyim b'raḥamim. | זוֹכֵר יְצוּרָיו לְחַיִּים בְּרַחֲמִים. |

| | |
|---|---|
| v'ne·eman Atah | וְנֶאֱמָן אַתָּה |
| l'haḥayot meitim. | לְהַחֲיוֹת מֵתִים. |
| Barukh Atah Adonai, | בָּרוּךְ אַתָּה יְיָ, |
| m'ḥayeih ha-meitim. | מְחַיֵּה הַמֵּתִים. |

## G'VUROT

### *God's benevolent power*

You are mighty forever, Adonai, giving life to the dead with Your great saving power.

*From Sh'mini Atzeret until Pesaḥ, we pray for rain:*

You cause the wind to blow and the rain to fall.

You support the living with kindness, you give life to the dead with great mercy. You support the fallen, heal the sick and set free those in prison. You keep faith with those who sleep in the dust. Who is like You, Sovereign of mighty deeds, and who can compare to You, Ruler of life and death who causes salvation to bloom.

*On Shabbat Shuvah, the Shabbat between Rosh Hashanah and Yom Kippur:*

Who is like you, Merciful Parent? You remember those You created with the merciful gift of life.

You are trustworthy in giving life to the dead. Praised are You, who gives life to the dead.

## K'DUSHAH

### *We praise God's holiness*

| | |
|---|---|
| N'kadeish | נְקַדֵּשׁ |
| et shimkha ba-olam | אֶת שִׁמְךָ בָּעוֹלָם, |
| k'sheim she-makdishim oto | כְּשֵׁם שֶׁמַּקְדִּישִׁים אוֹתוֹ |
| bish'mei marom, | בִּשְׁמֵי מָרוֹם, |
| kakatuv al yad n'vi·ekha | כַּכָּתוּב עַל יַד נְבִיאֶךָ, |
| v'kara zeh el zeh v'amar. | וְקָרָא זֶה אֶל זֶה וְאָמַר: |
| | |
| *Kadosh kadosh kadosh | *קָדוֹשׁ, קָדוֹשׁ, קָדוֹשׁ, |
| Adonai Tz'va·ot, | יְיָ צְבָאוֹת, |
| m'lo khol ha-aretz k'vodo. | מְלֹא כָל הָאָרֶץ כְּבוֹדוֹ. |
| | |
| L'umatam barukh yomeiru. | לְעֻמָּתָם בָּרוּךְ יֹאמֵרוּ: |
| | |
| *Barukh k'vod Adonai mimkomo. | *בָּרוּךְ כְּבוֹד יְיָ מִמְּקוֹמוֹ. |
| | |
| U-v'divrei kodsh'kha katuv leimor: | וּבְדִבְרֵי קָדְשְׁךָ כָּתוּב לֵאמֹר: |
| | |
| *Yimlokh Adonai l'olam, | *יִמְלֹךְ יְיָ לְעוֹלָם, |
| Elohayikh Tziyon | אֱלֹהַיִךְ צִיּוֹן, |
| l'dor va-dor. Hall'luyah. | לְדֹר וָדֹר, הַלְלוּיָהּ. |
| | |
| L'dor va-dor | לְדוֹר וָדוֹר |
| nagid godlekha | נַגִּיד גָּדְלֶךָ, |
| u-l'netzaḥ n'tzaḥim | וּלְנֵצַח נְצָחִים |
| k'dushatkha nakdish. | קְדֻשָּׁתְךָ נַקְדִּישׁ, |
| v'shivḥakha Eloheinu | וְשִׁבְחֲךָ, אֱלֹהֵינוּ, |
| mipinu lo yamush | מִפִּינוּ לֹא יָמוּשׁ |
| l'olam va·ed, | לְעוֹלָם וָעֶד, |
| ki Eil Melekh gadol v'kadosh Atah. | כִּי אֵל מֶלֶךְ גָּדוֹל וְקָדוֹשׁ אָתָּה. |
| Barukh Atah Adonai, | בָּרוּךְ אַתָּה יְיָ, |
| he-Eil ha-kadosh | הָאֵל הַקָּדוֹשׁ |

*On Shabbat Shuvah, the Shabbat between Rosh Hashanah and Yom Kippur:*

| | |
|---|---|
| [ha-Melekh ha-kadosh]. | הַמֶּלֶךְ הַקָּדוֹשׁ. |

## K'DUSHAH

***We praise God's holiness.***

We shall tell of Your holiness on earth just as it is told in the heavens above. As Your prophet wrote, the angels called to one another, saying

"Holy, holy, holy is *Adonai Tzeva'ot*, the whole world is filled with God's glory." (Isaiah 6:3)

Those [angels] facing them say "Barukh":

"Praised is God's glory from God's place." (Ezekiel 3:12)

And in Your holy words it is written:

Adonai will rule forever, your God, O Zion, for all generations. Halleluyah. (Psalm 146:10)

For all generations we will tell Your greatness, and we will add our holiness to Yours forever and ever. We will never stop praising you, for You are a great and holy God.

*When reading the Amidah silently, substitute this blessing for the Kedushah:*

You are holy and Your Name is holy and holy beings praise You every day.

Praised are You Adonai, holy God.

*On Shabbat Shuvah, the Shabbat between Rosh Hashanah and Yom Kippur:*

Praised are You Adonai, the Holy Ruler.

## K'DUSHAT HA-YOM

| | |
|---|---|
| Atah ehad v'shimkha ehad, | אַתָּה אֶחָד וְשִׁמְךָ אֶחָד, |
| u-mi K'amkha Yisra·el goy eḥad | וּמִי כְּעַמְּךָ יִשְׂרָאֵל גּוֹי אֶחָד |
| ba-aretz, Tif·eret g'ulah, | בָּאָרֶץ, תִּפְאֶרֶת גְּדֻלָּה, |
| va-ateret y'shu·ah, | וַעֲטֶרֶת יְשׁוּעָה, |
| Yom m'nuḥah u-k'dushah | יוֹם מְנוּחָה וּקְדֻשָּׁה |
| l'amkha natata, | לְעַמְּךָ נָתָתָּ, |
| Avraham yageil, Yitzḥak y'ranein, | אַבְרָהָם יָגֵל, יִצְחָק יְרַנֵּן, |
| Ya·akov u-vanav yanuḥu vo, | יַעֲקֹב וּבָנָיו יָנוּחוּ בוֹ, |
| m'nuḥat ahavah u-n'davah, | מְנוּחַת אַהֲבָה וּנְדָבָה, |
| m'nuḥat emet ve-emunah, | מְנוּחַת אֱמֶת וֶאֱמוּנָה, |
| m'nuḥat shalom v'shalvah | מְנוּחַת שָׁלוֹם וְשַׁלְוָה |
| v'hashkeit va-vetaḥ, | וְהַשְׁקֵט וָבֶטַח, |
| m'nuḥah sh'leimah | מְנוּחָה שְׁלֵמָה |
| she-Atah rotzeh bah, | שָׁאַתָּה רוֹצֶה בָּהּ, |
| yakiru vanekha | יַכִּירוּ בָנֶיךָ |
| v'yeid·u | וְיֵדְעוּ |
| ki mei-it'kha hi m'nuḥatam, | כִּי מֵאִתְּךָ הִיא מְנוּחָתָם, |
| v'al m'nuḥatam | וְעַל מְנוּחָתָם |
| yakdishu et sh'mekha. | יַקְדִּישׁוּ אֶת שְׁמֶךָ. |

| | |
|---|---|
| Eloheinu vEilohei avoteinu, | אֱלֹהֵינוּ וֵאלֹהֵי אֲבוֹתֵינוּ, |
| r'tzei vim'nuhateinu, | רְצֵה בִמְנוּחָתֵנוּ, |
| Kad'sheinu b'mitz-votekha | קַדְּשֵׁנוּ בְּמִצְוֹתֶיךָ, |
| v'tein helkeinu b'Toratekha, | וְתֵן חֶלְקֵנוּ בְּתוֹרָתֶךָ, |
| sab·einu mi-tuvekha | שַׂבְּעֵנוּ מִטּוּבֶךָ, |
| v'samheinu bishu·atekha, | וְשַׂמְּחֵנוּ בִּישׁוּעָתֶךָ, |
| v'taheir libeinu l'ov-d'kha be·emet. | וְטַהֵר לִבֵּנוּ לְעָבְדְּךָ בֶּאֱמֶת, |
| V'hanhileinu Adonai Eloheinu | וְהַנְחִילֵנוּ יְיָ אֱלֹהֵינוּ |
| b'ahavah u-v'ratzon | בְּאַהֲבָה וּבְרָצוֹן |
| Shabbat kod-shekha. | שַׁבַּת קָדְשֶׁךָ, |
| V'yanuhu vam Yisra·el | וְיָנוּחוּ בָם יִשְׂרָאֵל |
| m'kadshei sh'mekha. | מְקַדְּשֵׁי שְׁמֶךָ. |
| Barukh Atah Adonai, | בָּרוּךְ אַתָּה יְיָ, |
| m'kadeish ha-Shabbat. | מְקַדֵּשׁ הַשַּׁבָּת. |

## K'DUSHAT HA-YOM

You are One and Your Name is One, and who is like Your people Israel, a unique people in the world? Magnificent in greatness, crown of salvation – a day of rest and holiness You gave to your people. Abraham rejoices, Isaac sang with joy, Jacob and his sons rested on it – a rest of love freely given, a rest of truth and faithfulness, a rest of peace and tranquility, quiet and security, a perfect rest that is pleasing to You. May Your children know and understand that their rest comes from You, and that through their rest, they sanctify Your Name.

Our God and God of our ancestors, be pleased with our Shabbat rest, make us holy with Your mitzvot and let us share in Your Torah. Satisfy us with Your goodness and make us happy with Your help. Purify our hearts so that we can serve you truly. Adonai our God, let us receive Your holy Shabbat with love and favor, so that Your people Israel who make Your Name holy will rest on it. Praised are You Adonai, who makes the Shabbat holy.

**Atah Eḥad:** On Shabbat afternoon, as the shadows lengthen and our souls blossom with Shabbat holiness and rest, we say these lovely words. We thank God for the gift of Shabbat rest, with many synonyms for rest and tranquility, because Shabbat rest – *menuḥah* – is unique. It's not only stopping work. It's more than a day off. It is a positive experience of God's blessing and love, our soul's beauty, and sacred time.

Another thought: In the Friday night Kabbalat service, the K'dushat Ha-yom has the Va-y'khulu passage from the Creation story, tying the Amidah to the theme of Creation. In the Shabbat Shaḥarit Amidah, we refer to Moses bringing down the two Tablets of the Commandments with the mitzvah of Shabbat written on them. This ties in with the theme of Revelation. Here, on Shabbat afternoon, we find the theme of Redemption, a time when Shabbat will be fulfilled with perfection. There are several clues to this redemption theme. "You are One and Your Name is One" reminds us of the quote from Zechariah at the end of Aleinu, "On that day God will be One and God's name will be One," which is a vision of the End of Days. Also, the reference to the Ancestors can also be read in the future tense to refer to the time that will be one of "perfect rest." So consider this idea of redemption. What would a redeemed world look like? What would be changed? And we Jews also like to ask, "What can I do to bring the world close to redemption?

## AVODAH

***We pray to God to accept our prayers.***

| | |
|---|---|
| R'tzeih Adonai Eloheinu | רְצֵה, יְיָ אֱלֹהֵינוּ, |
| b'am'kha Yisra·el u-vit'filatam, | בְּעַמְּךָ יִשְׂרָאֵל וּבִתְפִלָּתָם, |
| v'hasheiv et ha-avodah | וְהָשֵׁב אֶת הָעֲבוֹדָה |
| li-d'vir beitekha, | לִדְבִיר בֵּיתֶךָ, |
| u-t'filatamn b'ahavah | וּתְפִלָּתָם בְּאַהֲבָה |
| t'kabeil b'ratzon. | תְקַבֵּל בְּרָצוֹן, |
| U-t'hi l'ratzon tamid | וּתְהִי לְרָצוֹן תָּמִיד |
| avodat Yisra·el amekha. | עֲבוֹדַת יִשְׂרָאֵל עַמֶּךָ. |

*On Rosh Ḥodesh and on Ḥol Ha-mo·ed,*
*we add the prayer known as Ya·aleh v'yavo.*

אֱלֹהֵינוּ וֵאלֹהֵי אֲבוֹתֵינוּ, יַעֲלֶה וְיָבֹא, וְיַגִּיעַ, וְיֵרָאֶה, וְיֵרָצֶה, וְיִשָּׁמַע, וְיִפָּקֵד, וְיִזָּכֵר זִכְרוֹנֵנוּ וּפִקְדוֹנֵנוּ, וְזִכְרוֹן אֲבוֹתֵינוּ, וְזִכְרוֹן מָשִׁיחַ בֶּן דָּוִד עַבְדֶּךָ, וְזִכְרוֹן יְרוּשָׁלַיִם עִיר קָדְשֶׁךָ, וְזִכְרוֹן כָּל עַמְּךָ בֵּית יִשְׂרָאֵל לְפָנֶיךָ, לִפְלֵיטָה, לְטוֹבָה, לְחֵן וּלְחֶסֶד וּלְרַחֲמִים, לְחַיִּים וּלְשָׁלוֹם, בְּיוֹם

רֹאשׁ הַחֹדֶשׁ הַזֶּה.
חַג הַמַּצּוֹת הַזֶּה.
חַג הַסֻּכּוֹת הַזֶּה.

| | |
|---|---|
| Zokhreinu Adonai Eloheinu | זָכְרֵנוּ, יְיָ אֱלֹהֵינוּ, |
| bo l'tovah Amen! | בּוֹ לְטוֹבָה, |
| U'fokdeinu vo liv'rakha Amen! | וּפָקְדֵנוּ בוֹ לִבְרָכָה, |
| v'hoshi·einu vo l'ḥayyim Amen! | וְהוֹשִׁיעֵנוּ בוֹ לְחַיִּים. |

| | |
|---|---|
| V'teḥezenah eineinu | וְתֶחֱזֶינָה עֵינֵינוּ |
| b'shuv'kha l'Tziyon b'raḥamim. | בְּשׁוּבְךָ לְצִיּוֹן בְּרַחֲמִים. |
| Barukh Atah Adonai | בָּרוּךְ אַתָּה יְיָ, |
| ha-maḥazir sh'khinato l'Tziyon. | הַמַּחֲזִיר שְׁכִינָתוֹ לְצִיּוֹן. |

## AVODAH

***We pray to God to accept our prayers.***

Adonai, be pleased with Your people Israel and with their prayer. Restore worship to Your Temple. May the prayer of Your people Israel always be accepted with love and favor.

*On Rosh ḥodesh and on ḥol Ha-mo•ed, we add the prayer known as Yàaleh v'yavo.*

Our God and God of our ancestors, may [what we pray for] ascend, come, and reach, appear, be accepted and heard, counted and remembered: our memory and our record, the memory of our ancestors, and the memory of the Messiah, the son of David Your servant; the memory of Jerusalem, Your holy city, and the memory of Your entire people, before You, for survival, for good, for grace, for lovingkindness, for mercy, for life and for peace on this…

The first day of the month
The festival of Matzah
The Festival of Sukkot

Remember us on it, Adonai our God, for good; take note of us on it for blessing; and save us on it for life. In this matter of salvation and mercy, spare us and be gracious to us, and have mercy upon us and save us, for our eyes are turned toward You, for you are God, sovereign, gracious and merciful.

May we see Your merciful return to Zion. Praised are You, Adonai, who restores Your presence to Zion.

## MODIM

### *Thank You, God.*

מוֹדִים אֲנַֽחְנוּ לָךְ, שָׁאַתָּה הוּא, יְיָ אֱלֹהֵֽינוּ וֵאלֹהֵי אֲבוֹתֵֽינוּ, לְעוֹלָם וָעֶד, צוּר חַיֵּֽינוּ, מָגֵן יִשְׁעֵֽנוּ, אַתָּה הוּא לְדוֹר וָדוֹר, נוֹדֶה לְּךָ וּנְסַפֵּר תְּהִלָּתֶֽךָ, עַל חַיֵּֽינוּ הַמְּסוּרִים בְּיָדֶֽךָ, וְעַל נִשְׁמוֹתֵֽינוּ הַפְּקוּדוֹת לָךְ, וְעַל נִסֶּֽיךָ שֶׁבְּכָל יוֹם עִמָּֽנוּ, וְעַל נִפְלְאוֹתֶֽיךָ וְטוֹבוֹתֶֽיךָ שֶׁבְּכָל עֵת, עֶֽרֶב וָבֹֽקֶר וְצָהֳרָֽיִם, הַטּוֹב, כִּי לֹא כָלוּ רַחֲמֶֽיךָ, וְהַמְרַחֵם, כִּי לֹא תַֽמּוּ חֲסָדֶֽיךָ, מֵעוֹלָם קִוִּֽינוּ לָךְ מוֹדִים אֲנַֽחְנוּ לָךְ,

*On Ḥanukah:*

| | |
|---|---|
| עַל הַנִּסִּים, וְעַל הַפֻּרְקָן, | Al ha-nisim v'al ha-purkan, |
| וְעַל הַגְּבוּרוֹת, | v'al ha-g'vurot, |
| וְעַל הַתְּשׁוּעוֹת, | v'al ha-t'shu·ot, |
| וְעַל הַמִּלְחָמוֹת, | v'al ha-milḥamot |
| שֶׁעָשִֽׂיתָ לַאֲבוֹתֵֽינוּ | she-asita la-avoteinu |
| בַּיָּמִים הָהֵם בַּזְּמַן הַזֶּה. | ba-yamim ha-heim z'man ha-zeh. |

בִּימֵי מַתִּתְיָֽהוּ בֶּן יוֹחָנָן כֹּהֵן גָּדוֹל, חַשְׁמוֹנַאי וּבָנָיו, כְּשֶׁעָמְדָה מַלְכוּת יָוָן הָרְשָׁעָה עַל עַמְּךָ יִשְׂרָאֵל לְהַשְׁכִּיחָם תּוֹרָתֶֽךָ, וּלְהַעֲבִירָם מֵחֻקֵּי רְצוֹנֶֽךָ, וְאַתָּה בְּרַחֲמֶֽיךָ הָרַבִּים עָמַֽדְתָּ לָהֶם בְּעֵת צָרָתָם, רַֽבְתָּ אֶת רִיבָם, דַּֽנְתָּ אֶת דִּינָם, נָקַֽמְתָּ אֶת נִקְמָתָם, מָסַֽרְתָּ גִבּוֹרִים בְּיַד חַלָּשִׁים, וְרַבִּים בְּיַד מְעַטִּים, וּטְמֵאִים בְּיַד טְהוֹרִים, וּרְשָׁעִים בְּיַד צַדִּיקִים, וְזֵדִים בְּיַד עוֹסְקֵי תוֹרָתֶֽךָ. וּלְךָ עָשִֽׂיתָ שֵׁם גָּדוֹל וְקָדוֹשׁ בְּעוֹלָמֶֽךָ, וּלְעַמְּךָ יִשְׂרָאֵל עָשִֽׂיתָ תְּשׁוּעָה גְדוֹלָה וּפֻרְקָן כְּהַיּוֹם הַזֶּה. וְאַחַר כֵּן בָּֽאוּ בָנֶֽיךָ לִדְבִיר בֵּיתֶֽךָ, וּפִנּוּ אֶת הֵיכָלֶֽךָ, וְטִהֲרוּ אֶת מִקְדָּשֶֽׁךָ, וְהִדְלִֽיקוּ נֵרוֹת בְּחַצְרוֹת קָדְשֶֽׁךָ, וְקָבְעוּ שְׁמוֹנַת יְמֵי חֲנֻכָּה אֵֽלּוּ, לְהוֹדוֹת וּלְהַלֵּל לְשִׁמְךָ הַגָּדוֹל.

וְעַל כֻּלָּם יִתְבָּרַךְ וְיִתְרוֹמַם שִׁמְךָ מַלְכֵּֽנוּ תָּמִיד לְעוֹלָם וָעֶד.

## MODIM

### *Thank You, God.*

We give thanks for God's daily miracles

We thank You for being our God and God of our ancestors forever and ever. You are the Rock of our lives and our saving Shield. In every generation we will thank and praise You for our lives which are in Your power, for our souls which are in Your keeping, for Your miracles which are with us every day, and for your wonders and good things that are with us at all times, evening, morning, and noon. O Good One, Your mercies have never stopped. O Merciful One, your kindness has never stopped. We have always placed our hope in You. For all these things, our Ruler, may Your Name be blessed and honored forever.

*On Ḥanukah:*

We thank You, God, for the miracles, for the rescues, for the mighty deeds, for the saving acts, and for the wars that you fought for our ancestors long ago at this time of year.

In the days of Mattathias son of Yochanan, the High Priest, of the Hasmonean family, and his sons, when the evil Greek government rose up against Your people Israel, they tried to make them forget Your Torah and break Your laws. You, in Your great mercy, stood firm for them in their time of trouble. You defended them, you judged in their favor, you punished their enemies. You helped the weak to defeat the strong, the few to defeat the many, the pure to defeat the impure, the righteous to defeat the wicked, and the followers of Your Torah to defeat the sinners. Because you did this, Your Name was made great and holy before all the world. You won a great victory for Your people Israel that lasted until this day. Afterwards, Your children came into the holiest part of Your House, cleaned and purified Your Palace, and lit lights in the courtyards of Your Holy Place. They set these eight days of Hanukah as a time for thanking and Praising You.

For all these things, our Ruler, may Your name be blessed and honored forever.

*On Shabbat Shuvah, the Shabbat between Rosh Hashanah and Yom Kippur, add:*

וּכְתוֹב לְחַיִּים טוֹבִים כָּל בְּנֵי בְרִיתֶךָ.

וְכֹל הַחַיִּים יוֹדְוּךָ סֶּלָה, וִיהַלְלוּ אֶת שִׁמְךָ בֶּאֱמֶת, הָאֵל יְשׁוּעָתֵנוּ וְעֶזְרָתֵנוּ סֶלָה. בָּרוּךְ אַתָּה יְיָ, הַטּוֹב שִׁמְךָ וּלְךָ נָאֶה לְהוֹדוֹת.

## BIRKAT SHALOM

### *The Blessing of Peace*

| | |
|---|---|
| Shalom rav al Yisra·el amkha | שָׁלוֹם רָב עַל יִשְׂרָאֵל עַמְּךָ |
| Tasim l'olam. | תָּשִׂים לְעוֹלָם, |
| Ki atah hu Melekh Adon | כִּי אַתָּה הוּא מֶלֶךְ אָדוֹן |
| l'khol ha-olam. | לְכָל הַשָּׁלוֹם. |
| V'tov b'einekha l'vareikh | וְטוֹב בְּעֵינֶיךָ לְבָרֵךְ |
| et amkha Yisra·el | אֶת עַמְּךָ יִשְׂרָאֵל |
| b'khol eit uv'khol sha·ah | בְּכָל עֵת וּבְכָל שָׁעָה |
| bish'lomekha. | בִּשְׁלוֹמֶךָ. |

*On Shabbat Shuvah, the Shabbat between Rosh Hashanah and Yom Kippur, say these words instead of the next paragraph:.*

| | |
|---|---|
| B'seifer ḥayyim, b'rakhah v'shalom, | בְּסֵפֶר חַיִּים, בְּרָכָה וְשָׁלוֹם, |
| u-farnasah tovah, n'zakheir | וּפַרְנָסָה טוֹבָה, נִזָּכֵר |
| v'nikateiv l'fanekha, | וְנִכָּתֵב לְפָנֶיךָ, |
| anaḥnu v'khol amkha beit Yisra·el. | אֲנַחְנוּ וְכָל עַמְּךָ בֵּית יִשְׂרָאֵל, |
| L'ḥayyim tovim u-l'shalom. | לְחַיִּים טוֹבִים וּלְשָׁלוֹם. |
| Barukh atah Adonai | בָּרוּךְ אַתָּה יְיָ, |
| oseh ha-shalom. | עוֹשֵׂה הַשָּׁלוֹם |

| | |
|---|---|
| Barukh atah Adonai ha-m'vareikh | בָּרוּךְ אַתָּה יְיָ, הַמְבָרֵךְ |
| et amo Yisra·el ba-shalom. | אֶת עַמּוֹ יִשְׂרָאֵל בַּשָּׁלוֹם. |

*On Shabbat Shuvah, the Shabbat between Rosh Hashanah and Yom Kippur, add:*

Write us down for a good life.

May every living thing thank You and praise You sincerely, O God, our rescue and help. Praised are You, Your Name is "the Good One," and it is good to thank You.

## BIRKAT SHALOM

***We pray for peace, the ultimate blessing.***

Grant great peace to Your people Israel and to all who live on earth, for You are a Ruler and Sovereign of peace. May it be good in Your eyes to bless Your people Israel in every season at all times with peace.

*On Shabbat Shuvah, the Shabbat between Rosh Hashanah and Yom Kippur, say these words instead of the next paragraph:*

Remember us and write us down in the Book of life, blessing, peace, and support, along with the entire Jewish people, for a good life and for peace. Praised are You, Adonai, who makes peace.

Praised are You, Adonai, who blesses God's people Israel with peace.

## ELOHAI N'TZOR

*A prayer for self-mastery and purification.*

אֱלֹהַי, נְצוֹר לְשׁוֹנִי מֵרָע, וּשְׂפָתַי מִדַּבֵּר מִרְמָה, וְלִמְקַלְלַי נַפְשִׁי תִדֹּם, וְנַפְשִׁי כֶּעָפָר לַכֹּל תִּהְיֶה. פְּתַח לִבִּי בְּתוֹרָתֶךָ, וּבְמִצְוֹתֶיךָ תִּרְדּוֹף נַפְשִׁי. וְכָל הַחוֹשְׁבִים עָלַי רָעָה, מְהֵרָה הָפֵר עֲצָתָם וְקַלְקֵל מַחֲשַׁבְתָּם. עֲשֵׂה לְמַעַן שְׁמֶךָ, עֲשֵׂה לְמַעַן יְמִינֶךָ, עֲשֵׂה לְמַעַן קְדֻשָּׁתֶךָ, עֲשֵׂה לְמַעַן תּוֹרָתֶךָ. לְמַעַן יֵחָלְצוּן יְדִידֶיךָ, הוֹשִׁיעָה יְמִינְךָ וַעֲנֵנִי. יִהְיוּ לְרָצוֹן אִמְרֵי פִי וְהֶגְיוֹן לִבִּי לְפָנֶיךָ, יְיָ צוּרִי וְגוֹאֲלִי.

| | |
|---|---|
| Oseh shalom bimromav, | עֹשֶׂה שָׁלוֹם בִּמְרוֹמָיו, |
| Hu ya·aseh shalom aleinu | הוּא יַעֲשֶׂה שָׁלוֹם עָלֵינוּ, |
| v'al kol Yisra·el, | וְעַל כָּל יִשְׂרָאֵל, |
| v'imru Amen. | וְאִמְרוּ אָמֵן. |

*This prayer is not said when Taḥanun would be omitted during the week to come because of Rosh Ḥodesh or a Festival:*

צִדְקָתְךָ צֶדֶק לְעוֹלָם, וְתוֹרָתְךָ אֱמֶת. וְצִדְקָתְךָ אֱלֹהִים עַד מָרוֹם אֲשֶׁר עָשִׂיתָ גְדֹלוֹת, אֱלֹהִים מִי כָמוֹךָ. צִדְקָתְךָ כְּהַרְרֵי אֵל, מִשְׁפָּטֶיךָ תְּהוֹם רַבָּה, אָדָם וּבְהֵמָה תוֹשִׁיעַ, יְיָ.

## ELOHAI N'TZOR

***An additional prayer for self-mastery and purification.***

My God, help me not to say bad things or to tell lies. Help me to ignore people who say bad things about me. Open my heart to Your Torah, so that I can do Your mitzvot. If anyone wants to do me harm, quickly stop their ideas and spoil their plans. Do this because of Your love, Your holiness, and Your Torah: so that those You love will be free. May the words of my mouth and the thoughts of my heart find favor with You, my Rock and my Savior.

May the One who makes peace up above give peace to us and to all the people of Israel. Amen.

*This prayer is not said when Taḥanun would be omitted during the week to come because of Rosh Ḥodesh or a Festival:*

Your righteousness is righteous forever, and Your Torah is truth.
And Your righteousness, God, reaches the heights, where You did great things – O God, who is like You?
Your righteousness is like the mighty mountains; Your laws are like the great deep. You deliver humans and animals, Adonai.

## KADDISH SHALEIM

*Leader:*

| | |
|---|---|
| Yit-gadal v'yit-kadash sh'mei rabba, | יִתְגַּדַּל וְיִתְקַדַּשׁ שְׁמֵהּ רַבָּא. |
| b'al'ma di v'ra | בְּעָלְמָא דִּי בְרָא |
| khir'utei | כִרְעוּתֵהּ, |
| v'yam-likh malkhutei | וְיַמְלִיךְ מַלְכוּתֵהּ |
| b'ḥayeikhon u-v'yomei'khon | בְּחַיֵּיכוֹן וּבְיוֹמֵיכוֹן |
| u-v'ḥayei d'khol beit Yisra·el, | וּבְחַיֵּי דְכָל בֵּית יִשְׂרָאֵל, |
| ba·agala u-viz'man kariv, | בַּעֲגָלָא וּבִזְמַן קָרִיב, |
| v'imru, Amen. | וְאִמְרוּ אָמֵן. |

*Congregation and Leader:*

| | |
|---|---|
| Y'hei sh'mei rabba m'va-rakh, | יְהֵא שְׁמֵהּ רַבָּא מְבָרַךְ |
| l'alam ul-almei al'maya. | לְעָלַם וּלְעָלְמֵי עָלְמַיָּא. |

*Leader:*

| | |
|---|---|
| Yitbarakh v'yishtabaḥ | יִתְבָּרַךְ וְיִשְׁתַּבַּח |
| v'yitpa·ar v'yitromam v'yitnasei | וְיִתְפָּאַר וְיִתְרוֹמַם וְיִתְנַשֵּׂא |
| v'yithadar v'yit·aleh v'yithalal | וְיִתְהַדָּר וְיִתְעַלֶּה וְיִתְהַלָּל |
| sh'mei d'kud'sha, b'rikh Hu. | שְׁמֵהּ דְּקֻדְשָׁא בְּרִיךְ הוּא, |
| L'eila | לְעֵלָּא |
| [u-l'eila mi-kol] | (בעשי"ת לְעֵלָּא וּלְעֵלָּא מִכָּל) |
| min kol birkhata v'shirata | מִן כָּל בִּרְכָתָא וְשִׁירָתָא |
| tushb'ḥata v'neḥemata | תֻּשְׁבְּחָתָא וְנֶחֱמָתָא, |
| da·amiran b'al'ma, | דַּאֲמִירָן בְּעָלְמָא, |
| v'imru Amen. | וְאִמְרוּ אָמֵן. |
| Titkabel | תִּתְקַבֵּל |
| tz'lot'hon uva-ut'hon | צְלוֹתְהוֹן וּבָעוּתְהוֹן |
| d'khol Yisra·el | דְּכָל יִשְׂרָאֵל |
| kadam avuhon di vish'maya, | קֳדָם אֲבוּהוֹן דִּי בִשְׁמַיָּא |
| v'imru Amen. | וְאִמְרוּ אָמֵן. |
| Y'hei sh'lama rabba min shamaya | יְהֵא שְׁלָמָא רַבָּא מִן שְׁמַיָּא, |
| v'ḥayyim | וְחַיִּים |
| aleinu v'al kol Yisra·el, | עָלֵינוּ וְעַל כָּל יִשְׂרָאֵל, |
| v'imru Amen. | וְאִמְרוּ אָמֵן. |

*Take three steps back and bow to the left at the word "oseh", to the right at "hu", and to the center at "aleinu".*

| | |
|---|---|
| Oseh shalom bim'romav, | עֹשֶׂה שָׁלוֹם בִּמְרוֹמָיו, |
| Hu ya·aseh shalom | הוּא יַעֲשֶׂה שָׁלוֹם |
| aleinu v'al kol Yisra·el, | עָלֵינוּ וְעַל כָּל יִשְׂרָאֵל, |
| v'imru Amen. | וְאִמְרוּ אָמֵן. |

## KADDISH SHALEIM

May God's great name be made great and holy in the world that God created according to God's will. May God establish the Divine kingdom soon, in our days, quickly and in the near future, and let us say, Amen.

*Congregation and Leader together:*

May God's great name be praised forever and ever.

Blessed, praised, glorified and raised high, honored and elevated be the name of the Holy Blessed One, far beyond all blessings and songs, praises and comforts which people can say, and let us say: Amen.

May the prayers and pleas of the entire House of Israel be accepted before their Parent in heaven. And let us say: Amen.

May there be abundant peace from heaven and life for us and for all Israel, and let us say: Amen.

May the One who makes peace in the high heavens make peace for us and for all Israel, and let us say: Amen.

## ALEINU

***Praise and hope; the particular blessings of being a Jew and universal hopes for all mankind.***

| | |
|---|---|
| Aleinu l'shabei·aḥ | עָלֵינוּ לְשַׁבֵּחַ |
| la-Adon hakol, | לַאֲדוֹן הַכֹּל, |
| lateit g'dulah | לָתֵת גְּדֻלָּה |
| l'yotzeir b'reishit. | לְיוֹצֵר בְּרֵאשִׁית, |
| Shelo asanu | שֶׁלֹּא עָשָׂנוּ |
| k'goyei ha-aratzot | כְּגוֹיֵי הָאֲרָצוֹת, |
| v'lo samanu | וְלֹא שָׂמָנוּ |
| k'mishp'ḥot ha-adamah, | כְּמִשְׁפְּחוֹת הָאֲדָמָה, |
| shelo sam | שֶׁלֹּא שָׂם |
| ḥelkeinu kahem | חֶלְקֵנוּ כָּהֶם, |
| v'goraleinu k'khol hamonam. | וְגֹרָלֵנוּ כְּכָל הֲמוֹנָם, |
| Va-anaḥnu kor'im u-mishtaḥavim | וַאֲנַחְנוּ כּוֹרְעִים וּמִשְׁתַּחֲוִים |
| u-modim | וּמוֹדִים, |
| lifnei Melekh malkhei ham'lakhim | לִפְנֵי מֶלֶךְ מַלְכֵי הַמְּלָכִים, |
| Hakadosh Barukh Hu. | הַקָּדוֹשׁ בָּרוּךְ הוּא. |
| She-hu noteh shamayim | שֶׁהוּא נוֹטֶה שָׁמַיִם |
| v'yoseid aretz, | וְיֹסֵד אָרֶץ, |
| u-moshav y'karo | וּמוֹשַׁב יְקָרוֹ |
| ba-shamayim mima·al | בַּשָּׁמַיִם מִמַּעַל, |
| ush'khinat uzo | וּשְׁכִינַת עֻזּוֹ |
| b'govhei m'romim. | בְּגָבְהֵי מְרוֹמִים, |
| Hu Eloheinu ein od. | הוּא אֱלֹהֵינוּ אֵין עוֹד. |
| Emet Malkeinu | אֱמֶת מַלְכֵּנוּ, |
| efes zulato | אֶפֶס זוּלָתוֹ, |
| kakatuv b'Torato: | כַּכָּתוּב בְּתוֹרָתוֹ: |
| v'yada·ta hayom | וְיָדַעְתָּ הַיּוֹם |
| vahashevotah el l'vavekha, | וַהֲשֵׁבֹתָ אֶל לְבָבֶךָ, |
| ki Adonai Hu ha-Elohim | כִּי יְיָ הוּא הָאֱלֹהִים |
| ba-shamayim mima·al | בַּשָּׁמַיִם מִמַּעַל, |
| v'al ha-aretz mitaḥat | וְעַל הָאָרֶץ מִתָּחַת, |
| ein od. | אֵין עוֹד. |

## ALEINU

***Praise and hope; the particular blessings of being a Jew and universal hopes for all mankind.***

We should praise the Ruler of all,
tell the greatness of the Creator,
for not making us like the other peoples and
families of the earth, nor giving us the same destiny.
We bend the knee and bow and give thanks to the Ruler
of all earthly rulers, the Blessed Holy One.
God spread out the heavens and built the earth's
foundations, and lives in glory in the heavens.
God's mighty presence is high above.
God is our God – no one else.
Our Ruler is true, there is nothing besides God,
as it is written in His Torah: "You shall know, therefore,
this day and keep in mind that Adonai alone is
God in heaven above and on earth below;
there is no other."

| | |
|---|---|
| Al kein n'kaveh l'ka | עַל כֵּן נְקַוֶּה לְּךָ |
| Adonai Eloheinu | יְיָ אֱלֹהֵינוּ, |
| lir'ot m'heirah b'tif·eret uzekha, | לִרְאוֹת מְהֵרָה בְּתִפְאֶרֶת עֻזֶּךָ, |
| l'ha·avir gilulim min ha-aretz | לְהַעֲבִיר גִּלּוּלִים מִן הָאָרֶץ, |
| v'ha-elilim karot yikareitun, | וְהָאֱלִילִים כָּרוֹת יִכָּרֵתוּן, |
| l'takein olam | לְתַקֵּן עוֹלָם |
| b'malkhut Shadai | בְּמַלְכוּת שַׁדַּי, |
| v'khol b'nei vasar yikr'u vi-Sh'mekha, | וְכָל בְּנֵי בָשָׂר יִקְרְאוּ בִשְׁמֶךָ, |
| l'hafnot eilekha | לְהַפְנוֹת אֵלֶיךָ |
| kol rish·ei aretz. | כָּל רִשְׁעֵי אָרֶץ. |
| Yakiru v'yeid'u | יַכִּירוּ וְיֵדְעוּ |
| kol yoshvei teiveil | כָּל יוֹשְׁבֵי תֵבֵל, |
| ki l'kha tikhra kol berekh | כִּי לְךָ תִּכְרַע כָּל בֶּרֶךְ, |
| tishava kol lashon. | תִּשָּׁבַע כָּל לָשׁוֹן. |
| L'fanekha Adonai Eloheinu | לְפָנֶיךָ יְיָ אֱלֹהֵינוּ |
| yikhr'u v'yipolu. | יִכְרְעוּ וְיִפֹּלוּ, |
| v'likh'vod shimkha y'kar yiteinu, | וְלִכְבוֹד שִׁמְךָ יְקָר יִתֵּנוּ, |
| vikab'lu khulam | וִיקַבְּלוּ כֻלָּם |
| et ol malkhutekha | אֶת עוֹל מַלְכוּתֶךָ, |
| v'timlokh aleihem m'heirah | וְתִמְלֹךְ עֲלֵיהֶם מְהֵרָה |
| l'olam va·ed, | לְעוֹלָם וָעֶד. |
| ki ha-malkhut shel'kha hi | כִּי הַמַּלְכוּת שֶׁלְּךָ הִיא, |
| u-l'ol'mei ad timlokh b'khavod, | וּלְעוֹלְמֵי עַד תִּמְלוֹךְ בְּכָבוֹד, |
| kakatuv b'Toratekha: | כַּכָּתוּב בְּתוֹרָתֶךָ, |
| Adonai yimlokh l'olam va·ed. | יְיָ יִמְלֹךְ לְעוֹלָם וָעֶד. |
| v'ne·emar: | וְנֶאֱמַר, |
| v'hayah Adonai l'Melekh | וְהָיָה יְיָ לְמֶלֶךְ |
| al kol ha-aretz, | עַל כָּל הָאָרֶץ, |
| ba-yom ha-hu yih'yeh Adonai eḥad | בַּיּוֹם הַהוּא יִהְיֶה יְיָ אֶחָד, |
| ush'mo eḥad. | וּשְׁמוֹ אֶחָד. |

And so we hope in You, Adonai our God,
soon to see the glory of Your might,
removing idols from the earth, and banishing false gods,
fixing the brokenness of the world so that it will be God's kingdom.
All humanity will call Your Name,
and all the wicked of the earth will turn toward You.
All who live in the world will know and
understand that every knee must bend to You
and every tongue must promise loyalty.
They will bow to You,
Adonai our God,
honoring the glory of Your name.
All will accept Your authority,
and the time will come soon when You
will rule over them forever.
For the world is Your kingdom,
and you will always rule over it in glory.
As it is written in the Torah:
"Adonai shall rule forever and ever."
And the Prophet Zechariah said:
"God will be Ruler over all the earth. On that day God will be One and God's Name will be One."

## KADDISH YATOM (MOURNER'S KADDISH)

### *We remember the dead by praising God*

*Leader:*

| | |
|---|---|
| Yit-gadal v'yit-kadash sh'mei rabba, | יִתְגַּדַּל וְיִתְקַדַּשׁ שְׁמֵהּ רַבָּא. |
| b'al'ma di v'ra | בְּעָלְמָא דִּי בְרָא |
| khir'utei | כִרְעוּתֵהּ, |
| v'yam-likh malkhutei | וְיַמְלִיךְ מַלְכוּתֵהּ |
| b'ḥayeikhon u-v'yomeikhon | בְּחַיֵּיכוֹן וּבְיוֹמֵיכוֹן |
| u-v'ḥayei d'khol beit Yisra·el, | וּבְחַיֵּי דְכָל בֵּית יִשְׂרָאֵל, |
| ba·agala u-viz'man kariv, | בַּעֲגָלָא וּבִזְמַן קָרִיב, |
| v'imru, Amen. | וְאִמְרוּ אָמֵן. |

*Congregation and Leader:*

| | |
|---|---|
| Y'hei sh'mei rabba m'va-rakh, | יְהֵא שְׁמֵהּ רַבָּא מְבָרַךְ |
| l'alam ul'al'mei al'maya, | לְעָלַם וּלְעָלְמֵי עָלְמַיָּא. |

*Leader:*

| | |
|---|---|
| Yitbarakh v'yishtabaḥ | יִתְבָּרַךְ וְיִשְׁתַּבַּח |
| v'yitpa·ar v'yitromam v'yitnasei | וְיִתְפָּאַר וְיִתְרוֹמַם וְיִתְנַשֵּׂא |
| v'yit-hadar v'yit·aleh v'yit-halal | וְיִתְהַדָּר וְיִתְעַלֶּה וְיִתְהַלָּל |
| sh'mei d'kud'sha, b'rikh Hu. | שְׁמֵהּ דְּקֻדְשָׁא בְּרִיךְ הוּא, |
| L'eila [u-l'eila mi-kol] | לְעֵלָּא (לְעֵלָּא וּלְעֵלָּא מִכָּל) |
| min kol birkhata v'shirata | מִן כָּל בִּרְכָתָא וְשִׁירָתָא |
| tushb'ḥata v'neḥemata | תֻּשְׁבְּחָתָא וְנֶחֱמָתָא, |
| da·amiran b'al'ma, | דַּאֲמִירָן בְּעָלְמָא, |
| v'imru Amen. | וְאִמְרוּ אָמֵן. |
| Y'hei sh'lama rabba min shamaya | יְהֵא שְׁלָמָא רַבָּא מִן שְׁמַיָּא, |
| v'ḥayyim aleinu | וְחַיִּים עָלֵינוּ |
| v'al kol Yisra·el, | וְעַל כָּל יִשְׂרָאֵל, |
| v'imru Amen. | וְאִמְרוּ אָמֵן. |
| Oseh shalom bim'romav, | עֹשֶׂה שָׁלוֹם בִּמְרוֹמָיו, |
| hu ya·aseh shalom | הוּא יַעֲשֶׂה שָׁלוֹם |
| aleinu v'al kol Yisra·el, | עָלֵינוּ וְעַל כָּל יִשְׂרָאֵל, |
| v'imru Amen. | וְאִמְרוּ אָמֵן. |

## KADDISH YATOM (MOURNER'S KADDISH)

***We remember the dead by praising God.***

May God's great Name be made great and holy in the world that God created according to God's will. May God establish the Divine kingdom soon, in our days, quickly and in the near future, and let us say, Amen.

*Congregation and Leader together:*

May God's great Name be praised for ever and ever.

Blessed, praised, glorified and raised high, honored and elevated be the Name of the Holy Blessed One, far beyond all blessings and songs, praises and comforts which people can say, and let us say: Amen.

May there be abundant peace from heaven and life for us and for all Israel, and let us say: Amen.

May the One who makes peace in the high heavens make peace for us and for all Israel, and let us say: Amen.

# Havdalah

| | |
|---|---|
| Hinei Eil y'shu·ati | הִנֵּה אֵל יְשׁוּעָתִי, |
| evtaḥ v'lo efḥad, | אֶבְטַח וְלֹא אֶפְחָד, |
| ki azi v'zimrat Yah Adonai, | כִּי עָזִּי וְזִמְרָת יָהּ יְיָ, |
| va-y'hi li li-shu'ah. | וַיְהִי לִי לִישׁוּעָה. |
| U-sh'avtem mayim b'sasson, | וּשְׁאַבְתֶּם מַיִם בְּשָׂשׂוֹן, |
| mi-ma·ayanei ha-y'shu·ah. | מִמַּעַיְנֵי הַיְשׁוּעָה. |
| Ladonai ha-y'shu·ah | לַייָ הַיְשׁוּעָה, |
| al amkha virkhatekha selah. | עַל עַמְּךָ בִרְכָתֶךָ סֶּלָה. |
| Adonai tz'va·ot imanu | יְיָ צְבָאוֹת עִמָּנוּ, |
| misgav lanu Elohei Ya·akov selah. | מִשְׂגָּב לָנוּ אֱלֹהֵי יַעֲקֹב סֶלָה. |
| Adonai tz'va·ot | יְיָ צְבָאוֹת, |
| ashrei adam botei·aḥ bakh. | אַשְׁרֵי אָדָם בֹּטֵחַ בָּךְ. |
| Adonai hoshi·ah | יְיָ הוֹשִׁיעָה, |
| ha-melekh ya·aneinu v'yom koreinu. | הַמֶּלֶךְ יַעֲנֵנוּ בְיוֹם קָרְאֵנוּ. |
| La-y'hudim hai'ta orah | לַיְּהוּדִים הָיְתָה אוֹרָה |
| v'simḥah v'sasson vikar. | וְשִׂמְחָה וְשָׂשׂוֹן וִיקָר. |
| Kein ti-h'yeh lanu. | כֵּן תִּהְיֶה לָּנוּ. |
| Kos y'shu·ot esa, | כּוֹס יְשׁוּעוֹת אֶשָּׂא, |
| u-v'sheim Adonai ekra. | וּבְשֵׁם יְיָ אֶקְרָא. |

*(Over the wine, but don't drink it yet:)*

| | |
|---|---|
| Barukh atah Adonai, | בָּרוּךְ אַתָּה יְיָ, |
| Eloheinu melekh ha-olam, | אֱלֹהֵינוּ מֶלֶךְ הָעוֹלָם, |
| borei p'ri ha-gafen. | בּוֹרֵא פְּרִי הַגָּפֶן. |

*After the blessing over the wine, the cup is transferred to the left hand, the spices are taken in the right hand, and the blessing is recited.*

| | |
|---|---|
| Barukh atah Adonai, | בָּרוּךְ אַתָּה יְיָ, |
| Eloheinu melekh ha-olam, | אֱלֹהֵינוּ מֶלֶךְ הָעוֹלָם, |
| borei minei v'samim. | בּוֹרֵא מִינֵי בְשָׂמִים. |

# Havdalah

*The word Havdalah means "separation." We mark the boundary between the Shabbat and the rest of the week. Havdalah is recited at the end of Shabbat, with the appearance of the stars. It is recited standing, with the cup of wine in the right hand and the spices in the left hand, or they may be placed on the table or held by another person. We begin with a selection of Bible verses on the common theme of God's help and deliverance.*

Behold!
God is my salvation – I will trust and will not fear; for the strength and song of Adonai God have become my salvation.
You will draw water with joy from the wellsprings of salvation.
To Adonai belongs salvation;upon Your people is Your blessing, Selah.

*Adonai Tziva'ot* is with us ; the God of Jacob is a stronghold for us.
*Adonai Tziva'ot*, fortunate is the one who trusts in You.
Adonai, deliver [us], the Ruler will answer us on the day we call.
For the Jews there was light and joy, gladness and honor.
So may it be for us.
I will raise the cup of salvation and call upon the Name of Adonai.

*(Over the wine, but don't drink it yet:)*

Praised are You, Adonai our God Ruler of the Universe, Creator of the fruit of the vine.

Praised are You, Adonai our God, Ruler of the Universe, Creator of all kinds of spices.

*Now the leader puts down the wine and spices, and says the blessing over he light. In order to link the blessing to an action, we look at our hands. Some cup their hands, look at their fingernails, and make a shadow. This constitutes the first "use" of the light for the new week.*

| | |
|---|---|
| Barukh atah Adonai, | בָּרוּךְ אַתָּה יְיָ, |
| Eloheinu melekh ha-olam, | אֱלֹהֵינוּ מֶלֶךְ הָעוֹלָם, |
| borei m'orei ha-eish. | בּוֹרֵא מְאוֹרֵי הָאֵשׁ. |

*The wine is now taken in the right hand again and the last lessing is recited:*

| | |
|---|---|
| Barukh atah Adonai, | בָּרוּךְ אַתָּה יְיָ, |
| Eloheinu melekh ha-olam, | אֱלֹהֵינוּ מֶלֶךְ הָעוֹלָם, |
| ha-mavdil bein kodesh l'ḥol, | הַמַּבְדִּיל בֵּין קֹדֶשׁ לְחוֹל, |
| bein or l'ḥoshekh, | בֵּין אוֹר לְחֹשֶׁךְ, |
| bein Yisra·el la-amim, | בֵּין יִשְׂרָאֵל לָעַמִּים, |
| bein yom ha-sh'vi·i | בֵּין יוֹם הַשְּׁבִיעִי |
| l'sheishet y'mei ha-ma·aseh. | לְשֵׁשֶׁת יְמֵי הַמַּעֲשֶׂה. |
| Barukh atah Adonai, | בָּרוּךְ אַתָּה יְיָ, |
| ha-mavdil bein kodesh l'ḥol. | הַמַּבְדִּיל בֵּין קֹדֶשׁ לְחוֹל. |

*Drink the wine. Some people extinguish the candle at this point. Some do this by pouring some wine into a dish and dousing it there, others by using the wine cup.*

| | |
|---|---|
| *Ha-mavdil bein kodesh l'ḥol,* | הַמַּבְדִּיל בֵּין קֹדֶשׁ לְחוֹל. |
| *ḥatoteinu hu yimḥol,* | חַטֹּאתֵינוּ הוּא יִמְחֹל |
| *zar·aynu v'khaspeinu yarbeh ka-ḥol,* | זַרְעֵנוּ וְכַסְפֵּנוּ יַרְבֶּה כַּחוֹל |
| *v'kha-kokhavim ba-lailah.* | וְכַכּוֹכָבִים בַּלָּיְלָה. |
| *Yom panah* | יוֹם פָּנָה |
| *k'tzeil tomer,* | כְּצֵל תֹּמֶר |
| *ekra la-El ah-lai gomer,* | אֶקְרָא לָאֵל עָלַי גּוֹמֵר |
| *amar shomeir,* | אָמַר שֹׁמֵר, |
| *atah vokeir, v'gam lailah.* | אָתָא בֹקֶר, וְגַם לָיְלָה |

*Some put out the candle at this point.*

| | |
|---|---|
| *Shavu·ah tov!* | שָׁבוּעַ טוֹב! |
| *Eliyahu ha-navi, Eliyahu ha-tishbi,* | אֵלִיָּהוּ הַנָּבִיא, אֵלִיָּהוּ הַתִּשְׁבִּי, |
| *Eliyahu, Eliyahu, Eliyahu ha-gil·adi.* | אֵלִיָּהוּ, אֵלִיָּהוּ, אֵלִיָּהוּ הַגִּלְעָדִי, |
| *Bim'heirah v'yameinu, yavo eilaynu,* | בִּמְהֵרָה בְיָמֵינוּ, יָבוֹא אֵלֵינוּ |
| *im mashi·aḥ ben David.* | עִם מָשִׁיחַ בֶּן דָּוִד. |

*Now the leader puts down the wine and spices, and says the blessing over he light. In order to link the blessing to an action, we look at our hands. Some cup their hands, look at their fingernails, and make a shadow. This constitutes the first "use" of the light for the new week.*

Praised are You, Adonai our God, Ruler of the Universe, Creator of the lights of fire.

*The wine is now taken in the right hand again and the last blessing is recited:*

Praised are You, Adonai our God, Ruler of the Universe, Who makes a distinction between sacred and profane, between light and darkness, between Israel and the peoples, between the seventh day and the six work days. Praised are You, Adonai, Who makes a distinction between sacred and profane.

*Drink the wine. Some people extinguish the candle at this point. Some do this by pouring some wine into a dish and dousing it there, others by using the wine cup.*

*The following are not part of the formal havdalah ceremony itself, but are traditionally sung. The first is from an 11th century liturgical poem.*

May the One who separates between holy and profane forgive our sins; May God increase our offspring and our wealth like dust and like the nighttime stars.
The day moved on like a date-palm's shadow – I shall cry out to God to fulfill for me what the watchman said: "The dawn has come, and also night." (Isaiah 21:12)

*Some put out the candle at this point.*

A good week!

Elijah the prophet, Elijah the Tishbite, Elijah the Gileadite, may he come quickly to us with the Messiah, son of David.

# Special Occasion and Holiday Readings

## יזכור

### YIZKOR SERVICE

*Yizkor began as an act of collective memory, to honor the communities that were martyred during the First Crusade. Individual memorials were added later. The power of Yizkor comes from the joining of individual and communal memory. To read the words at home in solitude would not be the same. When we stand shoulder to shoulder with a community of remembrance and mourning, we are comforted. We understand that everyone knows loss, that we are bound together by a complex network of memory, and that those memories are the basis for our shared future as well.*

יְיָ מָה־אָדָם וַתֵּדָעֵהוּ. בֶּן־אֱנוֹשׁ וַתְּחַשְּׁבֵהוּ:
אָדָם לַהֶבֶל דָּמָה. יָמָיו כְּצֵל עוֹבֵר:
בַּבֹּקֶר יָצִיץ וְחָלָף. לָעֶרֶב יְמוֹלֵל וְיָבֵשׁ:
תָּשֵׁב אֱנוֹשׁ עַד־דַּכָּא. וַתֹּאמֶר שׁוּבוּ בְנֵי אָדָם:
שׁוּבָה יְהוָה עַד־מָתָי וְהִנָּחֵם עַל־עֲבָדֶיךָ:

Adonai, what are human beings that You take note of them;
Humanity that You think of them.
A person is like a transient breath; our days like a fleeting shadow.
In the morning it blossoms; by evening it withers and dries up.
You return humanity to the dust. You decree, "Return, O humans!"
Turn, O Lord, "How long?" Have mercy on Your servants.

As we remember our beloved dead, we realize that their lives are more than a memory. We are who we are because of their influence on our thought, character and behavior. Memories leave their imprint. They affect our lives and our characters every day.

Memory is essential to being a Jew. Our festivals carry a historical cargo, recalling the exodus from Egypt, the giving of the Torah, and desert wanderings. Later events in Jewish history called forth new days of commemoration. Even the High Holy Days, which do not commemorate a historical event, involve memory, urging us to recall our past deeds on Rosh Hashanah, and our departed on Yom Kippur.

Today, we stand as a community, finding support in our common human condition of loss. At the same time, we stand as individuals, each of us with his or her own stories, our unique memories of those we mourn.

Judaism helps us to find holiness and joy within the limitations and flaws of human existence. Death is the ultimate limit, and we have been given wise and nurturing practices and teachings to help us cope. By telling of the passing of every major figure, the Torah teaches us that death is not a punishment, but a necessary part of life. By having us stand together in a congregation of memory, Yizkor reminds us that everyone knows bereavement. Rather than curse our finitude, we gather to bless the gift of life. Those we remember lived, loved, created, and taught their life lessons within the framework of mortality – and so do we.

שִׁוִּיתִי יְיָ לְנֶגְדִּי תָמִיד, כִּי מִימִינִי בַּל אֶמּוֹט.
לָכֵן | שָׂמַח לִבִּי וַיָּגֶל כְּבוֹדִי, אַף בְּשָׂרִי יִשְׁכֹּן לָבֶטַח.

I have placed Adonai before me constantly.
God is at my right hand; I will never be shaken.
Therefore my heart rejoices, my whole being rejoices, and my body rests secure.

As we rise for Yizkor, we affirm our links with our personal chains of memory created by family history and relationships. Yizkor brings us memories of beauty and joy as well as pain and loss, smiles along with tears. We link our memories with God's memory: just as we remember our beloved dead, we know that they are in God's mind as well. May this give us some measure of comfort. For a few moments we will immerse ourselves in memory. We will recall family members and all they meant to us. We may struggle with memories of difficult relationships, or bask in the warmth of treasured lives, but in every case we will acknowledge that those we recall are still part of us. The great Israeli poet Yehudah Amichai wrote:

> When a person dies, they say of him, "He was
> gathered unto his ancestors."
> As long as he is alive, his ancestors are gathered
> within him;
> each and every cell of his body and soul
> is an emissary
> of one of his countless ancestors from
> the beginning of all the generations.

Yizkor is not words on a page – it is memories, influences, and stories, in our minds, in our hearts, in our souls. Let us remember.

*Please rise for a time of silent prayer and remembrance.*

*For male relatives:*

| | |
|---|---|
| Yizkor Elohim | יִזְכּוֹר אֱלֹהִים |
| et nishmat__________ | אֶת נִשְׁמַת__________ |
| she-halakh l'olamo. | שֶׁהָלַךְ לְעוֹלָמוֹ. |
| Hin'ni nodeir (noderet) tz'dakah | הִנְנִי נוֹדֵר (נוֹדֶרֶת) צְדָקָה |
| b'ad hazkarat nishmato. | בְּעַד הַזְכָּרַת נִשְׁמָתוֹ. |
| Ana t'hi nafsho | אָנָא תְּהִי נַפְשׁוֹ |
| tz'rurah bi-tz'ror ha-ḥayyim | צְרוּרָה בִּצְרוֹר הַחַיִּים |
| u-t'hi m'nuḥato kavod, | וּתְהִי מְנוּחָתוֹ כָּבוֹד, |
| S'va s'maḥot et panekha, | שֹׂבַע שְׂמָחוֹת אֶת פָּנֶיךָ, |
| n'imot biminekha netzaḥ. Amen | נְעִמוֹת בִּימִינְךָ נֶצַח. אָמֵן. |

May God remember the soul of __________ who has gone to his eternal home. I vow to give to tzedakah in his memory. May his soul be bound up in the bond of life, and may he rest with honor, full of joy in Your presence, abiding in pleasantness at Your right hand, forever. Amen.

*For male relatives:*

| | |
|---|---|
| Yizkor Elohim | יִזְכּוֹר אֱלֹהִים |
| et nishmat__________ | אֶת נִשְׁמַת__________ |
| she-halkhah l'olamah. | שֶׁהָלְכָה לְעוֹלָמָהּ. |
| Hin'ni nodeir (noderet) tz'dakah | הִנְנִי נוֹדֵר (נוֹדֶרֶת) צְדָקָה |
| ba'ad hazkarat nishmatah. | בַּעַד הַזְכָּרַת נִשְׁמָתָהּ. |
| Ana t'hi nafshah | אָנָּא תְּהִי נַפְשָׁהּ |
| tz'rurah bi-tz'ror ha-ḥayyim | צְרוּרָה בִּצְרוֹר הַחַיִּים |
| u-t'hi m'nuḥatah kavod, | וּתְהִי מְנוּחָתָהּ כָּבוֹד, |
| S'va s'maḥot et panekha, | שֹׂבַע שְׂמָחוֹת אֶת פָּנֶיךָ, |
| n'imot biminekha netzaḥ. Amen | נְעִמוֹת בִּימִינְךָ נֶצַח. אָמֵן. |

May God remember the soul of __________ who has gone to her eternal home. I vow to give to tzedakah in her memory. May her soul be bound up in the bond of life, and may she rest with honor, full of joy in Your presence, abiding in pleasantness at Your right hand, forever. Amen.

*In memory of all the dead:*

| | |
|---|---|
| Eil malei raḥamim, | אֵל מָלֵא רַחֲמִים. |
| shokhein ba-m'romim, | שׁוֹכֵן בַּמְּרוֹמִים. |
| hamtzei m'nuḥah n'khonah | הַמְצֵא מְנוּחָה נְכוֹנָה |
| taḥat kanfei ha-shekhinah. | תַּחַת כַּנְפֵי הַשְּׁכִינָה. |
| b'ma·alot k'doshim u-t'horim | בְּמַעֲלוֹת קְדוֹשִׁים וּטְהוֹרִים |
| k'zohar ha-rakiáa mazhirim, | כְּזֹהַר הָרָקִיעַ מַזְהִירִים, |
| et nishmot kol eileh | אֶת־נִשְׁמוֹת כָּל אֵלֶּה |
| she-hizkarnu ha-yom li-v'rakhah | שֶׁהִזְכַּרְנוּ הַיּוֹם לִבְרָכָה |
| she-halkhu l'olamam, | שֶׁהָלְכוּ לְעוֹלָמָם, |
| b'Gan Eiden t'hi m'nuḥatam. | בְּגַן עֵדֶן תְּהִי מְנוּחָתָם. |
| Ana ba·al ha-raḥamim hastireim | אָנָּא בַּעַל הָרַחֲמִים הַסְתִּירֵם |
| b'seiter k'nafekha l'olamim. | בְּסֵתֶר כְּנָפֶךָ לְעוֹלָמִים. |
| U-tz'ror bi-tz'ror ha-ḥayyim | וּצְרוֹר בִּצְרוֹר הַחַיִּים |
| et nishmoteihem. | אֶת נִשְׁמוֹתֵיהֶם. |
| Adonai hu naḥalatam, | יְיָ הוּא נַחֲלָתָם, |
| v'yanuḥu b'shalom al | וְיָנוּחוּ בְּשָׁלוֹם עַל |
| mishk'voteihem. | מִשְׁכְּבוֹתֵיהֶם. |
| V'nomar: Amen | וְנֹאמַר: אָמֵן. |

God full of mercy who dwells on high, grant perfect rest under the protecting wings of Your Presence among the holy and pure who shine like the glow of the heavenly canopy, to the souls of all those who have gone to their eternal rest whom we have remembered today for a blessing. May they find eternal rest in the Garden of Eden. Please, Sovereign of Mercy, embrace them in the shelter of Your wings forever. May their souls be bound up in the bond of life. God is their portion. May they rest in peace. And let us say: Amen.

## PRAYERS FOR SUKKOT

| | |
|---|---|
| Barukh atah Adonai, | בָּרוּךְ אַתָּה יְיָ |
| Eloheinu melekh ha-olam, | אֱלֹהֵינוּ מֶלֶךְ הָעוֹלָם, |
| asher kid'shanu b'mitzvotav, | אֲשֶׁר קִדְּשָׁנוּ בְּמִצְוֹתָיו, |
| v'tzi-vanu al n'tilat lulav. | וְצִוָּנוּ עַל נְטִילַת לוּלָב. |

*When taking the lulav for the first time this Sukkot:*

| | |
|---|---|
| Barukh atah Adonai, | בָּרוּךְ אַתָּה יְיָ |
| Eloheinu melekh ha-olam, | אֱלֹהֵינוּ מֶלֶךְ הָעוֹלָם, |
| she-heḥeya-nu, v'kiy'manu, | שֶׁהֶחֱיָנוּ וְקִיְּמָנוּ |
| v'higiy·anu la-z'man hazeh. | וְהִגִּיעָנוּ לַזְּמַן הַזֶּה. |

## PRAYERS FOR SUKKOT

The Torah commands us, *You shall **take** for yourselves on the first day the fruit of a beautiful* [*etrog*] *tree, the branches of date palms, twigs of leafy trees, and brook willows, and you shall rejoice before Adonai your God seven days.* (Leviticus 23:40) Usually when we say a blessing over a mitzvah that involves an object, we hold it in our hand while saying the blessing (for example, on Hanukah, you hold the *shammash* while saying the blessings, then light the candles). But, once you take the Four Species in your hand, you've fulfilled the mitzvah! Our Rabbis cleverly solved this problem: they defined "taking" the Four Species as positioning them in the direction in which they grow. Therefore, if you hold the *etrog* with the *pitam* (the remnant of the flower, not the stem) facing down, you have not "taken" it. So grasp the four species with the *etrog* in your left hand, (some take the *etrog* first because it appears first in the Torah) and the *lulav* in the right, holding them so that the Species are all close together. Hold the *lulav* with its "spine" facing you, the willows to the left and the myrtles to the right. Say the blessing, and then turn the etrog so that the *pitam* is on top. Then wave the species by stretching your arms away from your body, and drawing them back toward your chest, three times, to the compass points – east, south, west, north – and then up and down. This totals 18 wavings (chai).

Praised are You, Adonai our God, Ruler of the universe, who made us holy with mitzvot, and who gave us the mitzvah to take the *lulav*.

*When taking the lulav for the first time this Sukkot:*

Praised are You, Adonai our God, Ruler of the Universe, Who has kept us alive, sustained us, and brought us to this season.

## A Prayer for Giving Thanks on Sukkot

Say thank you to God who does great wonders
God's kindness and love last forever.

God prepares rain and dew for the earth.
God makes mountains that are green with grass.

Our God is good to the fields and green meadows
God blesses us with the rich harvest of the earth's bounties.

The valleys of the earth overflow
And the hills sing praises of joy.

Blessed is Adonai for the precious gifts of the earth's harvest
For the abundance of food that is given to us.
May God always give us the gifts of creation.
And may God always bless us with peace and fulfilment.

## Kohelet: A Responsive Reading

*It is the custom to read the Book of Kohelet, also called Ecclesiastes, on the intermediate Shabbat of Sukkot. Much of the book looks around at the things of this world and declares, "They are all worthless." One reason we may read these words on Sukkot is so that we don't feel too satisfied with ourselves after the harvest, when we might be tempted to feel proud and smug.*

For everything there is a season,
A time for everything under the sun.

A time to be born, a time to die,
A time to plant, and a time to uproot.

A time to kill and a time to heal,
A time to tear down and a time to build up,

A time to cry and a time to laugh,
A time to mourn and a time to dance,

A time to cast away stones and a time to gather stones together,
A time to love and a time to hate.

A time to search and a time to lose,
A time to tear and a time to sew.

A time to be quiet and a time to speak,
A time to keep and a time to throw away,

A time for war and a time for peace.

## GESHEM: THE PRAYER FOR RAIN

*On Shemini Atzeret, the last day of Sukkot, we pray for rain. We do this no matter where we live. Even if we were on the Hawaiian island of Kauai, which is the wettest spot in the world – 460 inches of rain a year! – we would still say this prayer, because it is really tied to the rainy season in the Land of Israel. The prayer is part of Gevurot, the second blessing of the Amidah, which tells of God's lovingkindness, expressed through helping deeds, including bringing rain. There are six parts of the prayer, each of which refers to events involving water in the lives of Abraham, Isaac, Jacob, Moses, Aaron, and the Twelve Tribes.*

בָּרוּךְ אַתָּה יְיָ אֱלֹהֵינוּ וֵאלֹהֵי אֲבוֹתֵינוּ, אֱלֹהֵי אַבְרָהָם, אֱלֹהֵי יִצְחָק, וֵאלֹהֵי יַעֲקֹב, (אֱלֹהֵי שָׂרָה, אֱלֹהֵי רִבְקָה, אֱלֹהֵי רָחֵל, וֵאלֹהֵי לֵאָה,) הָאֵל הַגָּדוֹל הַגִּבּוֹר וְהַנּוֹרָא, אֵל עֶלְיוֹן, גּוֹמֵל חֲסָדִים טוֹבִים, וְקֹנֵה הַכֹּל, וְזוֹכֵר חַסְדֵי אָבוֹת, וּמֵבִיא גוֹאֵל לִבְנֵי בְנֵיהֶם, לְמַעַן שְׁמוֹ בְּאַהֲבָה. מֶלֶךְ עוֹזֵר וּמוֹשִׁיעַ וּמָגֵן. בָּרוּךְ אַתָּה יְיָ, מָגֵן אַבְרָהָם (וּפוֹקֵד שָׂרָה). אַתָּה גִּבּוֹר לְעוֹלָם אֲדֹנָי, מְחַיֵּה מֵתִים אַתָּה, רַב לְהוֹשִׁיעַ.

אֱלֹהֵינוּ וֵאלֹהֵי אֲבוֹתֵינוּ,

זְכוֹר אָב נִמְשַׁךְ אַחֲרֶיךָ כַּמַּיִם, בֵּרַכְתּוֹ כְּעֵץ שָׁתוּל עַל פַּלְגֵי מַיִם,
גְּנַנְתּוֹ הִצַּלְתּוֹ מֵאֵשׁ וּמִמַּיִם, דְּרַשְׁתּוֹ בְּזָרְעוֹ עַל כָּל מָיִם.
בַּעֲבוּרוֹ אַל תִּמְנַע מָיִם.

זְכוֹר הַנּוֹלָד בִּבְשׂוֹרַת יֻקַּח נָא מְעַט מַיִם, וְשַׂחְתָּ לְהוֹרוֹ לְשָׁחֲטוֹ לִשְׁפֹּךְ דָּמוֹ כַּמַּיִם, זְהֵר גַּם הוּא לִשְׁפֹּךְ לֵב כַּמַּיִם, חָפַר וּמָצָא בְּאֵרוֹת מָיִם.
בְּצִדְקוֹ חֹן חַשְׁרַת מָיִם.

זְכוֹר טָעַן מַקְלוֹ וְעָבַר יַרְדֵּן מַיִם, יִחַד לֵב וְגָל אֶבֶן מִפִּי בְאֵר מַיִם, כְּנֶאֱבַק לוֹ בָּלוּל מֵאֵשׁ וּמִמַּיִם, לָכֵן הִבְטַחְתּוֹ הֱיוֹת עִמּוֹ בָּאֵשׁ וּבַמָּיִם.
בַּעֲבוּרוֹ עַל תִּמְנַע מָיִם.

## GESHEM: THE PRAYER FOR RAIN

*On Shemini Atzeret, the last day of Sukkot, we pray for rain. We do this no matter where we live. Even if we were on the Hawaiian island of Kauai, which is the wettest spot in the world – 460 inches of rain a year! – we would still say this prayer, because it is really tied to the rainy season in the Land of Israel. The prayer is part of Gevurot, the second blessing of the Amidah, which tells of God's lovingkindness, expressed through helping deeds, including bringing rain. There are six parts of the prayer, each of which refers to events involving water in the lives of Abraham, Isaac, Jacob, Moses, Aaron, and the Twelve Tribes.*

Praised are You, Adonai our God and God of our ancestors, God of Abraham, God of Isaac, and God of Jacob, [God of Sarah, God of Rebecca, God of Rachel and God of Leah], the great, strong and awe-inspiring God, God on high. You act with lovingkindness and create everything. God remembers the loving deeds of our ancestors, and will bring a redeemer to their children's children because that is God's loving nature. You are a helping, saving and shielding Ruler. Praised are You, Adonai, Shield of Abraham (and Guardian of Sarah). You are mighty forever, Adonai, giving life to the dead with Your great saving power.

Our God and God of our ancestors:

Remember Abraham who flowed to You like water.
You blessed him like a tree planted by streams of water.
You rescued him from fire and water.
He passed Your test by planting good deeds by every water source.
For Abraham's sake, do not keep back water.

Remember Isaac, whose birth was foretold when Abraham offered the angels "a little water."
You asked his father to spill his blood like water.
In the desert, Isaac dug and found wells of water.
For Isaac's sake, do not keep back water.

Remember Jacob who crossed the Jordan's water.
He bravely rolled the stone off the mouth of the well of water.
He wrestled with an angel made of fire and water,
and therefore You promised to be with him through fire and water.
For Jacob's sake do not keep back water!

זְכוֹר מָשׁוּי בְּתֵבַת גֹּמֶא מִן הַמַּיִם, נָמוּ דָּלֹה דָלָה וְהִשְׁקָה צֹאן
מָיִם, סְגוּלֶיךָ עֵת צָמְאוּ לְמַּיִם, עַל הַסֶּלַע הָךְ וַיֵּצְאוּ מָיִם.
בְּצִדְקוֹ חֹן חַשְׁרַת מָיִם.

זְכוֹר פְּקִיד שָׁתוֹת טוֹבֵל חָמֵשׁ טְבִילוֹת בְּמַּיִם, צוֹעֶה וּמַרְחִיץ כַּפָּיו בְּקִדּוּשׁ
מַיִם, קוֹרֵא וּמַזֶּה טָהֳרַת מַיִם, רֻחַק מֵעַם פַּחַז כַּמָּיִם.
בַּעֲבוּרוֹ אַל תִּמְנַע מָיִם.

זְכוֹר שְׁנֵים עָשָׂר שְׁבָטִים שֶׁהֶעֱבַרְתָּ בְּגִזְרַת מַיִם, שֶׁהִמְתַּקְתָּ לָמוֹ מְרִירוּת
מַיִם, תּוֹלְדוֹתָם נִשְׁפַּךְ דָּמָם עָלֶיךָ כַּמַּיִם, תֵּפֶן, כִּי נַפְשֵׁנוּ אָפְפוּ מָיִם.
בְּצִדְקָם חֹן חַשְׁרַת מָיִם.

*Leader:*

שָׁאַתָּה הוּא יְיָ אֱלֹהֵינוּ מַשִּׁיב הָרוּחַ וּמוֹרִיד הַגָּשֶׁם.

*Each line is read first by the congregation and then by the leader.*
*The congregation responds Amen to each line by the leader.*

| | |
|---|---|
| L'v'rakhah v'lo li-k'lallah! Amen. | לִבְרָכָה וְלֹא לִקְלָלָה (אָמֵן). |
| L'ḥayyim v'lo la-mavet! Amen. | לְחַיִּים וְלֹא לְמָוֶת (אָמֵן). |
| L'sova v'lo l'razon! Amen | לְשֹׂבַע וְלֹא לְרָזוֹן (אָמֵן). |

*The Ark is closed and the service continues with*
*the M'khalkel Ḥayyim on page 138.*

Remember Moses, who was drawn out of the Nile's water in a reed basket,
Who helped Jethro's daughters: "He drew water and gave the sheep water."
He struck the rock and out came water.
For Moses' sake do not hold back water!

Remember Aaron, the High Priest, who, on Yom Kippur, washed himself five times with water,
He prayed and was sprinkled with purifying water,
He kept apart from a people who were as unstable as water.
For Aaron's sake do not hold back water.

Remember the Twelve Tribes whom You brought through the divided waters;
For whom You sweetened bitter waters;
Their descendants' blood was spilled like water.
Turn to us, God, who are surrounded by troubles like water.
For the Jewish people's sake, do not hold back water!

*Leader:*

You are Adonai our God,
Who causes the wind to blow and the rain to fall.

*Each line is read first by the congregation and then by the leader.*
*The congregation responds Amen to each line by the leader.*

For blessing and not for curse.
For life and not for death.
For plenty and not for lack.

*The Ark is closed and the service continues with* *the M'khalkel Ḥayyim on page 139.*

## SIMCHAT TORAH

*It is the custom for the leader, or a series of leaders, to chant each of these verses first, with the congregation repeating them:*

| | |
|---|---|
| Atah hareita la-da·at | אַתָּה הָרְאֵתָ לָדַעַת, |
| Ki Adonai hu ha-Elohim, | כִּי יְיָ הוּא הָאֱלֹהִים, |
| Ein od milvado. | אֵין עוֹד מִלְּבַדּוֹ. |
| L'oseh nifla·ot g'dolot l'vado, | לְעֹשֵׂה נִפְלָאוֹת גְּדֹלוֹת לְבַדּוֹ, |
| Ki l'olam hasdo. | כִּי לְעוֹלָם חַסְדּוֹ. |
| Ein kamokha va-Elohim, | אֵין כָּמוֹךָ בָאֱלֹהִים, |
| Adonai, v'ein k'ma·asekha. | אֲדֹנָי, וְאֵין כְּמַעֲשֶׂיךָ. |
| Y'hi kh'vod Adonai l'olam, | יְהִי כְבוֹד יְיָ לְעוֹלָם, |
| Yismah Adonai b'ma·asav. | יִשְׂמַח יְיָ בְּמַעֲשָׂיו. |
| Y'hi shem Adonai m'vorakh, | יְהִי שֵׁם יְיָ מְבֹרָךְ, |
| Mei-atah v'ad olam. | מֵעַתָּה וְעַד עוֹלָם. |
| T'hi Adonai Eloheinu imanu, | יְהִי יְיָ אֱלֹהֵינוּ עִמָּנוּ, |
| Ka·asher hayah im avoteinu, | כַּאֲשֶׁר הָיָה עִם אֲבֹתֵינוּ, |
| Al ya·azveinu v'al yit'sheinu. | אַל יַעַזְבֵנוּ וְאַל יִטְּשֵׁנוּ. |
| V'imru, hoshei·einu, | וְאִמְרוּ, הוֹשִׁיעֵנוּ, |
| Elohei yish·einu, | אֱלֹהֵי יִשְׁעֵנוּ, |
| V'kabtzeinu v'hatzileinu min ha-goyim, | וְקַבְּצֵנוּ וְהַצִּילֵנוּ מִן הַגּוֹיִם, |
| L'hodot l'shem kodshekha, | לְהֹדוֹת לְשֵׁם קָדְשֶׁךָ, |
| L'hishtabe·ah bit'hilatekha. | לְהִשְׁתַּבֵּחַ בִּתְהִלָּתֶךָ. |
| Adonai melekh, Adonai malakh, | יְיָ מֶלֶךְ, יְיָ מָלָךְ, |
| Adonai yimlokh l'olam va·ed. | יְיָ יִמְלֹךְ לְעוֹלָם וָעֶד. |
| Adonai oz l'amo yitein, | יְיָ עֹז לְעַמּוֹ יִתֵּן, |
| Adonai y'varekh et amo va-shalom. | יְיָ יְבָרֵךְ אֶת עַמּוֹ בַשָּׁלוֹם. |

*The ark is opened:*

| | |
|---|---|
| Va-y'hi binso·a ha-aron | וַיְהִי בִּנְסֹעַ הָאָרֹן, |
| Va-yomer Moshe, kumah Adonai | וַיֹּאמֶר מֹשֶׁה, קוּמָה יְיָ, |
| V'yafutzu oyvekha, | וְיָפֻצוּ אֹיְבֶיךָ, |
| v'yanusu m'san·ekha | וְיָנֻסוּ מְשַׂנְאֶיךָ |
| Mipanekha. | מִפָּנֶיךָ. |
| Kumah Adonai lim'nuhatekha, | קוּמָה יְיָ לִמְנוּחָתֶךָ, |
| Atah va-aron uzekha. | אַתָּה וַאֲרוֹן עֻזֶּךָ. |
| Kohanekha yilb'shu tzedek, | כֹּהֲנֶיךָ יִלְבְּשׁוּ צֶדֶק, |

## SIMCHAT TORAH

*It is the custom for the leader, or a series of leaders, to chant each of these verses first, with the congregation repeating them:*

It has been shown you that Adonai is
God, there is no one else. (Deut. 4:35)
Give praise to the One who does great, wonderful things
all alone, whose kindness lasts forever. (Psalm 136:4)
There is none like You, Adonai, and there is
nothing like Your deeds. (Psalm 86:8)
May Adonai's glory last forever; may You
rejoice in your deeds. (Ps. 104:31)
May Adonai's name be blessed, now and forever. (Ps. 113:2)
May Adonai our God be with us, as God was with our
ancestors. Do not abandon us or desert us. (1 Kings 8:57)
Say, "Save us, saving God, gather us together, rescuing us
from the nations, so that we will be able to thank Your
holy Name, to glory in Your praise. (1 Chronicles 16:35)
Adonai rules, Adonai has always
ruled, Adonai will rule forever.
Adonai will give strength to God's people.
Adonai will bless God's people with peace. (Ps. 29:11)
May our words find favor before the
Ruler of everything (Ps. 19:15)

*The ark is opened:*

Whenever the Ark would travel, Moses would say, "Arise, Adonai, and scatter Your enemies; may those that hate you flee from you." (Numbers 10:35)

Your priests are dressed in righteousness;

| | |
|---|---|
| Va-ḥasidekha y'raeinu. | וַחֲסִידֶיךָ יְרַנֵּנוּ. |
| Ba·avur David av'dekha, al tasheiv | בַּעֲבוּר דָּוִד עַבְדֶּךָ, אַל תָּשֵׁב |
| P'nei m'shiḥekha. | פְּנֵי מְשִׁיחֶךָ. |
| V'amar ba-yom ha-hu, hineih | וְאָמַר בַּיּוֹם הַהוּא, הִנֵּה |
| Eloheinu zeh, kivinu lo v'yoshi·einu, | אֱלֹהֵינוּ זֶה, קִוִּינוּ לוֹ וְיוֹשִׁיעֵנוּ, |
| Zeh Adonai kivinu lo nagilah | זֶה יְיָ קִוִּינוּ לוֹ נָגִילָה |
| v'nism'k-ḥah Bishu·ato. | וְנִשְׂמְחָה בִּישׁוּעָתוֹ. |
| Malkhut'kha malkhut kol olamim, | מַלְכוּתְךָ מַלְכוּת כָּל עֹלָמִים, |
| u-memshalt'kha b'khol dor va-dor. | וּמֶמְשַׁלְתְּךָ בְּכָל דּוֹר וָדֹר. |
| Ki mi-Tziyon teitzei Torah, | כִּי מִצִּיּוֹן תֵּצֵא תוֹרָה, |
| u-d'var Adonai Mirushalayim. | וּדְבַר יְיָ מִירוּשָׁלָיִם. |
| Av ha-raḥamim, heitivah | אַב הָרַחֲמִים, הֵיטִיבָה |
| Vir'tzonkha et Tziyon, tivneh | בִרְצוֹנְךָ אֶת צִיּוֹן, תִּבְנֶה |
| Ḥomot Y'rushalayim. Ki v'kha l'vad | חוֹמוֹת יְרוּשָׁלָיִם. כִּי בְךָ לְבַד |
| Bataḥnu, Melekh Eil ram va-nisa | בָּטָחְנוּ, מֶלֶךְ אֵל רָם וְנִשָּׂא, |
| Adon Olamim. | אֲדוֹן עוֹלָמִים. |

*The Torah scrolls are taken out of the ark to be carried around the synagogue for seven Hakafot, seven circlings:*

| | |
|---|---|
| Ana Adonai, hoshi·ah na. | אָנָּא יְיָ, הוֹשִׁיעָה נָּא. |
| Ana Adonai, hatzlihah na. | אָנָּא יְיָ, הַצְלִיחָה נָא. |
| Ana Adonai, aneinu v'yom kor·einu. | אָנָּא יְיָ, עֲנֵנוּ בְיוֹם קָרְאֵנוּ. |
| Elohei ha-ruhot, hoshi·ah na. | אֱלֹהֵי הָרוּחוֹת, הוֹשִׁיעָה נָּא. |
| Bohein l'vavot, hatzliha na. | בּוֹחֵן לְבָבוֹת, הַצְלִיחָה נָא. |
| Go·eil hazak, aneinu v'yom kor·einu. | גּוֹאֵל חָזָק, עֲנֵנוּ בְיוֹם קָרְאֵנוּ. |

| | |
|---|---|
| Doveir tz'dakot, hoshi·ah na. | דּוֹבֵר צְדָקוֹת, הוֹשִׁיעָה נָּא. |
| Hadur bil'vusho, hatzliha | הָדוּר בִּלְבוּשׁוֹ, הַצְלִיחָה נָא. |
| Na. Vatik v'hasid, aneinu v'yom | וָתִיק וְחָסִיד, עֲנֵנוּ בְיוֹם |
| Kor·einu. | קָרְאֵנוּ. |

| | |
|---|---|
| Zakh va-yashar, hoshi·a na. | זַךְ וְיָשָׁר, הוֹשִׁיעָה נָּא. |
| Ḥomeil Dalim, hatzliha na. | חוֹמֵל דַּלִּים, הַצְלִיחָה נָא. |
| Tov u-meitiv, aneinu v'yom kor·einu. | טוֹב וּמֵטִיב, עֲנֵנוּ בְיוֹם קָרְאֵנוּ. |

Your loyal ones sing for joy. For the sake of David Your servant, do not turn away from Your anointed one. (Ps. 132:8–10)

They shall say on that day, "This is our God, whom we hoped for and who saved us. Let us rejoice and be glad because of God's saving power. (Isaiah. 25:9)

God, You rule eternally, Your kingdom lasts for all generations. (Psalm 145:13)

For Torah shall come from Zion, the word of Adonai from Jerusalem. (Isaiah 2:3)

Merciful parent, favor Zion with Your goodness.
Rebuild the walls of Jerusalem. (Psalm 51:20)
For we trust only You, Ruler, God on high, Sovereign of worlds.

*The Torah scrolls are taken out of the ark to be carried around the synagogue for seven Hakafot, seven circlings:*

Please Adonai, save us now!
Please, Adonai, give us success now!
Please, Adonai, answer us when we call to you!
God of spirits, save us now!
Who knows our thoughts, bring us success now!
Mighty Redeemer, answer us when we call to you!

Speaker of righteousness, save us now!
God, dressed in beauty, Long-time loyal
Friend, answer us when we call to you!

Pure and honest One, save us now!
Who pities the poor, give us success now!
Good One who does good, answer us when we call to you!

One who knows our thoughts, save us now!
Mighty Source of light, give us success now!
One who is dressed in righteousness,
answer us when we call to you!

| | |
|---|---|
| Yodei·a mahashavot, hoshi·a na. | יוֹדֵעַ מַחֲשָׁבוֹת, הוֹשִׁיעָה נָּא. |
| Kabir v'na·or, hatzlihah na. | כַּבִּיר וְנָאוֹר, הַצְלִיחָה נָא. |
| Loveish tz'dakot, | לוֹבֵשׁ צְדָקוֹת, |
| Aneinu v'yom kor·einu. | עֲנֵנוּ בְיוֹם קָרְאֵנוּ. |
| Melekh olamim, hoshi·a na. | מֶלֶךְ עוֹלָמִים, הוֹשִׁיעָה נָּא. |
| Na·or v'adir, hatzliha na. | נָאוֹר וְאַדִּיר, הַצְלִיחָה נָא. |
| Someikh noflim, aneinu v'yom | סוֹמֵךְ נוֹפְלִים, עֲנֵנוּ בְיוֹם |
| Kor·einu. | קָרְאֵנוּ. |
| | |
| Ozeir dalim, hoahi·a na. | עוֹזֵר דַּלִּים, הוֹשִׁיעָה נָּא. |
| Podeh, u-matzil, hatzliha na. | פּוֹדֶה וּמַצִּיל, הַצְלִיחָה נָא. |
| Tzur olmim, aneinu v'yom | צוּר עוֹלָמִים, עֲנֵנוּ בְיוֹם |
| Kor·einu. | קָרְאֵנוּ. |
| | |
| Kadosh v'nora, hoshi·a na. | קָדוֹשׁ וְנוֹרָא, הוֹשִׁיעָה נָּא. |
| Rahum v'hanun, hatzliha na. | רַחוּם וְחַנּוּן, הַצְלִיחָה נָא. |
| Shomeir ha-b'rit, aneinu v'yom | שׁוֹמֵר הַבְּרִית, עֲנֵנוּ בְיוֹם |
| Kor·einu. | קָרְאֵנוּ. |
| | |
| Tomeikh t'mimim, hoshi·a na. | תּוֹמֵךְ תְּמִימִים, הוֹשִׁיעָה נָּא. |
| Takif la-ad, hatzliha na. | תַּקִּיף לָעַד, הַצְלִיחָה נָא. |
| Tamim b'ma·asav, aneinu v'yom | תָּמִים בְּמַעֲשָׂיו, עֲנֵנוּ בְיוֹם |
| Kor·einu. | קָרְאֵנוּ. |

Ruler of worlds, save us now!
Bright and powerful One, give us success now!
Who supports those who are falling,
answer us when we call to you!

Helper of the poor, save us now!
Who frees and rescues, give us success now!
Eternal Rock, answer us when we call to you!

Holy and awesome, save us now!
Merciful and gracious One, give us success now!
Keeper of the covenant, answer us when we call to you!
One who supports the innocent, save us now!
Strong One forever, give us success now!
Perfect in deeds, answer us when we call to you!

## SHABBAT ḤANUKAH

### *Additional Reading for the Amidah*

| | |
|---|---|
| Al ha-nisim v'al ha-purkan, | עַל הַנִּסִּים, וְעַל הַפֻּרְקָן, |
| v'al ha-g'vurot, | וְעַל הַגְּבוּרוֹת, |
| v'al ha-t'shu·ot, | וְעַל הַתְּשׁוּעוֹת, |
| v'al ha-milḥamot | וְעַל הַמִּלְחָמוֹת, |
| she-asita la-avoteinu | שֶׁעָשִׂיתָ לַאֲבוֹתֵינוּ |
| ba-yamim ha-heim z'man ha-zeh | בַּיָּמִים הָהֵם בַּזְּמַן הַזֶּה. |

בִּימֵי מַתִּתְיָהוּ בֶּן יוֹחָנָן כֹּהֵן גָּדוֹל, חַשְׁמוֹנַאי וּבָנָיו, כְּשֶׁעָמְדָה מַלְכוּת יָוָן
הָרְשָׁעָה עַל עַמְּךָ יִשְׂרָאֵל לְהַשְׁכִּיחָם תּוֹרָתֶךָ, וּלְהַעֲבִירָם מֵחֻקֵּי רְצוֹנֶךָ, וְאַתָּה
בְּרַחֲמֶיךָ הָרַבִּים עָמַדְתָּ לָהֶם בְּעֵת צָרָתָם, רַבְתָּ אֶת רִיבָם, דַּנְתָּ אֶת דִּינָם,
נָקַמְתָּ אֶת נִקְמָתָם, מָסַרְתָּ גִבּוֹרִים בְּיַד חַלָּשִׁים, וְרַבִּים בְּיַד מְעַטִּים, וּטְמֵאִים
בְּיַד טְהוֹרִים, וּרְשָׁעִים בְּיַד צַדִּיקִים, וְזֵדִים בְּיַד עוֹסְקֵי תוֹרָתֶךָ. וּלְךָ עָשִׂיתָ
שֵׁם גָּדוֹל וְקָדוֹשׁ בְּעוֹלָמֶךָ, וּלְעַמְּךָ יִשְׂרָאֵל עָשִׂיתָ תְּשׁוּעָה גְדוֹלָה וּפֻרְקָן
כְּהַיּוֹם הַזֶּה. וְאַחַר כֵּן בָּאוּ בָנֶיךָ לִדְבִיר בֵּיתֶךָ, וּפִנּוּ אֶת הֵיכָלֶךָ, וְטִהֲרוּ אֶת
מִקְדָּשֶׁךָ, וְהִדְלִיקוּ נֵרוֹת בְּחַצְרוֹת קָדְשֶׁךָ, וְקָבְעוּ שְׁמוֹנַת יְמֵי חֲנֻכָּה אֵלּוּ,
לְהוֹדוֹת וּלְהַלֵּל לְשִׁמְךָ הַגָּדוֹל.

## SHABBAT ḤANUKAH

### *Additional Reading for the Amidah*

We thank You, God, for the miracles, for the rescues, for the mighty deeds, for the saving acts, and for the wars that you fought for our ancestors long ago at this time of year:

In the days of Mattathias son of Yochanan, the High Priest, of the Hasmonean family, and his sons, when the evil Greek government rose up against Your people Israel, they tried to make them forget Your Torah and break Your laws. You, in Your great mercy, stood firm for them in their time of trouble. You defended them, you judged in their favor, you punished their enemies. You helped the weak to defeat the strong, the few to defeat the many, the pure to defeat the impure, the righteous to defeat the wicked, and the followers of Your Torah to defeat the sinners. Because you did this, Your Name was made great and holy before all the world. You won a great victory for Your people Israel that lasted until this day. Afterwards, Your children came into the holiest part of Your House, cleaned and purified Your Palace, and lit lights in the courtyards of Your Holy Place. They set these eight days of Hanukah as a time for thanking and praising You.

## TAL: THE PRAYER FOR DEW

| | |
|---|---|
| Barukh Atah Adonai, | בָּרוּךְ אַתָּה יְיָ |
| Eloheinu vEilohei avoteinu, | אֱלֹהֵינוּ וֵאלֹהֵי אֲבוֹתֵינוּ, |
| Elohei Avraham, Elohei Yitzhak, | אֱלֹהֵי אַבְרָהָם, אֱלֹהֵי יִצְחָק, |
| vEilohei Ya'akov, | וֵאלֹהֵי יַעֲקֹב, |
| [Elohei Sarah, Elohei Rivkah, | (אֱלֹהֵי שָׂרָה, אֱלֹהֵי רִבְקָה, |
| Elohei Rahel vEilohei Le·ah] | אֱלֹהֵי רָחֵל, וֵאלֹהֵי לֵאָה,) |
| ha-Eil ha-gadol ha-gibor v'ha-nora | הָאֵל הַגָּדוֹל הַגִּבּוֹר וְהַנּוֹרָא, |
| Eil elyon, | אֵל עֶלְיוֹן, |
| Gomeil hasadim tovim v'koneih | גּוֹמֵל חֲסָדִים טוֹבִים, וְקֹנֵה |
| ha-kol v'zokheir hasdei avot, | הַכֹּל, וְזוֹכֵר חַסְדֵי אָבוֹת, |
| u-meivi go·eil liv'nei | וּמֵבִיא גוֹאֵל לִבְנֵי |
| v'neihem l'ma·an sh'mo b'ahavah. | בְנֵיהֶם, לְמַעַן שְׁמוֹ בְּאַהֲבָה. |
| Melekh ozeir | מֶלֶךְ עוֹזֵר |
| u-moshi·a u-magein. | וּמוֹשִׁיעַ וּמָגֵן. |

| | |
|---|---|
| Barukh Atah Adonai, | בָּרוּךְ אַתָּה יְיָ, |
| magein Avraham [u-fokeid Sarah]. | מָגֵן אַבְרָהָם (וּפֹקֵד שָׂרָה). |

| | |
|---|---|
| Atah gibor l'olam Adonai, | אַתָּה גִּבּוֹר לְעוֹלָם אֲדֹנָי, |
| *m'ḥayeih* meitim Atah, | מְחַיֵּה מֵתִים אַתָּה, |
| rav l'hoshi·a. | רַב לְהוֹשִׁיעַ. |

אֱלֹהֵינוּ וֵאלֹהֵי אֲבוֹתֵינוּ,

| | |
|---|---|
| טַל תֵּן לִרְצוֹת אַרְצָךְ | שִׁיתֵנוּ בְרָכָה בְּדִיצָךְ, |
| רֹב דָּגָן וְתִירוֹשׁ בְּהַפְרִיצָךְ | קוֹמֵם עִיר בָּהּ חֶפְצָךְ, בְּטָל. |

| | |
|---|---|
| טַל צַוֵּה שָׁנָה טוֹבָה וּמְעֻטֶּרֶת | פְּרִי הָאָרֶץ לְגָאוֹן וּלְתִפְאֶרֶת, |
| עִיר כַּסֻּכָּה נוֹתֶרֶת | שִׂימָהּ בְּיָדְךָ עֲטֶרֶת, בְּטָל. |

| | |
|---|---|
| טַל נוֹפֵף עֲלֵי אֶרֶץ בְּרוּכָה | מִמֶּגֶד שָׁמַיִם שַׂבְּעֵנוּ בְרָכָה, |
| לְהָאִיר מִתּוֹךְ חֲשֵׁכָה | כַּנָּה אַחֲרֶיךָ מְשׁוּכָה, בְּטָל. |

## TAL: THE PRAYER FOR DEW

*On the first day of Pesaḥ we say a prayer for dew during the musaf serice. In the Land of Israel, there are very clear rainy and dry seasons. the dry season is long and hot, but it is lessened by breezes that come in from the Mediterranean Sea bringing dew at night. This bit of moisture is very important, and so Jews say this prayer wherever we are. Because dew appears at night and helps plants to grow though there is no rain, it is a symbol of revival, and so the prayer for dew also tells of our hopes for a fully rebuilt Jerusalem and Land of Israel.*

*The ark is opened:*

Praised are You, Adonai our God and God of our ancestors, God of Abraham, God of Isaac, and God of Jacob, [God of Sarah, God of Rebecca. God of Rachel and God of Leah], the great, strong and awe-inspiring God, God on high. You act with lovingkindness and create everything. God remembers the loving deeds of our ancestors, and will bring a redeemer to their children's children because that is God's loving natu. re.You are a helping, saving and shielding Ruler. Praised are You, Adonai, Shield of Abraham (and Guardian of Sarah). You are mighty forever, Adonai, giving life to the dead with Your great saving power.

Our God and God of our ancestors:

Give us dew to favor Your land, grant us a blessing of Your joy: Make us strong with plentiful grain and wine. Restore Jerusalem, Your delight, as flowers are renewed by dew.

Let this be a good year for dew, crowned with proud and beautiful fruit. May the city of Jerusalem, once empty, be turned into a crown that sparkles like the dew.

May dew fall upon the blessed land. Fill us up with heaven's finest blessings. May a light come out of the darkness to draw Israel to you as a root finds water from dew.

טַל יַעֲסִיס צוּף הָרִים
טְעַם בִּמְאוֹדֶיךָ מֻבְחָרִים,
חֲנוּנֶיךָ חַלֵּץ מִמַּסְגֵּרִים,
זִמְרָה נַנְעִים וְקוֹל נָרִים, בְּטָל.

טַל וָשֹׂבַע מַלֵּא אֲסָמֵינוּ
הֲכָעֵת תְּחַדֵּשׁ יָמֵינוּ,
דּוֹד, כְּעֶרְכְּךָ הַעֲמֵד שְׁמֵנוּ
גַּן רָוֶה שִׂימֵנוּ, בְּטָל.

טַל בּוֹ תְּבָרֵךְ מָזוֹן
בְּמִשְׁמַנֵּינוּ אַל יְהִי רָזוֹן,
אֲיֻמָּה אֲשֶׁר הִסַּעְתָּ כַּצֹּאן
אָנָּא תָּפֵק לָהּ רָצוֹן, בְּטָל.

שָׁאַתָּה הוּא יְיָ אֱלֹהֵינוּ, מַשִּׁיב הָרוּחַ וּמוֹרִיד הַטָּל,

לִבְרָכָה וְלֹא לִקְלָלָה (אָמֵן).
לְחַיִּים וְלֹא לְמָוֶת (אָמֵן).
לְשֹׂבַע וְלֹא לְרָזוֹן (אָמֵן).

Li-v'rakhah v'lo li-klalah (Amen).
L'ḥayyim v'lo l'mavet (Amen).
Li-sova v'lo l'razon (Amen).

*The Ark is closed and the service continues with the M'khalkel Ḥayyim on page 138.*

May dew sweeten the mountains. May Your chosen people taste Your bounty. Free those You favor from their chains. Then we will raise our voices in harmony pure as dew.

May dew fill up our silos with grain. If only You would now renew our days! Loving One, make our name last long like Yours. Make us like a garden well-watered by dew.

May You bless our food with dew. May we enjoy plenty with nothing lacking. Grant the wish of the people that followed you through the desert like sheep – with dew.

*Leader:*

You are Adonai our God,  
Who causes the wind to blow  
and the dew to fall.

*Each line is read first by the congregation and then by the leader. The congregation responds Amen to each line by the leader.*

For blessing and not for curse.  
For life and not for death.  
For plenty and not for lack.

*The Ark is closed and the service continues with the M'khalkel Ḥayyim on page 139.*

## THE SONG OF SONGS

*Shir ha-Shirim*

*We read the Song of Songs on the intermediate Shabbat of Pesaḥ. This is because it is a poem full of images of springtime, and Pesaḥ is a spring holiday. It is also because our Rabbis read the Song of Songs as a love poem between God and the Jewish people, and the Exodus is one of the greatest signs of that love.*

Let me have a kiss from your lips,
For your love is sweeter than wine.

*As a lily among thorns,*
*So is my love among the other young women.*

As an apple tree among the trees of the forest,
So is my beloved among the other young men.

*The winter has long passed, the rain is over and gone.*
*Flowers appear on the earth, the time of singing has come,*
*And the voice of the turtledove is heard in our land.*

I am my beloved's and my beloved is mine.

*Write my name upon your heart and upon your arm.*
*For love is as strong as death.*

It burns with flames so hot that floods cannot put it out,
Rivers cannot drown it.

## YOM HA-ATZMÀUT

***Israel Independance Day***

We thank you, God for Israel, the Jewish State.
We are happy that our people have a safe place
Where all Jews can feel at home.

*For two thousand years we were in exile,*
*Yet we never forgot Zion and Jerusalem.*

We prayed for rain and dew wherever we were, thinking of our Land.
We remembered Israel in our prayers every day, morning, noon and night,
At meals and at weddings; on every holiday.

*Whevever we could, Jews travelled there,*
*But it was not until our times that the miracle of Return took place.*

We thank You, God, for Zionist leaders like Herzl, Ben-Gurion, Golda Meir and Henrietta Szold, who inspired our people to rebuild our land.

We look forward to the day when we can travel to Israel,
To see our history come alive; to greet our fellow Jews
From the four corners of the earth.

Bless our Land, our Jewish State, with happiness and prosperity,
With well-being and harmony, but above all, with shalom, with peace.

## HATIKVAH

Kol ode baleivav p'nimah
Nefesh Yehudi homiyah
U-l'fa·atey mizraḥ kadimah
Ayin l'tziyon tzofiyah.
Od lo avdah tikvatenu
Hatikvah bat sh'not alpayim:
Lih'iyot am ḥofshi b'artzeinu
Eretz Tziyon v'Yerushalayim.

כָּל עוֹד בַּלֵּבָב פְּנִימָה
נֶפֶשׁ יְהוּדִי הוֹמִיָּה.
וּלְפַאֲתֵי מִזְרָח קָדִימָה
עַיִן לְצִיּוֹן צוֹפִיָּה.
עוֹד לֹא אָבְדָה תִּקְוָתֵנוּ
הַתִּקְוָה בַּת שְׁנוֹת אַלְפַּיִם
לִהְיוֹת עַם חָפְשִׁי בְּאַרְצֵנוּ,
אֶרֶץ צִיּוֹן וִירוּשָׁלַיִם.

## HATIKVAH

As long as the Jewish spirit is yearning deep in the heart,
With eyes turned toward the East, looking toward Zion,
Then our hope – the two-thousand-year-old hope – will not be lost:
To be a free people in our land,
The land of Zion and Jerusalem

# Shavuot

## THE TEN COMMANDMENTS

In the third month after the children of Israel left Egypt they came to the Sinai desert.

*And God came down to the mountain and spoke these words:*

I am Adonai your God, who brought you out of the land of Egypt and the house of slavery.

*You shall have no other god beside Me.*

You shall not misuse the name of God.

*Remember the Sabbath day and keep it holy.*

Honor your father and your mother.

*You shall not murder.*

You shall not commit adultery.

*You shall not steal.*

You shall not bear false witness against your neighbor.

*You shall not covet or crave another's possessions.*

# Concluding Service for Shabbat

## מעריב

### BARKHU

וְהוּא רַחוּם יְכַפֵּר עָוֹן וְלֹא יַשְׁחִית, וְהִרְבָּה לְהָשִׁיב אַפּוֹ, וְלֹא יָעִיר כָּל חֲמָתוֹ. יְיָ הוֹשִׁיעָה, הַמֶּלֶךְ יַעֲנֵנוּ בְיוֹם קָרְאֵנוּ.

*Leader*

בָּרְכוּ אֶת יְיָ הַמְבֹרָךְ.

*Congregation, then Leader*

בָּרוּךְ יְיָ הַמְבֹרָךְ לְעוֹלָם וָעֶד.

בָּרוּךְ אַתָּה יְיָ, אֱלֹהֵינוּ מֶלֶךְ הָעוֹלָם, אֲשֶׁר בִּדְבָרוֹ מַעֲרִיב עֲרָבִים, בְּחָכְמָה פּוֹתֵחַ שְׁעָרִים, וּבִתְבוּנָה מְשַׁנֶּה עִתִּים, וּמַחֲלִיף אֶת הַזְּמַנִּים, וּמְסַדֵּר אֶת הַכּוֹכָבִים בְּמִשְׁמְרוֹתֵיהֶם בָּרָקִיעַ כִּרְצוֹנוֹ. בּוֹרֵא יוֹם וָלָיְלָה, גּוֹלֵל אוֹר מִפְּנֵי חֹשֶׁךְ, וְחֹשֶׁךְ מִפְּנֵי אוֹר. וּמַעֲבִיר יוֹם וּמֵבִיא לָיְלָה, וּמַבְדִּיל בֵּין יוֹם וּבֵין לָיְלָה, יְיָ צְבָאוֹת שְׁמוֹ. אֵל חַי וְקַיָּם, תָּמִיד יִמְלוֹךְ עָלֵינוּ לְעוֹלָם וָעֶד. בָּרוּךְ אַתָּה יְיָ, הַמַּעֲרִיב עֲרָבִים.

אַהֲבַת עוֹלָם בֵּית יִשְׂרָאֵל עַמְּךָ אָהָבְתָּ, תּוֹרָה וּמִצְוֹת, חֻקִּים וּמִשְׁפָּטִים אוֹתָנוּ לִמַּדְתָּ. עַל כֵּן יְיָ אֱלֹהֵינוּ, בְּשָׁכְבֵנוּ וּבְקוּמֵנוּ נָשִׂיחַ בְּחֻקֶּיךָ, וְנִשְׂמַח בְּדִבְרֵי תוֹרָתֶךָ וּבְמִצְוֹתֶיךָ לְעוֹלָם וָעֶד. כִּי הֵם חַיֵּינוּ וְאֹרֶךְ יָמֵינוּ, וּבָהֶם נֶהְגֶּה יוֹמָם וָלָיְלָה, וְאַהֲבָתְךָ אַל תָּסִיר מִמֶּנּוּ לְעוֹלָמִים. בָּרוּךְ אַתָּה יְיָ, אוֹהֵב עַמּוֹ יִשְׂרָאֵל.

### SH'MA

(אֵל מֶלֶךְ נֶאֱמָן)

שְׁמַע יִשְׂרָאֵל, יְיָ אֱלֹהֵינוּ, יְיָ אֶחָד.

בָּרוּךְ שֵׁם כְּבוֹד מַלְכוּתוֹ לְעוֹלָם וָעֶד.

וְאָהַבְתָּ אֵת יְיָ אֱלֹהֶיךָ, בְּכָל לְבָבְךָ, וּבְכָל נַפְשְׁךָ, וּבְכָל מְאֹדֶךָ. וְהָיוּ הַדְּבָרִים הָאֵלֶּה, אֲשֶׁר אָנֹכִי מְצַוְּךָ הַיּוֹם, עַל לְבָבֶךָ. וְשִׁנַּנְתָּם לְבָנֶיךָ, וְדִבַּרְתָּ בָּם, בְּשִׁבְתְּךָ בְּבֵיתֶךָ, וּבְלֶכְתְּךָ בַדֶּרֶךְ, וּבְשָׁכְבְּךָ, וּבְקוּמֶךָ. וּקְשַׁרְתָּם לְאוֹת עַל יָדֶךָ, וְהָיוּ לְטֹטָפֹת בֵּין עֵינֶיךָ. וּכְתַבְתָּם עַל מְזֻזוֹת בֵּיתֶךָ וּבִשְׁעָרֶיךָ.

וְהָיָה אִם שָׁמֹעַ תִּשְׁמְעוּ אֶל מִצְוֹתַי, אֲשֶׁר אָנֹכִי מְצַוֶּה אֶתְכֶם הַיּוֹם, לְאַהֲבָה אֶת יְיָ אֱלֹהֵיכֶם וּלְעָבְדוֹ, בְּכָל לְבַבְכֶם וּבְכָל נַפְשְׁכֶם. וְנָתַתִּי מְטַר אַרְצְכֶם בְּעִתּוֹ, יוֹרֶה וּמַלְקוֹשׁ, וְאָסַפְתָּ דְגָנֶךָ וְתִירֹשְׁךָ וְיִצְהָרֶךָ. וְנָתַתִּי עֵשֶׂב בְּשָׂדְךָ לִבְהֶמְתֶּךָ, וְאָכַלְתָּ וְשָׂבָעְתָּ. הִשָּׁמְרוּ לָכֶם פֶּן יִפְתֶּה לְבַבְכֶם, וְסַרְתֶּם וַעֲבַדְתֶּם אֱלֹהִים אֲחֵרִים וְהִשְׁתַּחֲוִיתֶם לָהֶם. וְחָרָה אַף יְיָ בָּכֶם, וְעָצַר אֶת הַשָּׁמַיִם וְלֹא יִהְיֶה מָטָר, וְהָאֲדָמָה לֹא תִתֵּן אֶת יְבוּלָהּ, וַאֲבַדְתֶּם מְהֵרָה מֵעַל הָאָרֶץ הַטֹּבָה אֲשֶׁר יְיָ נֹתֵן לָכֶם. וְשַׂמְתֶּם אֶת דְּבָרַי אֵלֶּה עַל לְבַבְכֶם וְעַל נַפְשְׁכֶם, וּקְשַׁרְתֶּם אֹתָם לְאוֹת עַל יֶדְכֶם, וְהָיוּ לְטוֹטָפֹת בֵּין עֵינֵיכֶם. וְלִמַּדְתֶּם אֹתָם אֶת בְּנֵיכֶם לְדַבֵּר בָּם, בְּשִׁבְתְּךָ בְּבֵיתֶךָ, וּבְלֶכְתְּךָ בַדֶּרֶךְ, וּבְשָׁכְבְּךָ, וּבְקוּמֶךָ. וּכְתַבְתָּם עַל מְזוּזוֹת בֵּיתֶךָ וּבִשְׁעָרֶיךָ. לְמַעַן יִרְבּוּ יְמֵיכֶם וִימֵי בְנֵיכֶם עַל הָאֲדָמָה אֲשֶׁר נִשְׁבַּע יְיָ לַאֲבֹתֵיכֶם לָתֵת לָהֶם, כִּימֵי הַשָּׁמַיִם עַל הָאָרֶץ.

וַיֹּאמֶר יְיָ אֶל מֹשֶׁה לֵּאמֹר. דַּבֵּר אֶל בְּנֵי יִשְׂרָאֵל וְאָמַרְתָּ אֲלֵהֶם, וְעָשׂוּ לָהֶם צִיצִת עַל כַּנְפֵי בִגְדֵיהֶם לְדֹרֹתָם, וְנָתְנוּ עַל צִיצִת הַכָּנָף פְּתִיל תְּכֵלֶת. וְהָיָה לָכֶם לְצִיצִת, וּרְאִיתֶם אֹתוֹ וּזְכַרְתֶּם אֶת כָּל מִצְוֹת יְיָ, וַעֲשִׂיתֶם אֹתָם, וְלֹא תָתוּרוּ אַחֲרֵי לְבַבְכֶם וְאַחֲרֵי עֵינֵיכֶם, אֲשֶׁר אַתֶּם זֹנִים אַחֲרֵיהֶם. לְמַעַן תִּזְכְּרוּ וַעֲשִׂיתֶם אֶת כָּל מִצְוֹתָי, וִהְיִיתֶם קְדֹשִׁים לֵאלֹהֵיכֶם. אֲנִי יְיָ אֱלֹהֵיכֶם, אֲשֶׁר הוֹצֵאתִי אֶתְכֶם מֵאֶרֶץ מִצְרַיִם, לִהְיוֹת לָכֶם לֵאלֹהִים, אֲנִי יְיָ אֱלֹהֵיכֶם.

## EMET V'EMUNAH

אֱמֶת וֶאֱמוּנָה כָּל זֹאת, וְקַיָּם עָלֵינוּ, כִּי הוּא יְיָ אֱלֹהֵינוּ וְאֵין זוּלָתוֹ, וַאֲנַחְנוּ יִשְׂרָאֵל עַמּוֹ. הַפּוֹדֵנוּ מִיַּד מְלָכִים, מַלְכֵּנוּ הַגּוֹאֲלֵנוּ מִכַּף כָּל הֶעָרִיצִים. הָאֵל הַנִּפְרָע לָנוּ מִצָּרֵינוּ, וְהַמְשַׁלֵּם גְּמוּל לְכָל אֹיְבֵי נַפְשֵׁנוּ, הָעֹשֶׂה גְדוֹלוֹת עַד אֵין חֵקֶר, וְנִפְלָאוֹת עַד אֵין מִסְפָּר. הַשָּׂם נַפְשֵׁנוּ בַּחַיִּים, וְלֹא נָתַן לַמּוֹט רַגְלֵנוּ. הַמַּדְרִיכֵנוּ עַל בָּמוֹת אוֹיְבֵינוּ, וַיָּרֶם קַרְנֵנוּ עַל כָּל שׂוֹנְאֵינוּ. הָעֹשֶׂה לָּנוּ נִסִּים וּנְקָמָה בְּפַרְעֹה, אוֹתוֹת וּמוֹפְתִים בְּאַדְמַת בְּנֵי חָם. הַמַּכֶּה בְעֶבְרָתוֹ כָּל בְּכוֹרֵי מִצְרָיִם, וַיּוֹצֵא אֶת עַמּוֹ יִשְׂרָאֵל מִתּוֹכָם לְחֵרוּת עוֹלָם. הַמַּעֲבִיר בָּנָיו בֵּין גִּזְרֵי יַם סוּף, אֶת רוֹדְפֵיהֶם וְאֶת שׂוֹנְאֵיהֶם בִּתְהוֹמוֹת טִבַּע. וְרָאוּ בָנָיו גְּבוּרָתוֹ, שִׁבְּחוּ וְהוֹדוּ לִשְׁמוֹ. וּמַלְכוּתוֹ בְּרָצוֹן קִבְּלוּ עֲלֵיהֶם, מֹשֶׁה וּבְנֵי יִשְׂרָאֵל לְךָ עָנוּ שִׁירָה בְּשִׂמְחָה רַבָּה, וְאָמְרוּ כֻלָּם:

## MI KAAMOKHA

מִי כָמֹכָה בָּאֵלִם יְיָ, מִי כָּמֹכָה נֶאְדָּר בַּקֹּדֶשׁ, נוֹרָא תְהִלֹּת, עֹשֵׂה פֶלֶא. מַלְכוּתְךָ רָאוּ בָנֶיךָ, בּוֹקֵעַ יָם לִפְנֵי מֹשֶׁה, זֶה אֵלִי עָנוּ וְאָמְרוּ: יְיָ יִמְלוֹךְ לְעוֹלָם וָעֶד. וְנֶאֱמַר: כִּי פָדָה יְיָ אֶת יַעֲקֹב, וּגְאָלוֹ מִיַּד חָזָק מִמֶּנּוּ. בָּרוּךְ אַתָּה יְיָ, גָּאַל יִשְׂרָאֵל.

## HASHKIVENU

הַשְׁכִּיבֵנוּ יְיָ אֱלֹהֵינוּ לְשָׁלוֹם, וְהַעֲמִידֵנוּ מַלְכֵּנוּ לְחַיִּים, וּפְרוֹשׂ עָלֵינוּ סֻכַּת שְׁלוֹמֶךָ, וְתַקְּנֵנוּ בְּעֵצָה טוֹבָה מִלְּפָנֶיךָ, וְהוֹשִׁיעֵנוּ לְמַעַן שְׁמֶךָ. וְהָגֵן בַּעֲדֵנוּ, וְהָסֵר מֵעָלֵינוּ אוֹיֵב, דֶּבֶר, וְחֶרֶב, וְרָעָב, וְיָגוֹן, וְהָסֵר שָׂטָן מִלְּפָנֵינוּ וּמֵאַחֲרֵינוּ, וּבְצֵל כְּנָפֶיךָ תַּסְתִּירֵנוּ, כִּי אֵל שׁוֹמְרֵנוּ וּמַצִּילֵנוּ אָתָּה, כִּי אֵל מֶלֶךְ חַנּוּן וְרַחוּם אָתָּה, וּשְׁמוֹר צֵאתֵנוּ וּבוֹאֵנוּ, לְחַיִּים וּלְשָׁלוֹם, מֵעַתָּה וְעַד עוֹלָם. בָּרוּךְ אַתָּה יְיָ, שׁוֹמֵר עַמּוֹ יִשְׂרָאֵל לָעַד.

בָּרוּךְ יְיָ לְעוֹלָם, אָמֵן וְאָמֵן. בָּרוּךְ יְיָ מִצִּיּוֹן שֹׁכֵן יְרוּשָׁלָיִם הַלְלוּיָהּ. בָּרוּךְ יְיָ אֱלֹהִים אֱלֹהֵי יִשְׂרָאֵל, עֹשֵׂה נִפְלָאוֹת לְבַדּוֹ. וּבָרוּךְ שֵׁם כְּבוֹדוֹ לְעוֹלָם, וְיִמָּלֵא כְבוֹדוֹ אֶת כָּל הָאָרֶץ, אָמֵן וְאָמֵן. יְהִי כְבוֹד יְיָ לְעוֹלָם, יִשְׂמַח יְיָ בְּמַעֲשָׂיו. יְהִי שֵׁם יְיָ מְבֹרָךְ, מֵעַתָּה וְעַד עוֹלָם. כִּי לֹא יִטֹּשׁ יְיָ אֶת עַמּוֹ בַּעֲבוּר שְׁמוֹ הַגָּדוֹל, כִּי הוֹאִיל יְיָ לַעֲשׂוֹת אֶתְכֶם לוֹ לְעָם. וַיַּרְא כָּל הָעָם וַיִּפְּלוּ עַל פְּנֵיהֶם, וַיֹּאמְרוּ, יְיָ הוּא הָאֱלֹהִים, יְיָ הוּא הָאֱלֹהִים. וְהָיָה יְיָ לְמֶלֶךְ עַל כָּל הָאָרֶץ, בַּיּוֹם הַהוּא יִהְיֶה יְיָ אֶחָד וּשְׁמוֹ אֶחָד. יְהִי חַסְדְּךָ יְיָ עָלֵינוּ, כַּאֲשֶׁר יִחַלְנוּ לָךְ. הוֹשִׁיעֵנוּ יְיָ אֱלֹהֵינוּ, וְקַבְּצֵנוּ מִן הַגּוֹיִם, לְהוֹדוֹת לְשֵׁם קָדְשֶׁךָ, לְהִשְׁתַּבֵּחַ בִּתְהִלָּתֶךָ. כָּל גּוֹיִם אֲשֶׁר עָשִׂיתָ יָבוֹאוּ וְיִשְׁתַּחֲווּ לְפָנֶיךָ אֲדֹנָי, וִיכַבְּדוּ לִשְׁמֶךָ. כִּי גָדוֹל אַתָּה וְעֹשֵׂה נִפְלָאוֹת, אַתָּה אֱלֹהִים לְבַדֶּךָ. וַאֲנַחְנוּ עַמְּךָ וְצֹאן מַרְעִיתֶךָ, נוֹדֶה לְּךָ לְעוֹלָם, לְדוֹר וָדוֹר נְסַפֵּר תְּהִלָּתֶךָ. בָּרוּךְ יְיָ בַּיּוֹם, בָּרוּךְ יְיָ בַּלָּיְלָה, בָּרוּךְ יְיָ בְּשָׁכְבֵנוּ, בָּרוּךְ יְיָ בְּקוּמֵנוּ. כִּי בְיָדְךָ נַפְשׁוֹת הַחַיִּים וְהַמֵּתִים, אֲשֶׁר בְּיָדוֹ נֶפֶשׁ כָּל חָי וְרוּחַ כָּל בְּשַׂר אִישׁ. בְּיָדְךָ אַפְקִיד רוּחִי, פָּדִיתָה אוֹתִי, יְיָ, אֵל אֱמֶת. אֱלֹהֵינוּ שֶׁבַּשָּׁמַיִם, יַחֵד שִׁמְךָ, וְקַיֵּם מַלְכוּתְךָ תָּמִיד, וּמְלוֹךְ עָלֵינוּ לְעוֹלָם וָעֶד.

יִרְאוּ עֵינֵינוּ, וְיִשְׂמַח לִבֵּנוּ, וְתָגֵל נַפְשֵׁנוּ בִּישׁוּעָתְךָ בֶּאֱמֶת, בֶּאֱמוֹר לְצִיּוֹן, מָלַךְ אֱלֹהָיִךְ. יְיָ מֶלֶךְ, יְיָ מָלָךְ, יְיָ יִמְלוֹךְ לְעוֹלָם וָעֶד. כִּי הַמַּלְכוּת שֶׁלְּךָ הִיא, וּלְעוֹלְמֵי עַד תִּמְלוֹךְ בְּכָבוֹד, כִּי אֵין לָנוּ מֶלֶךְ אֶלָּא אָתָּה. בָּרוּךְ אַתָּה יְיָ, הַמֶּלֶךְ בִּכְבוֹדוֹ, תָּמִיד יִמְלוֹךְ עָלֵינוּ לְעוֹלָם וָעֶד, וְעַל כָּל מַעֲשָׂיו.

## HATZI KADDISH

*Leader*

יִתְגַּדַּל וְיִתְקַדַּשׁ שְׁמֵהּ רַבָּא. בְּעָלְמָא דִּי בְרָא כִרְעוּתֵהּ, וְיַמְלִיךְ מַלְכוּתֵהּ בְּחַיֵּיכוֹן וּבְיוֹמֵיכוֹן וּבְחַיֵּי דְכָל בֵּית יִשְׂרָאֵל, בַּעֲגָלָא וּבִזְמַן קָרִיב, וְאִמְרוּ אָמֵן.

יְהֵא שְׁמֵהּ רַבָּא מְבָרַךְ לְעָלַם וּלְעָלְמֵי עָלְמַיָּא.

יִתְבָּרַךְ וְיִשְׁתַּבַּח וְיִתְפָּאַר וְיִתְרוֹמַם וְיִתְנַשֵּׂא וְיִתְהַדָּר וְיִתְעַלֶּה וְיִתְהַלָּל שְׁמֵהּ דְּקֻדְשָׁא בְּרִיךְ הוּא, לְעֵלָּא מִן כָּל (לְעֵלָּא וּלְעֵלָּא מִכָּל) בִּרְכָתָא וְשִׁירָתָא תֻּשְׁבְּחָתָא וְנֶחֱמָתָא, דַּאֲמִירָן בְּעָלְמָא, וְאִמְרוּ אָמֵן.

## AMIDAH

אֲדֹנָי שְׂפָתַי תִּפְתָּח וּפִי יַגִּיד תְּהִלָּתֶךָ.

בָּרוּךְ אַתָּה יְיָ אֱלֹהֵינוּ וֵאלֹהֵי אֲבוֹתֵינוּ, אֱלֹהֵי אַבְרָהָם, אֱלֹהֵי יִצְחָק, וֵאלֹהֵי יַעֲקֹב, שָׂרָה רִבְקָה רָחֵל וְלֵאָה, הָאֵל הַגָּדוֹל הַגִּבּוֹר וְהַנּוֹרָא, אֵל עֶלְיוֹן, גּוֹמֵל חֲסָדִים טוֹבִים, וְקֹנֵה הַכֹּל, וְזוֹכֵר חַסְדֵי אָבוֹת, וּמֵבִיא גּוֹאֵל לִבְנֵי בְנֵיהֶם, לְמַעַן שְׁמוֹ בְּאַהֲבָה.

*Ten Days of Penitence* זָכְרֵנוּ לְחַיִּים, מֶלֶךְ חָפֵץ בַּחַיִּים, וְכָתְבֵנוּ בְּסֵפֶר הַחַיִּים, לְמַעַנְךָ אֱלֹהִים חַיִּים.

מֶלֶךְ עוֹזֵר וּמוֹשִׁיעַ וּמָגֵן. בָּרוּךְ אַתָּה יְיָ, מָגֵן אַבְרָהָם.

אַתָּה גִּבּוֹר לְעוֹלָם אֲדֹנָי, מְחַיֵּה מֵתִים אַתָּה, רַב לְהוֹשִׁיעַ.

*In the winter* מַשִּׁיב הָרוּחַ וּמוֹרִיד הַגָּשֶׁם.

מְכַלְכֵּל חַיִּים בְּחֶסֶד, מְחַיֵּה מֵתִים בְּרַחֲמִים רַבִּים, סוֹמֵךְ נוֹפְלִים, וְרוֹפֵא חוֹלִים, וּמַתִּיר אֲסוּרִים, וּמְקַיֵּם אֱמוּנָתוֹ לִישֵׁנֵי עָפָר, מִי כָמוֹךָ בַּעַל גְּבוּרוֹת וּמִי דּוֹמֶה לָּךְ, מֶלֶךְ מֵמִית וּמְחַיֶּה וּמַצְמִיחַ יְשׁוּעָה.

*Ten Days of Penitence* מִי כָמוֹךָ אַב הָרַחֲמִים, זוֹכֵר יְצוּרָיו לְחַיִּים בְּרַחֲמִים.

וְנֶאֱמָן אַתָּה לְהַחֲיוֹת מֵתִים. בָּרוּךְ אַתָּה יְיָ, מְחַיֵּה הַמֵּתִים.

אַתָּה קָדוֹשׁ וְשִׁמְךָ קָדוֹשׁ,
וּקְדוֹשִׁים בְּכָל יוֹם יְהַלְלְוּךָ סֶּלָה.
בָּרוּךְ אַתָּה יְיָ, הָאֵל הַקָּדוֹשׁ (*Ten Days of Penitence* הַמֶּלֶךְ הַקָּדוֹשׁ).

אַתָּה חוֹנֵן לְאָדָם דַּעַת, וּמְלַמֵּד לֶאֱנוֹשׁ בִּינָה. אַתָּה חוֹנַנְתָּנוּ לְמַדַּע תּוֹרָתֶךָ, וַתְּלַמְּדֵנוּ לַעֲשׂוֹת חֻקֵּי רְצוֹנֶךָ, וַתַּבְדֵּל יְיָ אֱלֹהֵינוּ בֵּין קֹדֶשׁ לְחוֹל, בֵּין אוֹר לְחֹשֶׁךְ, בֵּין יִשְׂרָאֵל לָעַמִּים, בֵּין יוֹם הַשְּׁבִיעִי לְשֵׁשֶׁת יְמֵי הַמַּעֲשֶׂה. אָבִינוּ מַלְכֵּנוּ, הָחֵל עָלֵינוּ הַיָּמִים הַבָּאִים לִקְרָאתֵנוּ לְשָׁלוֹם, חֲשׂוּכִים מִכָּל חֵטְא, וּמְנֻקִּים מִכָּל עָוֹן, וּמְדֻבָּקִים בְּיִרְאָתֶךָ. וְחָנֵּנוּ מֵאִתְּךָ דֵּעָה בִּינָה וְהַשְׂכֵּל. בָּרוּךְ אַתָּה יְיָ, חוֹנֵן הַדָּעַת.

הֲשִׁיבֵנוּ אָבִינוּ לְתוֹרָתֶךָ, וְקָרְבֵנוּ מַלְכֵּנוּ לַעֲבוֹדָתֶךָ, וְהַחֲזִירֵנוּ בִּתְשׁוּבָה שְׁלֵמָה לְפָנֶיךָ. בָּרוּךְ אַתָּה יְיָ, הָרוֹצֶה בִּתְשׁוּבָה.

סְלַח לָנוּ, אָבִינוּ, כִּי חָטָאנוּ, מְחַל לָנוּ, מַלְכֵּנוּ, כִּי פָשָׁעְנוּ, כִּי מוֹחֵל וְסוֹלֵחַ אָתָּה. בָּרוּךְ אַתָּה יְיָ, חַנּוּן הַמַּרְבֶּה לִסְלֹחַ.

רְאֵה בְעָנְיֵנוּ, וְרִיבָה רִיבֵנוּ, וּגְאָלֵנוּ מְהֵרָה לְמַעַן שְׁמֶךָ, כִּי גוֹאֵל חָזָק אָתָּה. בָּרוּךְ אַתָּה יְיָ, גּוֹאֵל יִשְׂרָאֵל.

רְפָאֵנוּ, יְיָ, וְנֵרָפֵא, הוֹשִׁיעֵנוּ וְנִוָּשֵׁעָה, כִּי תְהִלָּתֵנוּ אָתָּה, וְהַעֲלֵה רְפוּאָה שְׁלֵמָה לְכָל מַכּוֹתֵינוּ. כִּי אֵל מֶלֶךְ רוֹפֵא נֶאֱמָן וְרַחֲמָן אָתָּה. בָּרוּךְ אַתָּה יְיָ, רוֹפֵא חוֹלֵי עַמּוֹ יִשְׂרָאֵל.

בָּרֵךְ עָלֵינוּ, יְיָ אֱלֹהֵינוּ, אֶת הַשָּׁנָה הַזֹּאת וְאֶת כָּל מִינֵי תְבוּאָתָהּ לְטוֹבָה,
(*In the Summer*) וְתֵן בְּרָכָה (*In the Winter*) וְתֵן טַל וּמָטָר לִבְרָכָה
עַל פְּנֵי הָאֲדָמָה, וְשַׂבְּעֵנוּ מִטּוּבֶךָ, וּבָרֵךְ שְׁנָתֵנוּ כַּשָּׁנִים הַטּוֹבוֹת. בָּרוּךְ אַתָּה יְיָ, מְבָרֵךְ הַשָּׁנִים.

תְּקַע בְּשׁוֹפָר גָּדוֹל לְחֵרוּתֵנוּ, וְשָׂא נֵס לְקַבֵּץ גָּלֻיּוֹתֵינוּ, וְקַבְּצֵנוּ יַחַד מֵאַרְבַּע כַּנְפוֹת הָאָרֶץ. בָּרוּךְ אַתָּה יְיָ, מְקַבֵּץ נִדְחֵי עַמּוֹ יִשְׂרָאֵל.

הָשִׁיבָה שׁוֹפְטֵינוּ כְּבָרִאשׁוֹנָה וְיוֹעֲצֵינוּ כְּבַתְּחִלָּה, וְהָסֵר מִמֶּנּוּ יָגוֹן וַאֲנָחָה, וּמְלוֹךְ עָלֵינוּ אַתָּה, יְיָ, לְבַדְּךָ בְּחֶסֶד וּבְרַחֲמִים, וְצַדְּקֵנוּ בַּמִּשְׁפָּט. בָּרוּךְ אַתָּה יְיָ, מֶלֶךְ אוֹהֵב צְדָקָה וּמִשְׁפָּט (*Ten Days of Penitence* הַמֶּלֶךְ הַמִּשְׁפָּט).

וְלַמַּלְשִׁינִים אַל תְּהִי תִקְוָה, וְכָל הָרִשְׁעָה כְּרֶגַע תֹּאבֵד, וְכָל אוֹיְבֶיךָ מְהֵרָה יִכָּרֵתוּ, וְהַזֵּדִים מְהֵרָה תְעַקֵּר וּתְשַׁבֵּר וּתְמַגֵּר וְתַכְנִיעַ בִּמְהֵרָה בְיָמֵינוּ. בָּרוּךְ אַתָּה יְיָ, שֹׁבֵר אֹיְבִים וּמַכְנִיעַ זֵדִים.

עַל הַצַּדִּיקִים וְעַל הַחֲסִידִים וְעַל זִקְנֵי עַמְּךָ בֵּית יִשְׂרָאֵל, וְעַל פְּלֵיטַת סוֹפְרֵיהֶם, וְעַל גֵּרֵי הַצֶּדֶק וְעָלֵינוּ, יֶהֱמוּ נָא רַחֲמֶיךָ, יְיָ אֱלֹהֵינוּ, וְתֵן שָׂכָר טוֹב לְכָל הַבּוֹטְחִים בְּשִׁמְךָ בֶּאֱמֶת, וְשִׂים חֶלְקֵנוּ עִמָּהֶם לְעוֹלָם, וְלֹא נֵבוֹשׁ כִּי בְךָ בָּטָחְנוּ. בָּרוּךְ אַתָּה יְיָ, מִשְׁעָן וּמִבְטָח לַצַּדִּיקִים.

וְלִירוּשָׁלַיִם עִירְךָ בְּרַחֲמִים תָּשׁוּב, וְתִשְׁכּוֹן בְּתוֹכָהּ כַּאֲשֶׁר דִּבַּרְתָּ, וּבְנֵה אוֹתָהּ בְּקָרוֹב בְּיָמֵינוּ בִּנְיַן עוֹלָם, וְכִסֵּא דָוִד מְהֵרָה לְתוֹכָהּ תָּכִין. בָּרוּךְ אַתָּה יְיָ, בּוֹנֵה יְרוּשָׁלָיִם.

אֶת צֶמַח דָּוִד עַבְדְּךָ מְהֵרָה תַצְמִיחַ, וְקַרְנוֹ תָּרוּם בִּישׁוּעָתֶךָ, כִּי לִישׁוּעָתְךָ קִוִּינוּ כָּל הַיּוֹם. בָּרוּךְ אַתָּה יְיָ, מַצְמִיחַ קֶרֶן יְשׁוּעָה.

שְׁמַע קוֹלֵנוּ, יְיָ אֱלֹהֵינוּ, חוּס וְרַחֵם עָלֵינוּ, וְקַבֵּל בְּרַחֲמִים וּבְרָצוֹן אֶת תְּפִלָּתֵנוּ, כִּי אֵל שׁוֹמֵעַ תְּפִלּוֹת וְתַחֲנוּנִים אָתָּה, וּמִלְּפָנֶיךָ, מַלְכֵּנוּ, רֵיקָם אַל תְּשִׁיבֵנוּ. כִּי אַתָּה שׁוֹמֵעַ תְּפִלַּת עַמְּךָ יִשְׂרָאֵל בְּרַחֲמִים. בָּרוּךְ אַתָּה יְיָ, שׁוֹמֵעַ תְּפִלָּה.

רְצֵה, יְיָ אֱלֹהֵינוּ, בְּעַמְּךָ יִשְׂרָאֵל וּבִתְפִלָּתָם, וְהָשֵׁב אֶת הָעֲבוֹדָה לִדְבִיר בֵּיתֶךָ, וְאִשֵּׁי יִשְׂרָאֵל, וּתְפִלָּתָם בְּאַהֲבָה תְקַבֵּל בְּרָצוֹן, וּתְהִי לְרָצוֹן תָּמִיד עֲבוֹדַת יִשְׂרָאֵל עַמֶּךָ.

*Say on Rosh Ḥodesh and Ḥol Ha-mo'ed*

אֱלֹהֵינוּ וֵאלֹהֵי אֲבוֹתֵינוּ, יַעֲלֶה וְיָבֹא, וְיַגִּיעַ, וְיֵרָאֶה, וְיֵרָצֶה, וְיִשָּׁמַע, וְיִפָּקֵד, וְיִזָּכֵר זִכְרוֹנֵנוּ וּפִקְדוֹנֵנוּ, וְזִכְרוֹן אֲבוֹתֵינוּ, וְזִכְרוֹן מָשִׁיחַ בֶּן דָּוִד עַבְדֶּךָ, וְזִכְרוֹן יְרוּשָׁלַיִם עִיר קָדְשֶׁךָ, וְזִכְרוֹן כָּל עַמְּךָ בֵּית יִשְׂרָאֵל לְפָנֶיךָ, לִפְלֵיטָה, לְטוֹבָה, לְחֵן וּלְחֶסֶד וּלְרַחֲמִים, לְחַיִּים וּלְשָׁלוֹם, בְּיוֹם

| *On Rosh Ḥodesh:* | *On Pesaḥ:* | *On Sukkot:* |
|---|---|---|
| רֹאשׁ הַחֹדֶשׁ הַזֶּה. | חַג הַמַּצּוֹת הַזֶּה | חַג הַסֻּכּוֹת הַזֶּה |

זָכְרֵנוּ, יְיָ אֱלֹהֵינוּ, בּוֹ לְטוֹבָה, וּפָקְדֵנוּ בוֹ לִבְרָכָה, וְהוֹשִׁיעֵנוּ בוֹ לְחַיִּים. וּבִדְבַר יְשׁוּעָה וְרַחֲמִים, חוּס וְחָנֵּנוּ, וְרַחֵם עָלֵינוּ וְהוֹשִׁיעֵנוּ, כִּי אֵלֶיךָ עֵינֵינוּ, כִּי אֵל מֶלֶךְ חַנּוּן וְרַחוּם אָתָּה.

וְתֶחֱזֶינָה עֵינֵינוּ בְּשׁוּבְךָ לְצִיּוֹן בְּרַחֲמִים. בָּרוּךְ אַתָּה יְיָ, הַמַּחֲזִיר שְׁכִינָתוֹ לְצִיּוֹן.

מוֹדִים אֲנַחְנוּ לָךְ, שָׁאַתָּה הוּא, יְיָ אֱלֹהֵינוּ וֵאלֹהֵי אֲבוֹתֵינוּ, לְעוֹלָם וָעֶד, צוּר חַיֵּינוּ, מָגֵן יִשְׁעֵנוּ, אַתָּה הוּא לְדוֹר וָדוֹר, נוֹדֶה לְּךָ וּנְסַפֵּר תְּהִלָּתֶךָ, עַל חַיֵּינוּ הַמְּסוּרִים בְּיָדֶךָ, וְעַל נִשְׁמוֹתֵינוּ הַפְּקוּדוֹת לָךְ, וְעַל נִסֶּיךָ שֶׁבְּכָל יוֹם עִמָּנוּ, וְעַל נִפְלְאוֹתֶיךָ וְטוֹבוֹתֶיךָ שֶׁבְּכָל עֵת, עֶרֶב וָבֹקֶר וְצָהֳרָיִם, הַטּוֹב, כִּי לֹא כָלוּ רַחֲמֶיךָ, וְהַמְרַחֵם, כִּי לֹא תַמּוּ חֲסָדֶיךָ, מֵעוֹלָם קִוִּינוּ לָךְ.

*On Ḥanukah and Purim*

עַל הַנִּסִּים, וְעַל הַפֻּרְקָן, וְעַל הַגְּבוּרוֹת, וְעַל הַתְּשׁוּעוֹת, וְעַל הַמִּלְחָמוֹת, שֶׁעָשִׂיתָ לַאֲבוֹתֵינוּ בַּיָּמִים הָהֵם בַּזְּמַן הַזֶּה.

*On Ḥanukah*

בִּימֵי מַתִּתְיָהוּ בֶּן יוֹחָנָן כֹּהֵן גָּדוֹל, חַשְׁמוֹנַאי וּבָנָיו, כְּשֶׁעָמְדָה מַלְכוּת יָוָן הָרְשָׁעָה עַל עַמְּךָ יִשְׂרָאֵל לְהַשְׁכִּיחָם תּוֹרָתֶךָ, וּלְהַעֲבִירָם מֵחֻקֵּי רְצוֹנֶךָ, וְאַתָּה בְּרַחֲמֶיךָ הָרַבִּים עָמַדְתָּ לָהֶם בְּעֵת צָרָתָם, רַבְתָּ אֶת רִיבָם, דַּנְתָּ אֶת דִּינָם, נָקַמְתָּ אֶת נִקְמָתָם, מָסַרְתָּ גִבּוֹרִים בְּיַד חַלָּשִׁים, וְרַבִּים בְּיַד מְעַטִּים, וּטְמֵאִים בְּיַד טְהוֹרִים, וּרְשָׁעִים בְּיַד צַדִּיקִים, וְזֵדִים בְּיַד עוֹסְקֵי תוֹרָתֶךָ. וּלְךָ עָשִׂיתָ שֵׁם גָּדוֹל וְקָדוֹשׁ בְּעוֹלָמֶךָ, וּלְעַמְּךָ יִשְׂרָאֵל עָשִׂיתָ תְּשׁוּעָה גְדוֹלָה וּפֻרְקָן כְּהַיּוֹם הַזֶּה. וְאַחַר כֵּן בָּאוּ בָנֶיךָ לִדְבִיר בֵּיתֶךָ, וּפִנּוּ אֶת הֵיכָלֶךָ, וְטִהֲרוּ אֶת מִקְדָּשֶׁךָ, וְהִדְלִיקוּ נֵרוֹת בְּחַצְרוֹת קָדְשֶׁךָ, וְקָבְעוּ שְׁמוֹנַת יְמֵי חֲנֻכָּה אֵלּוּ, לְהוֹדוֹת וּלְהַלֵּל לְשִׁמְךָ הַגָּדוֹל.

*On Purim*

בִּימֵי מָרְדְּכַי וְאֶסְתֵּר בְּשׁוּשַׁן הַבִּירָה, כְּשֶׁעָמַד עֲלֵיהֶם הָמָן הָרָשָׁע, בִּקֵּשׁ לְהַשְׁמִיד לַהֲרֹג וּלְאַבֵּד אֶת כָּל הַיְּהוּדִים, מִנַּעַר וְעַד זָקֵן, טַף וְנָשִׁים, בְּיוֹם אֶחָד, בִּשְׁלוֹשָׁה עָשָׂר לְחֹדֶשׁ שְׁנֵים עָשָׂר, הוּא חֹדֶשׁ אֲדָר, וּשְׁלָלָם לָבוֹז. וְאַתָּה בְּרַחֲמֶיךָ הָרַבִּים הֵפַרְתָּ אֶת עֲצָתוֹ, וְקִלְקַלְתָּ אֶת מַחֲשַׁבְתּוֹ, וַהֲשֵׁבוֹתָ לּוֹ גְּמוּלוֹ בְּרֹאשׁוֹ, וְתָלוּ אוֹתוֹ וְאֶת בָּנָיו עַל הָעֵץ.)

וְעַל כֻּלָּם יִתְבָּרַךְ וְיִתְרוֹמַם שִׁמְךָ מַלְכֵּנוּ תָּמִיד לְעוֹלָם וָעֶד.

*Ten Days of Penitence* וּכְתוֹב לְחַיִּים טוֹבִים כָּל בְּנֵי בְרִיתֶךָ.

וְכֹל הַחַיִּים יוֹדוּךָ סֶּלָה, וִיהַלְלוּ אֶת שִׁמְךָ בֶּאֱמֶת, הָאֵל יְשׁוּעָתֵנוּ וְעֶזְרָתֵנוּ סֶלָה. בָּרוּךְ אַתָּה יְיָ, הַטּוֹב שִׁמְךָ וּלְךָ נָאֶה לְהוֹדוֹת.

שָׁלוֹם רָב עַל יִשְׂרָאֵל עַמְּךָ תָּשִׂים לְעוֹלָם, כִּי אַתָּה הוּא מֶלֶךְ אָדוֹן לְכָל הַשָּׁלוֹם. וְטוֹב בְּעֵינֶיךָ לְבָרֵךְ אֶת עַמְּךָ יִשְׂרָאֵל בְּכָל עֵת וּבְכָל שָׁעָה בִּשְׁלוֹמֶךָ.

*Ten Days of Penitence* בְּסֵֽפֶר חַיִּים, בְּרָכָה, וְשָׁלוֹם, וּפַרְנָסָה טוֹבָה, נִזָּכֵר וְנִכָּתֵב לְפָנֶֽיךָ, אֲנַֽחְנוּ וְכָל עַמְּךָ בֵּית יִשְׂרָאֵל, לְחַיִּים טוֹבִים וּלְשָׁלוֹם

בָּרוּךְ אַתָּה יְיָ, הַמְבָרֵךְ אֶת עַמּוֹ יִשְׂרָאֵל בַּשָּׁלוֹם.

(יִהְיוּ לְרָצוֹן אִמְרֵי פִי וְהֶגְיוֹן לִבִּי לְפָנֶֽיךָ, יְיָ צוּרִי וְגוֹאֲלִי.)

אֱלֹהַי, נְצוֹר לְשׁוֹנִי מֵרָע, וּשְׂפָתַי מִדַּבֵּר מִרְמָה, וְלִמְקַלְלַי נַפְשִׁי תִדֹּם, וְנַפְשִׁי כֶּעָפָר לַכֹּל תִּהְיֶה. פְּתַח לִבִּי בְּתוֹרָתֶֽךָ, וּבְמִצְוֹתֶֽיךָ תִּרְדּוֹף נַפְשִׁי. וְכָל הַחוֹשְׁבִים עָלַי רָעָה, מְהֵרָה הָפֵר עֲצָתָם וְקַלְקֵל מַחֲשַׁבְתָּם. עֲשֵׂה לְמַֽעַן שְׁמֶֽךָ, עֲשֵׂה לְמַֽעַן יְמִינֶֽךָ, עֲשֵׂה לְמַֽעַן קְדֻשָּׁתֶֽךָ, עֲשֵׂה לְמַֽעַן תּוֹרָתֶֽךָ. לְמַֽעַן יֵחָלְצוּן יְדִידֶֽיךָ, הוֹשִֽׁיעָה יְמִינְךָ וַעֲנֵֽנִי. יִהְיוּ לְרָצוֹן אִמְרֵי פִי וְהֶגְיוֹן לִבִּי לְפָנֶֽיךָ, יְיָ צוּרִי וְגוֹאֲלִי. עֹשֶׂה שָׁלוֹם (*Ten Days of Penititence* הַשָּׁלוֹם) בִּמְרוֹמָיו, הוּא יַעֲשֶׂה שָׁלוֹם עָלֵֽינוּ, וְעַל כָּל יִשְׂרָאֵל, וְאִמְרוּ אָמֵן.

יְהִי רָצוֹן מִלְּפָנֶֽיךָ, יְיָ אֱלֹהֵֽינוּ וֵאלֹהֵי אֲבוֹתֵֽינוּ, שֶׁיִּבָּנֶה בֵּית הַמִּקְדָּשׁ בִּמְהֵרָה בְיָמֵֽינוּ, וְתֵן חֶלְקֵֽנוּ בְּתוֹרָתֶֽךָ, וְשָׁם נַעֲבָדְךָ בְּיִרְאָה כִּימֵי עוֹלָם וּכְשָׁנִים קַדְמוֹנִיּוֹת. וְעָרְבָה לַייָ מִנְחַת יְהוּדָה וִירוּשָׁלָֽיִם, כִּימֵי עוֹלָם וּכְשָׁנִים קַדְמוֹנִיּוֹת.

## KADDISH SHALEIM

*Leader*

יִתְגַּדַּל וְיִתְקַדַּשׁ שְׁמֵהּ רַבָּא. בְּעָלְמָא דִּי בְרָא כִרְעוּתֵהּ, וְיַמְלִיךְ מַלְכוּתֵהּ בְּחַיֵּיכוֹן וּבְיוֹמֵיכוֹן וּבְחַיֵּי דְכָל בֵּית יִשְׂרָאֵל, בַּעֲגָלָא וּבִזְמַן קָרִיב, וְאִמְרוּ אָמֵן.

*All*

יְהֵא שְׁמֵהּ רַבָּא מְבָרַךְ לְעָלַם וּלְעָלְמֵי עָלְמַיָּא.

*Leader*

יִתְבָּרַךְ וְיִשְׁתַּבַּח וְיִתְפָּאַר וְיִתְרוֹמַם וְיִתְנַשֵּׂא וְיִתְהַדָּר וְיִתְעַלֶּה וְיִתְהַלָּל שְׁמֵהּ דְּקֻדְשָׁא בְּרִיךְ הוּא, לְעֵלָּא מִן כָּל (*Ten Days of Penitence* לְעֵלָּא וּלְעֵלָּא מִכָּל) בִּרְכָתָא וְשִׁירָתָא תֻּשְׁבְּחָתָא וְנֶחֱמָתָא, דַּאֲמִירָן בְּעָלְמָא, וְאִמְרוּ אָמֵן.

תִּתְקַבַּל צְלוֹתְהוֹן וּבָעוּתְהוֹן דְּכָל (בֵּית) יִשְׂרָאֵל קֳדָם אֲבוּהוֹן דִּי בִשְׁמַיָּא וְאִמְרוּ אָמֵן.

יְהֵא שְׁלָמָא רַבָּא מִן שְׁמַיָּא, וְחַיִּים (טוֹבִים) עָלֵינוּ וְעַל כָּל יִשְׂרָאֵל, וְאִמְרוּ אָמֵן.

עֹשֶׂה שָׁלוֹם (*Ten Days of Penitence* הַשָּׁלוֹם) בִּמְרוֹמָיו, הוּא יַעֲשֶׂה שָׁלוֹם עָלֵינוּ וְעַל כָּל יִשְׂרָאֵל, וְאִמְרוּ אָמֵן.

## ALEINU

עָלֵינוּ לְשַׁבֵּחַ לַאֲדוֹן הַכֹּל, לָתֵת גְּדֻלָּה לְיוֹצֵר בְּרֵאשִׁית, שֶׁלֹּא עָשָׂנוּ כְּגוֹיֵי הָאֲרָצוֹת, וְלֹא שָׂמָנוּ כְּמִשְׁפְּחוֹת הָאֲדָמָה, שֶׁלֹּא שָׂם חֶלְקֵנוּ כָּהֶם, וְגֹרָלֵנוּ כְּכָל הֲמוֹנָם, וַאֲנַחְנוּ כּוֹרְעִים וּמִשְׁתַּחֲוִים וּמוֹדִים, לִפְנֵי מֶלֶךְ מַלְכֵי הַמְּלָכִים, הַקָּדוֹשׁ בָּרוּךְ הוּא. שֶׁהוּא נוֹטֶה שָׁמַיִם וְיֹסֵד אָרֶץ, וּמוֹשַׁב יְקָרוֹ בַּשָּׁמַיִם מִמַּעַל, וּשְׁכִינַת עֻזּוֹ בְּגָבְהֵי מְרוֹמִים, הוּא אֱלֹהֵינוּ אֵין עוֹד. אֱמֶת מַלְכֵּנוּ, אֶפֶס זוּלָתוֹ, כַּכָּתוּב בְּתוֹרָתוֹ: וְיָדַעְתָּ הַיּוֹם וַהֲשֵׁבֹתָ אֶל לְבָבֶךָ, כִּי יְיָ הוּא הָאֱלֹהִים בַּשָּׁמַיִם מִמַּעַל, וְעַל הָאָרֶץ מִתָּחַת, אֵין עוֹד.

עַל כֵּן נְקַוֶּה לְּךָ יְיָ אֱלֹהֵינוּ, לִרְאוֹת מְהֵרָה בְּתִפְאֶרֶת עֻזֶּךָ, לְהַעֲבִיר גִּלּוּלִים מִן הָאָרֶץ, וְהָאֱלִילִים כָּרוֹת יִכָּרֵתוּן, לְתַקֵּן עוֹלָם בְּמַלְכוּת שַׁדַּי, וְכָל בְּנֵי בָשָׂר יִקְרְאוּ בִשְׁמֶךָ, לְהַפְנוֹת אֵלֶיךָ כָּל רִשְׁעֵי אָרֶץ. יַכִּירוּ וְיֵדְעוּ כָּל יוֹשְׁבֵי תֵבֵל, כִּי לְךָ תִּכְרַע כָּל בֶּרֶךְ, תִּשָּׁבַע כָּל לָשׁוֹן. לְפָנֶיךָ יְיָ אֱלֹהֵינוּ יִכְרְעוּ וְיִפֹּלוּ, וְלִכְבוֹד שִׁמְךָ יְקָר יִתֵּנוּ, וִיקַבְּלוּ כֻלָּם אֶת עוֹל מַלְכוּתֶךָ, וְתִמְלֹךְ עֲלֵיהֶם מְהֵרָה לְעוֹלָם וָעֶד. כִּי הַמַּלְכוּת שֶׁלְּךָ הִיא, וּלְעוֹלְמֵי עַד תִּמְלוֹךְ בְּכָבוֹד, כַּכָּתוּב בְּתוֹרָתֶךָ, יְיָ יִמְלֹךְ לְעוֹלָם וָעֶד. וְנֶאֱמַר, וְהָיָה יְיָ לְמֶלֶךְ עַל כָּל הָאָרֶץ, בַּיּוֹם הַהוּא יִהְיֶה יְיָ אֶחָד, וּשְׁמוֹ אֶחָד.

## KADDISH YATOM (MOURNER'S KADDISH)

*Leader*

יִתְגַּדַּל וְיִתְקַדַּשׁ שְׁמֵהּ רַבָּא. בְּעָלְמָא דִּי בְרָא כִרְעוּתֵהּ, וְיַמְלִיךְ מַלְכוּתֵהּ בְּחַיֵּיכוֹן וּבְיוֹמֵיכוֹן וּבְחַיֵּי דְכָל בֵּית יִשְׂרָאֵל, בַּעֲגָלָא וּבִזְמַן קָרִיב, וְאִמְרוּ אָמֵן.

*All*

יְהֵא שְׁמֵהּ רַבָּא מְבָרַךְ לְעָלַם וּלְעָלְמֵי עָלְמַיָּא.

*Leader*

יִתְבָּרַךְ וְיִשְׁתַּבַּח וְיִתְפָּאַר וְיִתְרוֹמַם וְיִתְנַשֵּׂא וְיִתְהַדָּר וְיִתְעַלֶּה וְיִתְהַלָּל שְׁמֵהּ דְּקֻדְשָׁא בְּרִיךְ הוּא, לְעֵלָּא מִן כָּל (*Ten Days of Penitence* לְעֵלָּא וּלְעֵלָּא מִכָּל) בִּרְכָתָא וְשִׁירָתָא תֻּשְׁבְּחָתָא וְנֶחֱמָתָא, דַּאֲמִירָן בְּעָלְמָא, וְאִמְרוּ אָמֵן.

יְהֵא שְׁלָמָא רַבָּא מִן שְׁמַיָּא, וְחַיִּים (טוֹבִים) עָלֵינוּ וְעַל כָּל יִשְׂרָאֵל, וְאִמְרוּ אָמֵן.

עֹשֶׂה שָׁלוֹם (*Ten Days of Penitence* הַשָּׁלוֹם) בִּמְרוֹמָיו, הוּא יַעֲשֶׂה שָׁלוֹם עָלֵינוּ וְעַל כָּל יִשְׂרָאֵל, וְאִמְרוּ אָמֵן.